The Anthropology of Moralities

THE ANTHROPOLOGY OF MORALITIES

Edited by

Monica Heintz

berghahn
NEW YORK · OXFORD
www.berghahnbooks.com

First published in 2009 by

Berghahn Books

www.berghahnbooks.com

©2009, 2013 Monica Heintz
First paperback edition published in 2013

Library of Congress Cataloging-in-Publication Data

The anthropology of moralities / edited by Monica Heintz.
    p. cm.
  Includes bibliographical references and index.
  ISBN 978-1-84545-592-7 (hardback) -- ISBN 978-1-84545-938-3
(institutional ebook) -- ISBN 978-1-78238-319-2 (paperback) -- ISBN
978-1-78238-320-8 (retail ebook)
  1. Cultural relativism. 2. Social values. I. Heintz, Monica.
  GN345.5.A57 2009
  303.3'72--dc22

                                                                    2009027914

British Library Cataloguing in Publication Data

A catalogue record for this book is available from the British Library

Printed in the United States on acid-free paper.

ISBN: 978-1-78238-319-2 paperback
ISBN: 978-1-78238-320-8 retail ebook

CONTENTS

ACKNOWLEDGEMENTS

This volume originated in the conference 'Rethinking Moralities' co-organised with Johan Rasanayagam at the Max Planck Institute of Social Anthropology in Halle, Germany, on 15–16 December 2005. For encouragement and support in organising this conference, I would like to express my gratitude to Chris Hann, director of the Max Planck Institute, to the administrative staff of the Institute, as well as to my co-convener Johan Rasanayagam. I thank all conference participants, whose valuable insights during the meeting helped us advance our research, and notably Michael Carrithers, Patrick Pharo and Marian Burchard. Last but not least, I thank the students in the master's programme in social anthropology from the University of Paris X – Nanterre who were the first to examine and criticise the coherence and utility of this volume during the 'Problématiques anthropologiques' course in 2006–7.

Chapter 1

INTRODUCTION: WHY THERE SHOULD BE AN ANTHROPOLOGY OF MORALITIES

Monica Heintz

There is probably no other field of enquiry in which the 'otherness' of human beings is as difficult to conceptualise as in the field of morals and values. Sometimes striking and difficult to accept, sometimes resembling our principles to the point that we become blind to their differences, values that underpin the others' actions are difficult to grasp, understand and explain. Can we, as anthropologists, maintain both the distance required by objective science and the empathy required for the analysis of lived experiences when addressing the issue of morality? Can we preserve in our writings the dignity of other cultures even though we may perhaps – as individuals – disapprove of their values? These delicate questions lurk in postmodernist debates, but have often remained rhetorical. To them we can add an even more problematic question: could we describe and analyse the others' values as if they were a set of traditional, fixed, unproblematic rules of life, while we at the same time acknowledge the complexity of moral questions in western societies – amply developed in Western art and literature? If the awareness of the historicised and complex nature of the Other has been with us at least since Johannes Fabian's *Time and the Other* (1983), the methodological challenge of analysing accordingly the most fundamental aspects that underline social life – values – in non-Western societies has not been met.

The challenge that the authors of this volume are trying to meet is to render possible an anthropology of moralities that enables the recognition of the plurality and creativity of moral discourses and practices all over the world and simultaneously keeps them in dialogue. Our main concern is methodological and epistemological, while our approach remains firmly anchored in the ethnographic method and its intimate connection with local case studies.

Ten years ago it would have been difficult to foresee the popularity that the word moral was to gain in anthropology, maybe as an echo to the terms in which public debates were cast in Western media, and perhaps due to anthropology reaching a maturity level that enabled the development of this new field. The edited book *Ethnographies of Moralities* (Howell 1997b) has become a landmark for a new generation of anthropological enquiries exploring values, morals and ethics while discovering the complexity of a subject that challenged the traditional anthropological methods.[1] Unlike new information technologies or transnational business, moralities are not new cultural phenomena and their long-term neglect by anthropologists is explained by James Laidlaw (2002) as being due to the Durkheimian influence. Emile Durkheim, whose socialist sympathies and strong moral stances are well known, considered morality as a floating mantle over society, pervasive in all of its aspects. The very fact of living together in communion was a sacred and a moral thing; thus morality was just another name for culture, for the very thing that kept humans together. The corollary was that the sociologist, by studying actions and trends of culture, was simultaneously studying values and morals and thus it was both unnecessary and impossible to extract them from their social context in order to make a separate, more abstract, object of study. However, the modernism which grew concomitantly with industrial Taylorism has adopted the method of dividing and extracting an object from the whole in order to better analyse it, and then placing it back. In contrast, Malinowski's organic model of society, in which every social aspect was related to all others to the point that one did not know where to start the analysis from, was far less inspiring to researchers.

This is why in this volume we propose to define an anthropology of moralities as a distinct field of enquiry within anthropology, and we argue for the refinement of research methods on morality as a necessary step in the development of anthropology. As the contributors to the volume highlight in their chapters, moralities are entangled within social action and as such are difficult to pinpoint and analyse. For grasping the ways in which moralities are created and transmitted, or interpreted, negotiated and resisted, anthropologists have to struggle with several empirical difficulties, such as how to differentiate between a moral/immoral and a morally neutral fact, how to recognise the moral source that underpins a certain behaviour or how to interpret inconsistencies between statements of morality and observed deviant practices. The foundation of a field of study encourages researchers to pull together various methods, methodological approaches and theoretical tools available in anthropology, philosophy and sociology in order to achieve the challenge of describing what is not always spelt out, but often accepted as tacit or hidden knowledge. The first step in reaching this objective is confronting the main issues and difficulties that challenge the research on moralities: the unresolved universalism versus cultural relativism debate, the issue of freedom for ethical choice, the question of creativity (structural and situational) of moral values, the questions posed by changes in values within society and at the meeting point with other cultures, and the problem of collecting relevant data (what, how and why). A second step in defining the field is to enquire into the manner in which moral values are created and transmitted, by addressing themes such as the power of moral models, moral education, the creation of moral obligation and the role of emotions in moral discourse.

A Note on Terminology

'Morality' (in English) designs a set of principles and judgements based on cultural concepts and beliefs by which humans determine whether given actions are right or wrong. Beidelman notes that the world moral derives from the latin mos, which defines a way of comporting oneself, a custom or a practice (1993: 2), and he asserts that morality is defined within social interactions. What is right and what is wrong are culturally situated and the terminology that deals with this division varies from one language to another.[2] But we can take as a methodological starting point for field research that observing what is accepted or rejected in social interaction leads the observer as close as possible to the moral values of a community.

Among three concurrent English terms for defining the field of our research, we have chosen 'morality' for its extended popular use in English – in comparison, the term 'ethics' is too abstract, the term 'values' is polythetic.[3] These three terms are certainly not synonymous and they each emphasise different aspects of a common topic. 'Morality' often refers in common English language to evaluations and judgements that are obvious and unproblematic, while 'ethics' – 'the science of morals' according to the Concise Oxford Dictionary – refers to more codified and elaborated judgements. In academe 'morality' evokes the general discourse on what is good and has deterministic normative overtones; 'ethics' evokes the individual choice of virtues and way of living. (Quite typically, a Durkheimian approach would focus on moralities, a Weberian approach on ethics, as the titles of these authors' main works show.) In this volume our choice of the term 'morality' to define the field does not have this academic connotation. Operating a choice based on the holist/individualist dichotomy at this early stage would have meant presupposing how morality/ethics/moral values are experienced in various cultures – as determined by society or by an individual choice – while we need first to question the relevance of 'freedom' and 'choice' and even of the existence of a society/individual dichotomy in every cultural context.

We wish to avoid introducing here a pure terminological divide that might be artificially created by differing receptivity to the English language of individual anthropologists (whose mother tongue may not necessarily be English). Thus, while we certainly nuance the use of these three terms in our studies, we consider the research on ethics, moral values and moralities as belonging to the same field, which we have labelled the anthropology of moralities, in order to echo the most widespread term used in anthropology today.

When referring to values, 'norms' is the complementary term that comes to our minds. Indeed, values lead to the elaboration of social norms and norms in return shape values. But they are two separate categories, at least for analytical purposes. Norms are rules that are socially enforced and sanctioned; they are 'implemented' values. This 'implementation' makes them amenable to resistance in the name of new or different values. The existence of a norm is not the proof of the existence and endorsement of the value that has initially generated it; an action that is thus 'formatted' might be in dissonance with the actor's values: there is no need for values if there are enough whips. Thus, the study of norms by legal anthropologists and the study of beliefs by anthropologists of religion are constant sources of methodological inspiration and information for the anthropologist who studies values.

Though this is beyond the question of terminology, we would like to mention here that this volume is not primarily concerned with the ethics of the anthropologist. However this concern remains present, which is inevitable when the anthropologist encounters the ethics of others and chooses the way in which to engage with it and later write about it.

Universalism versus Cultural Relativism

How can we study the Other's morality without resorting to our own normative judgements? How can we account for intercultural clashes of values and the radical cultural changes that may result? The plurality of moralities has not received an explicit and focused attention until recently, when accelerated globalisation forced different value systems into a more or less successful dialogue, for instance around the issue of human rights. The part played by anthropologists in these societal debates has been modest.[4]

The scientific debate between supporters of universalism and supporters of cultural relativism is much older, and in the 1960s–1970s it was crystallised in a dialogue between philosophers and anthropologists over the question of rationality (Wilson 1970; Hollis and Lukes 1982; Geertz 1984). Universalism presupposes the existence of a common core of rationality/morality from which diversity emerges in response to different natural contexts and as a result of different historical developments. This assumption provides an easy methodological support for the anthropologist, who has the comfort of exploring differences through a rational lens (or measuring them against the same basic moral standard), which is supposed to be to some degree universal. Cultural relativism asserts that what we hold to be true/good in one culture can be held to be false/wrong in another culture without any possibility of deciding whether one or the other culture is mistaken in asserting it: each culture has its own rationality. In its strong form, cultural relativism implies that the rationality/morality can only be judged from within a culture and through its own criteria, thus rendering cross-cultural comparison impossible. In its weak form of 'methodological relativism', cultural relativism avoids ethnocentrism by recommending a 'thick description' of beliefs or values that would enable them to appear meaningful in their cultural context: the other is rational (or moral), but he sees the world differently and understands it differently.

Presented under the heading of 'rationality', questions asked within the universalism versus cultural relativism debate were mostly prompted by moral concerns.[5] Why, among the Dayak of Borneo, did a man have to offer the head of his enemy as a gift of marriage? Why did women undergo excision in several African societies, going through suffering towards a sexual life without pleasure? How to account for this suffering, which hurts our Western sensitivity, while preserving the reasons for ancestral customs? Under the threat of being accused of ethnocentrism, several interpretations emerged trying to delicately save the 'other' from the accusations of savagery, infantilism (Frazer, Taylor) or illogical thought (Levy-Bruhl 1951[1911]). The 'intellectualists' who believed in the universality of reason looked for common points between 'us' and 'them' that would diminish the contrast; the intellectualists who believed in the particularity of each culture comprehensively described each phenomenon so as to show its 'rationality in context'. Symbolists (such as Beattie 1964) considered that some actions that seemed irrational were purely metaphorical: thus the Hopi's dance for bringing the rain was pure poetry. Fideists (a position expressed by Wittgenstein in his criticism of Frazer's *Golden Bough*) presented controversial phenomena as being sacred, mystically beautiful, thus bound to stay out of the reach of scientific judgement.

While many arguments could be brought for and against the basic assumptions of both cultural relativism and universalism, today anthropologists tend to ignore the question altogether and even to switch unintentionally from one position to the other under the influence of the events observed. As long as they adopt an 'intellectualist' position, which requires the comprehensive description of a phenomenon within its cultural context, their readers can work around the universalist or relativist assumptions of the author to reach their own conclusions. The fideist position will retain our attention for a little longer, as it is understandably the position we oppose, by arguing for an anthropology of the moral world and by not surrendering the field of moral descriptions to the philosopher. As an example, let us consider the fideist position of Richard Shweder (1991) when he recounts how the Roop Kanwar case divided the Indian public in the late 1980s. In 1987 in the Sikar district in Rajasthan, an eighteen-year-old educated Rajput woman, Roop Kanwar, immolated herself with the corpse of her dead husband in front of a large audience, thus practising the traditional suttee. The act was considered one of unspeakable beauty and sacredness by the traditionalists, and the place where she immolated herself became a place of pilgrimage. On the contrary, Indian modernist opponents described it as a narrow-minded archaic obedience and asserted that her relatives and the public supporters of suttee had pushed the young woman to death.[6] Who was right and who was wrong? Was the belief which inspired this woman, her belief in love and reincarnation, irrational? Was this really her personal belief? Were the 'modern' thinkers in India entitled to judge a time-honoured tradition and maybe even a personal choice to fulfil a strong belief? Faced with these strikingly different attitudes, Shweder, who declares his admiration for the woman's self-abnegation, decides that her action could not be judged. 'For which world or counterworld should we speak? For they are different and inconsistently so.' (Schweder 1991) The only respectful attitude is silence. While we can accept that the artist surrenders in front of the 'beauty' of the gesture and the moral philosopher takes on judging its moral value, the social scientist has to take on a more positivistic position. Confronted with an event that has triggered a debate cast in terms of right and wrong in the society observed, the anthropologist has to confront facts and discourses, search for reasons behind the actors' positions (be they 'traditional' or 'modern' and 'Westernised'), measure their engagement in the debate and see how opinions are polarised within society. He cannot surrender to his own emotional and/or moral position, but has to account for the complexity of a phenomenon that reveals which beliefs, values and meanings underpin action in another society.

Methodological Choices 1: The Question of Freedom

In the Roop Kanwar case the notion of agency and freedom of choice is central to the debate, for the case divided Indian society into those who considered the woman a victim of her family's traditional beliefs and those who considered her the artisan of her own fate (and compared it to the suicides for love in the Western world). In judging this case, both holist and individualist positions were adopted by members of Indian society, whom we have been accustomed to think of as forming a holist society (Dumont 1985). In his Malinowski Memorial Lecture of 2001, James Laidlaw (2002) has argued for an anthropology of ethics and freedom by showing that we cannot pursue the study of morality and ethics without first analysing the freedom of the individual to choose or not his way of life in a given society (Laidlaw 2002). Freedom is not quantifiable. If absolute freedom is the absence of all constraints, then absolute freedom is already a chimera: physical constraints limit our freedom to fly, to disappear and reappear, etc. Symmetrically, total lack of freedom is unimaginable as well; the individual could be seen as retaining, even under the strongest constraints, a certain degree of freedom to think, hope or breathe. Between these two extremes, where does the individual stand with respect to collective constraints – be they laws or just the collective imaginary? For instance, how much freedom did individuals living in a totalitarian society have? The question was poignantly asked of intellectuals of the ex-Soviet bloc, who were accused of having collaborated with the regime despite their post-1989 claims that they did not approve of its abuses. The existence of a few dissidents brings testimony against the claim that there was no choice endorsing individual moral positions (opposed to that of the regime). Nonetheless, as Yurchak (1997) asserts in the case of the USSR, these dissidents were considered abnormal, somehow outside society – an outsideness which, in a Durkheimian sense, could also mean immorality.

For Laidlaw (2002), Emile Durkheim's wish to found a science of 'moral facts' based on empirical research (as opposed to Kant's science of the moral based on the intellectual speculation of 'practical reason') has been handicapped by his assimilation of the 'collective' with the 'good' (Durkheim 1953[1906]). Society is for Durkheim a moral being qualitatively different from each individual and represents the source of goodness – the individual recognises this superiority and respects societal norms and values, if the latter are coherent and if society manages to integrate most of its members. Laidlaw challenges this simple deterministic Durkheimian relation between society and the individual, in which society dictates the best possible norms and the individual respects them by conviction. He invokes Nietzsche's remark that morality is unnatural to the human being, as it frustrates basic desires: hunger, thirst, sexual appetite. Thus the individual is often exposed to a dilemma about following societal norms or surrendering to his own desires, and his action depends as much on his reasoning as on the freedom he enjoys for reasoning and acting according to it. (The individual could also be in a straightforward opposition to societal norms and values, in pursuit of his own moral model or to satisfy his basic desires.)

This potential individual conflict opens up a whole sphere of investigation for the anthropologist. Its analysis could show how deeply society's values are enshrined within the individual. It could show how individuals with different social positions and from different societies have their own ways of defining their personal values, working through societal constraints, and adopt their own ways of translating beliefs and personal values into action. It could show how the harmonisation of values between individuals takes place, by the confrontation with the others' solutions to moral dilemmas, and how this evolves towards a collective elaboration of values and norms. If this methodological individualism presupposes a certain degree of freedom of choice, if we consider that absolute lack of freedom has no more reality than absolute freedom, it is an assumption that could be easily granted. Being methodological, this individualism does not presuppose the existence of an individualist society; it only requires starting from the individual level in order to understand behaviour. Johan Rasanayagam's chapter in this volume describes the moral reasoning leading an Uzbek intellectual to choose his way of life according to a selection and mixture of several moral models he consciously examines; Helle Rydstrøm's chapter shows how North Vietnamese female teenagers choose how to behave according to the strong ideological moral models present in their society. Obviously, the two categories of individuals did not enjoy the same freedom of choice, due to their differences in age, education, gender and social position; they cannot be agents of their own lives to the same degree. However taking into account their ways of thinking, and in parallel their actions, rather than simply interpreting the ideological moral frame of the countries in which they live, even if this context has obviously shaped their 'personal' convictions, allows the anthropologist to capture the way in which (societal) values are actually embodied.

This methodological choice is clearly reflected in the biographical method proposed by Jarrett Zigon in this volume. Calling his method 'autobiographical' could be considered an improper term, given the dialogic character of the encounter with the anthropologist who triggers and catalyses the biographical narration, being perceived as an audience or even as an external judge. Zigon's chapter is an illustration of the richness of ethical dilemmas, multiple exposures to moral models and influences, strenuous rereading of one's life and reinterpretation of one's actions during lifetime as revealed in a dialogue around the life course of a Russian adult. Accounting for this richness is an important testimony of respect towards the Other and the Other's culture, as his life unfolds in a dimension proper to the social and historical particularities of this culture.

This method emphasises the importance of personal experience in shaping individual values. Indeed, the way in which different 'models' of moral life and public virtues are adopted or rejected by the individual depends on his life experience, with its lived moral dilemmas and personal encounters. The biographical account delivered by the individual feeds in simultaneously at multiple levels of interrogation. First, the way in which the individual presents himself in front of the 'public' (internal or external to his culture) informs us about the real and imagined constraints that the existence of a witnessing public places on individual discourse. The individual reinterprets his past choices and actions so that they can be accepted by the society in which he lives or by the anthropologist to whom he talks (for satisfying this last's expectations, he appeals to his imagination of the Other). Secondly, the way in which the individual presents his past actions reflects his views of a meaningful life. These views are a cultural as much as an individual product and the interplay between the two is not easy to disentangle. Thirdly, the biographical account is also – at times – a true account of the moral choices faced by the individual during his life, but seen through the prism of his present-day values. What can be daunting in the case of biographical narrations is that these multiple levels they inform are not easily separable, which leads us to wonder whether the values phrased are an exercise in rhetoric, a pledge towards society's values or truly endorsed beliefs; a true account of past actions, choices and constraint or a *post facto* justification in line with individual or social expectations. This is why only a parallel and open dialogical confrontation with observed individual actions during social interactions could inform us about the actual values an individual nourishes at the moment of the collection of the autobiographical account.[7]

Methodological Choices 2: The Creativity of Social Interactions

Does methodological individualism with its emphasis on freedom and choice and its implicit presupposition of a clear-cut society/individual dichotomy suit the ethnography of non-individualist societies? Analyses of personhood in non-Western societies have generated a typology that divides societies into three types: individualist, holist and relationist. Clifford Geertz's study of the Balinese and Moroccan societies (1985), Louis Dumont (1985) or Richard Shweder's study of the Indian (1991) and M. Leenhardt's study of the Melanesian society (1947) are just a few classic examples of anthropologists whose ethnographies have led to the establishment of this typology. The lack of awareness of the dichotomy individual/society encountered in holist and relationist societies might be incompatible with the neat and clear dialogue based on negotiation, adoption or resistance between individual and society sketched above. Indeed, if moral values were spontaneously and collectively created in a situated context by members of a community, how could we differentiate between individual and collective values? And should we differentiate them, even given the methodological purpose of describing their 'negotiation'? The individual can be said to act according to his own interpretation/exegesis of social values only if these values are somehow distant from him, have been elaborated prior to his arrival. If these values were constantly elaborated 'with him' and 'for him', his relation to them could hardly be described in terms of negotiation, resistance or acceptance.

In their quest for the origin of moral values, cognitive scientists have paid attention to the results of behavioural economists' experiments on cooperation/collaboration. The experiments provoke situated negotiations of values that show the role of creativity and spontaneity and the importance of context for the establishment of a cooperation that anthropologists often take for granted. Cooperation finally succeeds and is for us the norm, meaning conformity, but at the price of confrontations of contradictory views, negotiations, exchanges. In the course of these complex social interactions, individuals adapt, change their minds, get influenced, assert, transform and get transformed by the others. Individuals are not the blunt supporters of moral principles that could enter in harmony or in contradiction with their 'society'.

> Social life is both rewarding and constricting, our benefits secured at the price of accepting, even embracing limitations and some pain and frustration. These rewards and punishments are epitomised by choices, and in our concomitant expectations that others will make similar choices. These choices of action in turn derive from others, from judgments about what the world is and should be. (Beidelman 1993: 2)

How could anthropologists ethnographically explore this complex interplay of subjectivities that leads to what we term 'morality' in a given cultural context?

The method of moral dilemma elicitation proposed by Thomas Widlok in this volume focuses on the very moment when moral judgement is elaborated. The method consists in proposing several scenarios of moral (and morally neutral) dilemmas and collecting visual and audio material that documents the ways in which the individuals deal with a potential dilemma. Thomas Widlok applies it to the Bushmen of southern Africa, but its universalism goes far beyond the cultural particularities of Bushmen. Inspired by the field methods elaborated in Max Planck Institute to study Psycholinguistics in Nijmegen, the method of moral dilemma elicitation gets round the universalist/relativist debate (a Western moral dilemma might or might not belong to the moral realm of another society according to the holders of one position or the other) by opening the way to the thick description of the moral elicitation. Thus it overcomes a frequent bias (essentially a translation bias) in the study of morality, which is that of presupposing what is subjected to a right/wrong judgement in another society and thus what falls into the moral realm (on the centrality of this question, see also Baumard and Sperber 2007: 6).

The method overcomes another bias in the study of morality, which is that of limiting the field of the moral to explicit moral statements and moral justifications, the so-called 'encoded morality'. While Zigon's method allows us to dig into the outspoken personal interpretations of the moral frames available in one society, Widlok's method allows the capturing of personal unspoken and unconscious moral values, the 'spontaneous ethical demands'. Widlok refers to Løgstrup's theory of 'ethical demand' (1997), which deals with universal aspects of the human condition and human interactions. 'Ethical demands' are silent demands, such as the demand placed on another individual through some basic interactions: asking a question, greeting, turning towards another individual. The person initiating this interaction trusts that he will get a response; the contrary will be a denial of his humanity. The ethical demands of an individual, the spoken as well as the unspoken, should be recognised as his moral values. By triggering spontaneous responses to a (morally problematic) scenario, the method of dilemma elicitation helps to reveal those ethical demands (ethical expectations) that would remain unspoken in the case of a typical post facto interview focused on a morally problematic act.

The analysis based on a corpus of data on dilemma elicitation has another important strength. As the site of the debate around a moral (or morally neutral) issue is the public space and not the private one-to-one dialogue between the anthropologist and the member of another society, we witness in fact an elaboration of collective values, the very elaboration and sharing of community norms. The way in which this is realised informs us about the power relations in a community, the modalities of dialogue, the forms of verbalised reasoning and the response to this reasoning by the audience. It brings us to the core of what it means to share a common value or to apply a certain value to a particular case (the scenario is always phrased in particularistic and not generalising terms).

This method has been designed for cross-cultural comparison and has the advantages of an experimental method – it gives the advantage of triggering and leading to a coherent corpus of data that can be used for comparison. In addition, it has enough flexibility to be adapted to different societies and different research interests, by adjusting translations and scenarios. The information obtained through audio and video recording captures the richness and creativity of moral reasoning 'in action'.

Clashes and Changes of Moral Frames

If the two methods detailed above allowed for a coherent record of moral stances and reasoning, they would remain far from the real actions of an individual if not complemented by the ethnographic observation of contextualised real behaviour. As such, these methods correspond to a set of provoked and punctual instances of moral reasoning, shaped by individuals' life experiences, the moral frames existing in the community and the challenge posed by the particular context of enunciation. But the analysis of moral values underpinning observed behaviour is more difficult, as the anthropologist can not easily determine (nor can the actor accurately express) what are the moral frames within which the actor is evaluating a situation and acting according to this evaluation. This issue is more pronounced at places and times of conflict between several moral frames or of change in moral frames (where the change is often, but not exclusively, the result of a confrontation between several existing moral frames). The chapters by Joel Robbins and Signe Howell invite us to understand moral frames during such encounters. At the same time, these places and times offer more insight into the moral phenomena, the saliency of the 'moral' being enhanced by the conflicting nature of the encounter.

Joel Robbins's account portrays the transformation of moral values following the Christianisation of the Urapmin in Papua New Guinea and shows how the moral system is struck by the radicalism and the complexity of a process that forces (in the long run) the passage from a traditional relationist type of society to a Christian individualistic society. To better understand such a profound change, Robbins elaborates a theory of values that is inspired by Dumont's structuralism but also adopts Weber's awareness of change and conflicts. Louis Dumont's theory of values establishes a hierarchy of values starting from a paramount value that dictates and subsumes 'lesser' values, each of which corresponds to a different domain of social life. While Dumont insists on the rational coherence of values in every domain – a coherence needed to allow non-conflicting actions to take place – Max Weber insists on the insurmountable conflicts existing between different value spheres (1949); these conflicts are typically the 'bread and butter' of the Western moral philosopher. This theoretical frame allows Robbins to analyse the whole chain of conflicts triggered by the Christianisation of the Urapmin. These are dramatic conflicts because they leave the Urapmin with the feeling of being in a permanent situation of sin: unable to act according to their newly found Christian values due to traditional cultural commitments towards another and discordant set of values.

Robbins observes both the discourses (moral enunciations and moral justifications) and practices, which allows him to understand the painful dissonance existing between the two. If practices dictated by the traditional culture were not taken into account, this dissonance would go unobserved and other central practices of the Urapmin (millenarianism, purification trance dances) would not be explained.

The Urapmin's new context is the result of increased globalisation. Globalisation, remarks Signe Howell in her chapter on transnational adoption, has simultaneously produced a need for common values and provoked conflicts of values. The process of local values readjusting in order to meet the requirements of dialogue between cultures, indispensable in global phenomena such as transnational adoption, is slow and is often preceded by the imposition of norms (in the form of governmental laws boosted by international agreements). In the field of childhood (as in many others), the imposed laws are Western laws that follow the evolution of Western values (for instance, the increased emphasis on the 'psy' factor in relation to personhood and citizenship). Signe Howell's chapter shows the way in which several countries, India, Ethiopia, China and Romania, respond to the Western demand for recognition of the special needs of the child. By doing this, she reveals the unequal balance of power between the Western tradition and the others, which depends on each country's availability and need for a dialogue with the West. Howell's chapter also reveals the interplay between norms and values at several levels: international agencies, local governments, Western and local families. The chapter portrays the way in which Western values are reflected in international laws, which lead in turn to local (governments') laws, which will probably end up changing local values – all transformations for the sake of international exchange and dialogue. In an increasingly global world, this mechanism, which is more the result of a certain balance of power rather than a genuine dialogue between different value systems, is frequently reproduced in different domains of social life. Social anthropologists' analyses of moral frames are expected to make an important contribution to understanding this transformation process.

In order to define the field of anthropology of moralities, we show in the first part of this volume the debates, questions and biases that shape the field and propose ways to face or overcome them. Concerning the concrete problems encountered when doing field research on moralities, we underline the difficulty of proceeding to the field with an underdetermined terminology – a consequence of the will to prevent the imposition of the observer's moral prejudices on the observed; the need to observe conflicting or deviant rather than harmonious phenomena – for, in the latter, moral reasoning is more salient; and the need to use methods that elicit moral stances rather than simply waiting for their occurrence – for circumventing the invisibility of the moral. In the second part of this volume, we define the field not by its specific problems and controversies, but by its specific themes: the transmission of moralities, moral obligation and moral responsibility, and the relation between morality and normativity more generally.

Main Themes

The transmission of moral values is the first object of research on morality, in the same way in which socialisation/enculturation remains the first object of research for anthropology: for Geertz, anthropology is primarily concerned with the way in which an individual acquires his cultural specificity (1973). While the question of the origin of the 'moral' interests is addressed by evolutionary anthropologists, social anthropologists are more concerned with the way in which moral values pass from one generation to the other within the same culture, or are borrowed from other cultures in the context of encounters, influences and imposition of values by other cultures. In other words, Geertz is more concerned with the subjectivisation and recreation of moral frames by the individual than with the origin of moral frames at the society level.

This is Johan Rasanayagam's approach to individual morality in this volume. He emphasises the way in which the individual evaluates, selects, adopts or rejects the moral frames available in society instead of simply surrendering to them. Asserting that the individual simply obeys or conforms to the moral frame enforced by the state would have been an easy temptation when referring to contemporary Uzbekistan under the dictatorship of Islam Karimov. But the long-term field observation of the discourses and practices of an experienced *mahalla* leader, Abdumajid-aka, showed how the individual recreates the moral frame of what a virtuous society should be from his own life experience, and acts accordingly. His definition of a moral person and of a moral community is inspired not only by traditional Uzbek values, imposed by Islam Karimov's ideology, but also by socialist values and individualist capitalist values. Abdumajid-aka's position as a leader of the local community entails his ideas of a virtuous society getting translated into local practices, influencing *mahalla* inhabitants' values and moving them away from the moral values imposed by the state. Thus Rasanayagam shows how a (locally influential) elaboration and recreation of values by the individual could spread among community members and succeed in subverting state-imposed ideologies and their influence on ordinary people.

If the *mahalla* leader's freedom of thought allows him to elaborate his own moral model of a virtuous life, the same cannot be so easily asserted about the female teenagers of rural Northern Vietnam observed by Helle Rydstrøm. The social context in Northern Vietnam is comparable to that of Uzbekistan, being characterised by a similar enforcement of moral values during dictatorship and by a similar appeal to traditional (but not overtly religious) values in a socialist/post-socialist context. What make female teenagers more vulnerable to the state ideology regarding sexuality (the field tackled by Helle Rydstrøm) are their gender, age and social position, which traditionally place them also in a situation of obedience towards their families. Girls' discourses betray a weak endorsement of traditional (and state) values but a strong will to behave as if these values were really endorsed, which proves that they do not have the social position that would allow the individual to assert a different view on the matter. Behaving as if these values were endorsed equates the girls with 'good' persons, while a deviant behaviour would mean they are 'bad' persons. The values they really hold appear less important in this context – their self-descriptions point to the importance of their image to be perceived as sensitive persons in relation to their bodies, not their inner beliefs. But in the northern Vietnamese case, as in the Uzbek case, it is not state ideology that dictates the 'good' (i.e. 'conforming') behaviour of the girls, but their concern about not hurting the feelings of their parents and making them lose face in the community.

Rydstrøm contributes with empirical evidence to Nietzsche's earlier-mentioned stance that morality is not natural to the human being. In the field of sexuality, the individual could be torn between moral models and bodily desires. While girls fear that inappropriate sexual behaviour would reflect on them and their families as being 'bad' and even declare their conviction that engaging in premarital sexual relations is not appropriate, they nonetheless happen to become pregnant and thus prejudice their image and their life prospects. In an 'all cultural' model, their behaviour would be considered to be the result of the confrontation between several moral models in which the model 'love before everything' prevails. This model does not seem to be available to Northern Vietnamese girls (no more than the model of protest against communities' values); thus, by freely engaging in sexual behaviour, they violate the models to which they adhere. The 'all cultural' model of explaining moral decisions fails and 'nature' overcomes (Elster 1999, Pharo 2004). The analysis of discourses and practices in fields such as sexuality and addiction forces us to take the bodily dimension into account.

Another bodily dimension that has a role in the successful transmission of moral values is constituted by emotions – complex reactions triggered by an external event that have physiological, neurophysiological, cognitive and motivational aspects. The strength of these reactions and their capacity to induce behavioural change make them a favourite tool in the discursive transmission of moral values. A father might appeal to his son's emotions in order to convince him of the rightfulness or wrongness of his actions. A dictator might use fear to induce certain beliefs. A painter may use his art to deliver a certain message through the emotional solicitation of his viewers.

Patrice Ladwig's case study of the emotional power of the Vessantara-Jataka recitation shows how emotions can be used in a much less didactic way, but with more subtly powerful effects. The story and performance of the Vessantara-Jataka by Lao Buddhist monks testify to certain aesthetic conceptions of sermon making and performances of narratives. Listening to these sermons is another method for lay people to gain merit, wisdom and virtue. The excessive character of the story could be thought to transmit, as in Jesus Christ's story, a hyperbolic model of behaviour. Ladwig's examination of the performance of the Vessantara-Jataka story, which complements the simple consideration of the story's content, leads him to hypothesise that what is actually transmitted in the context of the performance is not a moral model but an ethical ambivalence. This ethical ambivalence, which is a state of painfully awoken moral feelings, forces lay people into moral reasoning and not simply obedience to moral precepts, and, as such, its efficiency is increased. Vessantara's behaviour as recounted in the story provokes awe and admiration and leaves the listeners mystified, unsure about which path to follow, but deeply concerned about what counts as virtuous and what does not.

Karen Sykes's contribution to this volume shows how the transmission of moral values is not unidirectional, but goes along a complex bidirectional path from the keepers of moral virtues to their followers. Her account of the means by which New Irelanders induce moral obligation to the Papua New Guinea government is an example of collective action that uses the invocation of the moral to persuade the government to take upon itself the responsibility of providing social services for Bougainvillean children. They do so by engaging themselves in the virtuous but economically difficult task of adopting Bougainvillean children in order to give them access to social services. The reasoning behind adoption cannot be reduced to an act of persuasion of the Papua New Guinea government and in that respect Karen Sykes's chapter is a clear example of the extended case method and situational analysis in the Manchester tradition. Her chapter fully reveals the complexity of a trade-off, which is played out in moral discursive terms and is actually accompanied by moral actions.

In the last chapter of this volume, Mark Goodale asserts his belief that a different anthropological orientation for the normative can be pursued that combines the peculiar knowledge produced by the ethnographic encounter with normative practices and with knowledge that transcends the empirical data. These two dimensions, which he subsumes under the term 'ethical practice', are mutually and inseparably constitutive: a mere ethnographic understanding of normative practices is necessary but not sufficient, while the theorisation of normativity in such a way as not to be grounded in actual normative practices is merely an intellectual game. His illustration of the conversion of Bolivian moral imagination into concrete political action is the perfect example of the necessary intertwining of facts and theory for indigenous people. By opening up the reflection towards the impact of the moral imagination, Goodale touches on a sensitive point in anthropology: the need to reform the discipline in the context of globalisation of theories and ideas of the 'social' across the world.

Conclusion

Observing, describing and assessing values cross-culturally have given rise to strong methodological concerns, to which the anthropologists contributing to the present volume are giving voice. They are searching for ways in which to objectively identify and describe moral values, to analyse the compliance between discourses on values and practices and to explain the likely inconsistencies between discourse and practice. Contributors to this volume advance new ways of enquiring into the social construction of vices and virtues, the moral construction of sexuality, moral models and public rhetoric, local custom and transnational legislation. Their analyses are based on long-term field research in societies spreading from Europe to Melanesia and from South-east Asia to South America. Moreover, their analyses reflect a thorough engagement with the theoretical foundations of anthropology.

Is legislation the codification of morality? Is radical moral change possible? Is morality always a plural code of conduct? While addressing such questions with evidence provided by diverse and rich ethnography, the contributors to the volume elaborate the concept of moralities, employ new tools of investigation and propose solutions to issues and challenges that we hope will guide future research on the topic.

Notes

1. This edited volume has gradually replaced the only older explicit anthropological reference to the field of morality, Edel and Edel's *Anthropology and Ethics* (1968[1959]).
2. The fact that in Mongol there is no term that could be translated by 'morality' does not prevent Humphrey from identifing in Mongolian culture the field of moral discourses by looking at 'the evaluation of conduct in relation to esteemed or despised human qualities' (1997: 25).

3. A word that has several meanings is polythetic. Each pair, but not all meanings, has something in common: if meanings A and B are close, and meanings B and C are close, it is not necessarily true that A and C are close too. We can follow the analysis and difficulties encountered with a polythetic word in *Belief, Langage and Experience* (Needham, 1972), where the author explores the various meanings of the word 'belief' and decides that, in order to understand various forms of 'belief', one has to content oneself with the different phenomena introduced by the utterance 'I believe (that/in etc.)'.

4. Hauschild (2005) analyses how the American Anthropological Association was at first heavily engaged in the elaboration of the UN Declaration of Human Rights in 1946 and later abandoned this endeavour as not falling into their area of expertise – the rights defended by the declaration being individual and not collective/cultural.

5. In the philosophical/anthropological debate, rationality was intentionally discussed as much as possible off the field of *Homo economicus*, which had been amply investigated by economists and sociologists.

6. The case triggered the adoption by the central government of the Commission of Sati (Prevention) Act in 1987 and the prosecution of a dozen people, finally acquitted in 2004. The elaboration of a new legal act and the pursuit of suspects in court shows how moral values and social norms determine each other in society.

7. As Russia is a country that has undergone radical social and cultural changes in recent years, the historical moment when the interview was collected should also be taken into account.

Chapter 2

Norm and Spontaneity: Elicitation with Moral Dilemma Scenarios

Thomas Widlok

Introduction

Anthropology has a long record of comparing 'the mores and customs' in different places and of discovering specific moral biases in European thought (Widlok 2004a). Debates about cultural relativism and universalism are regularly (re)fuelled by the comparative ethnography of morality (Moody-Adams 1997).

However, the particular biases that an anthropology of morality faces are not only the misrepresentations of 'distant' forms of moral behaviour on the basis of specific norms and values of the observer (e.g. nationalism, liberalism or Eurocentrism). They are in a sense more general and more fundamental biases, such as blindness towards 'morality in action', the exaggeration of the importance of codified morality or the overemphasis of moral justifications in discussions of morality. Similar biases have been identified in other domains of anthropological enquiry. Gell has pointed out how a focus on art as the culturally relative standards of aesthetics has sidetracked a view that investigates the social agency of artworks (Gell 1998). Ingold has shown how a systematic bias on human skills as mental programmes requires to be redressed through a more balanced view of skills as being internal to the patterned movements of practitioners (Ingold 2000).

All these biases come at a cost. In this contribution I shall give examples of the costs involved in prevalent biases in the study of morality, I shall suggest some alternative theoretical and methodological approaches and outline new terms of analysis that may be gained through this mode of 'rethinking morality'. The region on which I draw in this contribution is the ethnography of southern African hunter-gatherer groups, commonly known as 'Bushmen' or 'San' but I maintain that the argument applies more generally across ethnographic regions.

Systematic Biases

Across regions there is a systemic bias in the anthropology of morality that exaggerates the importance of codified morality and overemphasises moral justifications. Even the classic textbook on 'anthropology and ethics' (Edel and Edel 1968) does not fully adhere to the productive programme of research set out by the authors, namely that of 'casting a wide net' when delimiting morality and ethics as a subject domain for anthropological research (Edel and Edel 1968: 12). It is remarkable that anthropologists have decided to focus on norm codification and on moral justifications, thereby following the main trend in neighbouring disciplines such as philosophy (see, for example, Ott 2001). They have rather narrowly concentrated on 'what people say when pressed about their judgements... what justifications they use' (Edel and Edel 1968: 16–17). Morality and ethics were thereby largely reduced to the investigation of *post facto* justifications and moreover to the systematic codification of these justifications in sets of prevalent norms.

When redressing this bias, there is more at stake than a legitimate focus and delimitation of a research area. Social systems differ in the degree to which they cultivate or require moral justification and codification. Misrepresentations regularly occur when there are less codification and elaborate justification than are expected. With regard to southern Africa numerous illustrations for this are to be found, for instance, in the work of Heinrich Vedder, an influential missionary and ethnologist who worked among 'Bushmen' at the beginning of the twentieth century. Vedder had a strong interest in morality and ethnic norms and seems to have been generally sympathetic to the subjects of his research. However, the forms of moral behaviour he dealt with were clearly 'distant' to him, primarily because they did not comply with European expectations of a moral *code*. In order to fill this 'lacuna', he saw his role, and the role of the ethnographer more generally, in providing the justification and in constructing the codification and rational justification that the 'Bushmen' could not or would not give. The result is a gross misrepresentation and denigration of the moral behaviour that he observed and represented in his writings. Addressing the white settler community in Namibia, he begins by defending an academic interest in the ethical dimension of 'Bushman' life:

> 'Ethical sentiments of the Bushmen!' Is it right to present an article about this? ... Naturally, it will not cross anyone's mind to write a doctoral thesis about this. That is not necessary, anyway. But if 'doctor' means nothing else than 'teacher', then anyone dealing with Bushmen [...] will contribute towards fitting the Bushmen in with the useful full human beings." (Vedder 1942: 97, my translation)

He then goes on to find traces in Bushman life of what he (or his audience) consider to be key human virtues of 'full human beings', namely gratitude, devotion, friendship, respect for property, thriftiness, religious sentiments, compassion, vindictiveness, honour/shame, and orderliness/cleanliness (Vedder 1942: 83ff.)[1] The culmination of his efforts, and at the same time an extreme case of exaggerating the importance of codified morality, is his attempt to formulate 'The ten commandments of the Bushman', which read as follows:

1. Be faithful to your parents
2. Be faithful to your spouse
3. Do bride service
4. Avoid your mother-in-law
5. Don't eat meat prohibited to you
6. Don't threaten an elder
7. Don't steal from another Bushman
8. Hide your cut-off hair from sorcerers
9. Bury your blood so that the dogs don't lick it
10. Don't point to a grave with your finger
(Vedder 1942: 19–20, my translation)

The main problem with this representation is not that there would be no correspondence to these rules in the attitudes or behaviour of 'Bushpeople' but that through such a compilation the readers are led to conclude that these people lacked a true correspondence to the ten commandments and had a deficient system of ethical attitudes and behaviour – and therefore needed to adopt the ethical canon suggested by the European missionaries.

Although Vedder's explicit interest is an 'applied' comparison between different moral behaviours, and translating and mediating between them wherever possible, he bases it on a comparison of ethical codes, which he had to distil for the 'San' since they apparently had not elaborated such a code themselves. To some extent, therefore, he complies with the distinction between 'descriptive ethics' (morals as social facts) and 'normative ethics' (reflecting between moralities), which is one of the basic and most widely cited analytical distinctions made by moral philosophers. But even at this level of basic distinctions there are costs involved, for instance that of overemphasising the difference between ethics and morality at the cost of distinguishing between moralism and the perception of concrete moral phenomena. This argument was developed by Knut Løgstrup (1989: 59–60), who distinguished between 'moralism' as any claim that is considered to be (or claimed to be) ethical because it is in concordance with a moral principle, and 'concrete moral phenomena', which come into play when pursuing the explication of the situation and the relations between persons involved. But, before I turn to the details of his argument, consider the following illustration, which is a hypothetical dialogue or scenario, a mode of representing arguments about morality to be commented on in the second half of this contribution. In the two following dialogues, entirely imaginary, professors are discussing the distribution of research money to associate researchers. In the first dialogue professor A's strategy is one of moralism, of invoking moral principles, whereas in the second dialogue professor B's strategy is one of foregrounding the concrete relationship and the obligations arising from it as a moral phenomenon:

A: I shall give researcher X half of this research money.

C: Why?

A: I promised.

C: Why stick to the promise?

A: Because one ought to keep one's promises.

C: Why?

A: Because it is a principle we should all adhere to.

B: I shall give researcher X half of this research money.

C: Why?

B: I promised.

C: Why stick to the promise?

B: X needs the money to continue his valuable work.

C: He could try to get it elsewhere.

B: But he wants to be at this intellectually stimulating institute.

C: Well, you worry too much about a single researcher.

B: But he counts on me and I don't want to jeopardise his trust and our relationship.

Note that the difference here is at the level of discourse, i.e. it is not a matter of contrasting narrative with behaviour. However, if we consider moral narrative and rhetoric as a mode of behaviour then the two short dialogues represent two different behavioural responses to the same problem or prompt (namely colleague C, who seems to question whether the money should be granted to the research associates at all). We may even go further by saying that there is a widely held bias that considers the first dialogue to represent a more prototypical ethical or moral response, because it refers back to principles of behaviour.

The combined effect of such systematic biases as those outlined in this section is that too much attention is paid to 'the daily bath of moralism' (Løgstrup 1989: xiii) while not enough attention is given to the ways in which ethnographic situations demand moral action from participants. In the following section, I shall suggest a theoretical and a methodological response for dealing with these biases. I suggest that by introducing new theoretical distinctions and by using moral dilemma elicitation as a method we can expand our ethnographic repertoire and redress the biases as spelled out above. The theoretical inspiration is drawn from the phenomenological philosophy of Knut Løgstrup and the methodological inspiration is drawn from the research toolkit of the Language and Cognition Group, formerly the Cognitive Anthropology Research Group (CARG) in Nijmegen. Behind each of these inspirations is a long tradition, that of phenomenological thought and of narratives dealing with moral dilemmas. The two sources base themselves on separate strands of research with independent origins and histories. Løgstrup made his theoretical arguments with examples drawn from European literature, not comparative ethnography. The researchers of CARG worked under a natural science-oriented analytical framework, not a phenomenological approach. In other words, readers with reservations regarding phenomenological theory may still find the methods suggested here to be productive for their own purposes and the same applies to those with reservations regarding comparative methods of elicitation. At the same time, I do think that the combination suggested here would help to improve both the methodological repertoire of phenomenological approaches and the reflective basis for a methodology centred on narratives and discourse. Moreover, I suggest that this combination promises to put the anthropology of morality in a good position for actively contributing to this interdisciplinary field and to develop a genuine anthropological approach instead of merely copying what other disciplines have suggested.

Basic Theoretical Distinctions

Before turning to the method of moral dilemma elicitation some theoretical considerations are in order lest the moral narratives under investigation here are confused with the moral scenarios commonly found in scholarly discussions of morality. The philosophy of morality, like popular discourse about ethical matters regularly uses (supposedly) real-life scenarios that are, however, not real in the ethnographic sense in that they are only used as illustrations and in that they are deemed interesting not because of the intricacies of real life but because they relate to a distinction or dilemma in philosophical reflection, i.e. they are used in a generalising mode of argument. The tacit assumption here is that morality issues in everyday practice follow – in a somewhat watered-down version – the idealised logic of philosophical reflections. From an anthropological point of view this assumption cannot be taken for granted, but the everyday practice does deserve to be investigated in its own right and not as an illustrative shadow of philosophical arguments. In a first step towards this aim, Løgstrup's distinction between generalising and universalising is promising (Løgstrup 1989). He argues that reservations with regard to a ready generalisation from a single case to all cases or to philosophical arguments and vice versa should not be confused with an argument against universalist assumptions.

Logstrup points out that there can be universalisation, the expectation that ethical rules apply without 'respect of person', without generalising from the single case into a rule that fits all cases categorised into a certain 'type' of situation, with its respective 'types' of ethical responses. Without curtailing the claim for universality, but without generalising either, it is possible to find out more details about the particulars of the moral situation in an attempt to come to an appropriate solution or response. The response found can still be rendered universal in the sense that any person under exactly these particular conditions would be expected to behave in a certain way. But the decision is not made on the grounds of a generalising operation, or through trying to find a general rule that would fit the situation, but through a particularising operation, by gaining more insights into the situation without singularising the case (see the infanticide scenario below). The following conceptual distinctions contribute towards this argument.

Spontaneous Demands and Encoded Morality

I have argued above that there is an imbalance in the attention given to encoded morality as opposed to what may be called 'spontaneous' ethical demands. What are the implications of this distinction? The term spontaneity in this context should not be associated with 'short-livedness' or 'contingency'. In Løgstrup's theory of morality these properties are more appropriately given to moral codes, historically contingent as they are, while the 'spontaneous' ethical phenomena are in fact based on a universal and continual aspect of the human condition and of all human interaction which he calls 'the ethical demand' (Løgstrup 1997). The basic ethical demand is a 'silent demand' in so far as it is not a formulated requirement but rather a given moral dimension of all human interaction. The interaction and relatedness on which all human life depends are based on the trust (or the demand) that the interactant, the other person I speak to or write for, will be willing to listen or read. The demand is that of turning towards, or not turning away from, someone who has addressed me through his actions, words or mere presence. The life of humans is generally so intertwined and dependent on one another's co-presence and cooperation that they constantly pose such 'silent' demands on one another, between generations and among peers alike. The presence of these demands are most strongly felt when the demand is met with a refusal, which in most cases would amount to a breakdown of communication and interaction. This breakdown is also the ultimate sanction faced by those who do not meet the demand. The advantage of this conception of 'spontaneous moral action' for ethnography is that it does not presuppose an elaborate or systematic moral code when investigating morality and ethics, while it is fundamentally grounded in social relationships.

There are, of course, also ethical demands that are not given, or silent, but which are arranged, proposed and made explicit in interaction. For instance, I may want others not only to listen to my words or to acknowledge my presence but also to take specific action as a consequence, such as buying my book, voting for me in an election or adopting my own political agenda. Løgstrup points out that, although both kinds of demands may be called ethical, the second type, that of an encoded morality, is derived from the first, the universal ethical demand of human interaction, and not vice versa. Overemphasising the importance of encoded morality is therefore also a misrepresentation of the sources of ethical behaviour, which Løgstrup sees as accessible not through the codes but through the phenomena of intertwined human existence. The question as to whether others comply with an encoded demand or not is predicated on one's skills and are a matter of individual achievement, while compliance with the spontaneous demand or trust in accepting one's co-presence or listening to one's words are ultimately enshrined in the phenomenon itself, a position known as 'moral realism'.

Predicates and Phenomena

How are we to distinguish the moral or ethical from any other dimension of behaviour, or how do we distinguish virtue from skill, if moral codification is not our starting point? In Løgstrup's moral realism, the occurrence of predicates such as 'ought' or 'must' or, indeed, 'good' or 'bad' is not in itself a promising guide for identifying what is moral or ethical. We are better advised to begin with the phenomena themselves and to see to what extent they enable or disenable the potentials of responding to the ethical demand intrinsic in human interaction. The advantage for ethnography, again, is that we do not presuppose an elaborated or systematic code as the source of moral behaviour and in fact we do not presuppose a process of encoding in language at all. Moral philosophers have tended to argue intensively about the terms 'good' or 'ought', a discussion that has its limits when it comes to cross-linguistic analysis but more severely when attempting to discuss moral behaviour when particular acts are not clearly marked in relation to these predicates. The phenomena themselves, whether they are named or not, need to be moved into the centre of the investigator's attention, as, arguably, they have always been from the point of view of the social agents who deal with them. Moreover, there are further implications with regard to the key anthropological contribution to the discussion of morality and ethics to date, namely that of moral relativism. If phenomena themselves are given some 'sovereignty' over the possible predicates and descriptions that may be made of them, then the issue of moral relativism that has fuelled, but also paralysed, anthropological contributions can be given a productive turn. Instead of enquiring about the meanings of predicates such as 'good' in changing contexts we begin to enquire about the properties of a phenomenon and its relevance in social relationships.

Sovereign Descriptions and Sovereign Phenomena

One of Løgstrup's example cases is a comparison between the phrases 'This letter box is yellow' and 'This man is meek' (Løgstrup 1989: 73). From a strict formal point of view the two phrases may be seen in absolute parallel since a noun (letter-box, man) is being attributed some predicate (being yellow, being meek). The descriptive form is near identical but the phenomena are very different. We may add to this example by recalling that cognitive anthropology has shown that languages have some scope in deciding whether something is called 'yellow' as opposed to 'green' or 'green-yellow' (d'Andrade 1995: 106ff.). There are, however, also limits as to where conventions draw the boundaries between colours. With regard to meekness (or trust, truthfulness, etc.) Løgstrup, and probably many anthropologists, would argue that we do not have the same sovereignty in our description, i.e. we are not completely free to draw boundaries here. The phenomena of meekness and trust resist misrepresentation to some extent. These are not neutral or passive 'things' to which any attribute can be assigned. To be sure, meekness or trust may be considered wrong, or not advisable, in some cases where the circumstances are such that others may take advantage of that meekness or trust by abusing it. However, these are exceptions and they are marked as exceptions on the basis of what is considered to be intrinsically good in meekness and trust, namely that it is supportive to human life and cooperation. Or, in terms of the distinctions already introduced above, there may be encoded recommendations, for example, for mistrust, but that does not change the intrinsic relation between trust as a response to the intrinsic ethical demand of human social interaction. The intricacies of a concrete situation of interaction may require being less trusting in some cases and in certain circumstances than in others, but this does not change the fact that the phenomenon trust resists some representations (for instance, that it would be generally damaging to human relations). In other words, as an observer of ethical phenomena, I am not completely sovereign, just as social agents are not completely sovereign in their morality under the premises of moral realism.

Moreover, observer and agent are ultimately in the same boat; they share enough common ground for ethical debate, for instance about the question as to when the circumstamces are such that one should not be trusting. Despite the possibility of radically different moral codes and conventions, there is therefore always the possibility of a shared common ground, and of negotiating these codes, based on the fact that human interaction and social life rely on a mutual demand (for trust, etc.). The separate worlds of moral codes do not in any immediate way reflect separate life worlds of social agents and of observers. Moral relativism in this view does not make understanding and negotiation impossible. Even awareness about the fact that norms are variable across time and space does not make them less imperative for the social agents who, due to their sociocultural embeddedness, do not have the power to simply 'switch' norms or to escape the conflicts they create (Løgstrup 1997: 100ff.). The approach taken here closes the gap between cultural worlds, without negating them, by invoking the shared world of phenomena. It also closes the gap between agent and observer since both ultimately face the same challenge.

We may now turn to the method of ethical dilemma elicitation, which is designed not for eliciting diverging moral codes but for eliciting different modes of reasoning about ethical phenomena. The basic concepts of moral realism, outlined above, do not deny the existence of moral disagreements. Rather, given that social agents occupy different positions in interaction, it is to be expected that this will lead to disputes around ethical demands, with diverging judgements about a certain situation and the appropriate response to it. Therefore the elicitation aims to render visible the ways in which particular situations are perceived and the ways in which they are reflected upon in terms of moral relations between humans.

The Method of Moral Dilemma Elicitation

Case situations or scenarios occupy a particular space in Western philosophical and public discourse. It is their single but rather clear-cut purpose to illustrate dilemmas of philosophical reflection. There is an implicit assumption of homology between case logic and reflective logic and there is an implicit or explicit judgement that transcending the individual case through generalisation is a superior mode of ethical behaviour.[2] However, there are other ways of using such dilemma situations for elicitation which are more open-ended, namely those developed in the linguistic tradition of using 'staged communicative events' in research. The methods described below take their initial inspiration from a toolkit for field research developed by the MPI Language and Cognition Group in Nijmegen (www.mpi.nl). The toolkit which has cumulatively brought together ideas for cross-cultural linguistic research has a section, developed primarily by Gunter Senft, entitled 'Reasoning in Language'. In its 2002 version of this field manual, Senft suggests six dilemmas for comparative research, introducing them in the following way:

> This project aims to investigate how speakers of various languages in indigenous cultures verbally reason about moral issues. The ways in which a solution for a moral problem is found, phrased and justified will be taken as the basis for researching reasoning processes that manifest themselves verbally in the speakers' arguments put forward to solve a number of moral problems which will be presented to them in the form of unfinished story plots or scenarios that ask for a solution. The plots chosen attempt to present common problems in human society and human behaviour. They should function to elicit moral discussion and/or moral arguments in groups of consultants of at least three persons. (Senft 2002)

Here is the original set of scenarios (described in more detail below in the Appendix):

- The abandoned and re-found child scenario. A dilemma in which discussions may be expected along the lines of the nature/nurture debate, i.e. whether children who grow up elsewhere are still considered 'proper' children with all rights and duties in their natal family.

- The chiefly authority scenario. A dilemma of weighing the authority of a chief against a pragmatic solution independently found by a subordinate agent.

- The troublesome partner scenario. The question of weighing commitment to a partner who him/herself is deceitful.

- The cheating rich man scenario. A question of how to deal with the abuse of trust and power.

- The lost son scenario. The question also raised in the Bible, about equal treatment and justice between a son who stayed with a family and a son who had been away.

- The infanticide scenario. The dilemma between saving the life of one child or the lives of the mother and the child's older siblings.

- The stealing out of hunger scenario. The question as to what extent pressing needs are allowed to overrule what is otherwise forbidden.

- The food for life scenario. The dilemma of sacrificing one life for many.

As Senft points out, researchers are encouraged to create more culture-specific scenarios of their own choosing, 'representing a moral dilemma based on the particularities of the local community' (Senft 2002). This may be based on a real event. To allow for comparability, these culture-specific scenarios should complement the above list of 'cross-cultural scenarios' (Senft 2002). The aim is to compare the moral discussions collected in response to all these scenarios.

For the purposes of my own field research I decided to allow for cultural diversity not primarily by adding a culturally specific scenario but by compiling a set of scenarios that would systematically vary around some of the underlying assumptions: first the notion of morally loaded scenarios versus scenarios without moral implications (from a Western philosophical perspective), secondly, the notion of a dilemma situation versus a less restrictive problematic situation, and, thirdly, with reference to one specific domain, namely land rights issues, creating a total of six scenarios.

Thus, in this set, for each moral scenario there is a non-moral one, for each land-related scenario there is a non-land-related ones etc., and within these two clusters all possible combinations of the dimensions dilemma and morality are contained. The idea behind this scheme is to be able to relate responses (and response patterns) across these scenarios within a single corpus of elicited narratives, independently of larger comparisons. Elicitation of all six scenarios was initially carried out with four discussion groups of =Akhoe Hai//om speakers (an all-male group, an all-female group and two mixed groups). I shall provide some of the results for a particular moral scenario, the infanticide dilemma, and compare them with the results gained using a non-moral dilemma situation (the snake-on-the-road dilemma).

Results of Moral Dilemma Elicitation in the Field

The discussion sessions that emerged from the narrative prompts were recorded on digital video and will be made available to researchers and the community of speakers as part of a multi-media archive (see www.mpi.nl/DOBES). Although video recording may in some settings not be acceptable to the speakers, the case at hand shows that it adds a whole dimension to the more traditional modes of recording such as audio or written records. Across all =Akhoe Hai//om instances an interactive style of reasoning about these problems emerged which in itself should be considered to be an integral part of the mode of (moral) reasoning. To begin with, the style was non-confrontational. Even though not all persons involved came up with the same comments or solutions to the problem, no confrontational argument evolved, contrary to what one might have expected given the seriousness and intricacy of the subject matter. No heated debate occurred with interruptions or other attempts to 'take the floor' from another speaker. Instead, echoing was the dominant mode of debate. Frequently, the narrative itself was retold by one or more of the participants, often adding more elements than were contained in the original prompt. As the discussion continued, echoing would also continue with participants repeating a phrase or part of the phrase uttered by previous speakers and by complementing their speech. For instance, one speaker would quote in direct speech one of the persons of the story, while another would add a phrase that frames direct speech, such as 'ti ra mi' ('it was said like this'). There is a striking resemblance here to the culturally specific storytelling style that has been documented for ≠Akhoe Hai//om folk tales (Widlok 2006).

The elaborate forms of concerted turn-taking in retelling the story are reinforced by mimicking the agents of the story which not only helps to make the situation 'come alive' but which also adds elements to the story. A summative transcript cannot capture this mimicry adequately but it shows the efforts of the speaker not to abstract from the situation but, on the contrary, to add more particulars that may help to solve the problem or at least to come to a grounded opinion about it.

Infanticide Dilemma

The infanticide dilemma that I used as a prompt is that of a woman who gives birth to a weak child in the bush and wonders whether to kill it because there was insufficient food for her other children and the newborn would make things even more difficult:

> There was a woman who had given birth to many children already, and she was pregnant again. But she had no food. She gave birth to her child in the bush, but the child was very small and weak. She thought that maybe she should kill the child because there was no food for all her children, and if this child would stay alive, all of them would suffer from hunger, the woman, her husband and their other children. What do you think the woman did?

The story of this dilemma was taken over almost unchanged from the original MPI set of scenarios, firstly because it seems to be particularly good for comparative purposes but also because infanticide is said to have been practised among San groups in southern Africa (as in many other hunter-gatherer groups). Since I had previously collected reports from ≠Akhoe Hai//om acknowledging infanticide 'in the old days' and had heard rumours about it happening at present, the chances were that a pro-infanticide position would be adopted by some discussants. In my version of the scenario I added that the woman gave birth in the bush since infanticide seems to have been only possible as part of a general practice and ideal of mothers giving birth unassisted by any others (Biesele 1997), so that she could in fact take a decision for infanticide but claim that the child was born dead or died shortly after the birth. In other words, since there is not, and probably never was, any public debate about this matter in practice, it could be expected that some debate might arise between men and women (as well as between older and younger women) on this issue when discussing the scenario, since the women might defend it as part of their self-determination while the men, who have a strong intrinsic interest in having and raising children (Hewlett 1991), might criticise it. However, in none of the four groups who were presented with the infanticide dilemma did any controversial discussion of the matter occur. There was acknowledgement that infanticide did indeed occur and that in that sense this was a realistic story worth discussing. The main strategy for discussing the dilemma, however, was not to accept it as a dilemma but rather to turn it into a problem. The problem could be dealt with if one were to insert oneself into the situation. Alternatively, it was felt that the situation remained difficult or impossible to resolve not due to it being an inescapable dilemma but due to a lack of adequate information – given that one was not able to be fully immersed in the situation on the premise of the ideal of unassisted/unaccompanied birth. Here is the comment of a young woman (who has two children herself):

> The baby does not have anything to drink and to eat. But you have got that baby … and you must try and feed him this water from the bush which you get from roots so that the baby can grow up. The baby is not chewing so that you must make things soft because it just swallows what you give to him. This way it will get some strength to put something in his stomach and become a person like us. You must struggle to give him food so that he can get energy and grow fast... As I think about that woman, we just don't know whether she killed the baby herself or not or maybe the woman did not have the strength to have that baby.

Note that the route towards utilitarian calculation of one life against another, which was planted in the original scenario, was not embarked upon (neither by this consultant nor by any of the others). Although there are indications from other contexts, for instance from funerals, that the loss of an adult or old person is considered more severe that that of a newborn child that may not have been given a name, such a calculation or ranking of lives did not occur in any of the debates I recorded in response to the infanticide dilemma. It seems that the life of a child, or any human, is considered to be so fundamental that it was excluded from calculations. This is so despite the fact that homicide does occur, and in fact probably occurs more often today than in the past. In other words, it is not the case that killings of these sorts are unthinkable or are always sanctioned from within the society. Rather, it is the conversion of the abstracted value of one life into another that people refuse to make.

The overall strategy that emerges from many of the transcription is that the situatedness of agents is being accounted for, hypotheses are being developed about the circumstances, the motives and the possible further developments arising from the story. Instead of relating the story to abstract rules and values, it is related to the concrete situation of those who are discussing the issue. They do not aim for an impartial view by taking themselves out of the picture but rather reflect by putting themselves into the picture in the double sense of the word. Despite this positioning with reference to the persons in the story there is little confrontational positioning. Rather, the sentiment seems to be that by immersing oneself as much as possible into the situation described, it will be obvious what the right thing to do would be. The discussion of moral issues here seems not to be categorically different from the everyday talk of decision-making among =Akhoe Hai//om. Here, too, decisions are commonly not made by arguing, weighing arguments or counting votes but by raising a host of points to be considered, which are then either echoed and repeated by others or dropped. Decisions for moving camp, for instance, come about in this manner. There is no formal debate with an agenda and a vote but the persons concerned will drop comments on the bad state of the current place (in terms of dirt, lack of resources, quarrels, etc.) and the desirable state of another place (in terms of availability of resources, etc.). As more and more comments of this kind are made and picked up by others it becomes clear whether (and by whom and when) there will be a move. It should therefore be instructive to see whether this pattern also holds with a scenario that in our view has no immediate moral implications (the snake-on-the-road dilemma).

The Snake-on-the-road Dilemma

The snake-on-the-road dilemma presents the listeners with the dilemma of a choice between a short but potentially dangerous route (a snake has been reported to be on that route) and a safer but longer route:

A family wanted to visit a cattle post to collect some food. One of the workers told them: 'Do not go through the bush, last time there was a snake in that area, take the car route'. But the family responded: 'The car route is a much longer way. If we take that we won't get to the post before sunset.' What do you think the family did?

The expectation was that there would be a negotiation between the avoidance of the snake and of a long road. The first thing to note when looking at the responses is that, although this dilemma was categorised as a 'non-moral' problem, it readily took on a moral dimension due to the fact that in the story another person is making a recommendation (which road to take) and is providing some information. Responses regularly questioned the motives of the person in the story, namely whether one could rely on his word, what the chances are of being lied to and what ulterior motives the other person may have. The recommendation of the person in the story did not, to my mind, when formulating the scenario, have a moral dimension to it, at least not a problematic one. From an ≠Akhoe Hai//om perspective, in contrast, the 'recommendation' as to which path to take was clearly verging on interference with personal autonomy, which is generally valued very highly. In a sense the inverse happened here in comparison with the infanticide dilemma which was meant to be clearly morally loaded but which was conceived of largely in practical terms of where to find food for a child under difficult circumstances. This supports the view that it is productive to cast a wide net, when setting up the anthropological agenda of investigating 'the moral'.

Despite this moral implication, the snake-on-the-road dilemma also regularly produced very different responses as to what people would or should do in such a situation (as did the other 'non-moral' problems). Although the majority said that they would go for the short road, their rationalisations covered a wide spectrum. Responses were to some extent informed by the local knowledge that snakes can cross your path everywhere, not only where they have previously been reported, and that they are mobile so that the chances are that the particular snake reported may not be there any more. For instance, one old woman responded: "Maybe that road has a snake he said. But if the snake is there than you don't have to worry if you believe in God: then that snake will go the other way. A middle-aged woman, commented on this in the following way":

I am thinking deeply and I think of something else. It is good to think like Granny. It is good but I am still thinking something [else]. On the main road there is no snake but on the footpath there is one. Then I shall walk with a dog so that the dog – if we do meet a snake – will fight the snake and I can get away in the meantime.

This response shows not only a creative extension of the problem, and an ingenious solution, but also the same tendency noted earlier that a solution is sought by adding more details and particulars rather than by abstracting from the situation. The first response shows that abstract responses do occur but that on the whole these are considered 'short cuts', which are not really satisfactory. Furthermore, in this, as well as in other cases, the strategy of expressing dissatisfaction with a solution suggested by someone else is not to engage in a hostile debate that seeks to establish the right solution in terms of an abstract principle (or as being derived from such a principle) but rather a morality of listening, of taking the other contribution seriously but without refraining from adding to it. Tolerance for heterodoxy is high in ≠Akhoe Hai//om society, as it is connected with a strong sense of personal autonomy in all matters. At the same time there is little respect or regard for accepting for oneself what someone else has suggested. Young people contradict old people, and women contradict men (and vice versa) by simply adding their view and their solution to the problem as another layer to a problem that takes on more and more detail as it is being discussed and as one moves from one situation to another.

Towards New Terms of Analysis

The method of moral dilemma elicitation that I have introduced in this contribution is, above all, a means for generating data on specific cultural systems of morality. The claim is that it redresses some of the systematic biases spelled out in the anthropology of morality to date and that it is therefore capable of producing a large spectrum of ethical phenomena and in a way that invites comparative study.

The question that remains is what other insights this case study may provide in the larger endeavour to rethink morality as set out in the workshop from which this volume arose. In conclusion I suggest that the combined theoretical and methodological approach introduced here leads us towards new terms of analysis and a reformulation of existing ones.

Modality of Moral Discourse

The methodology suggested here not only provides more information than a non-multimedia record would provide. More fundamentally it draws our attention to the modality of moral discourse. The record of ≠Akhoe Hai//om responses that I have introduced above not only establishes that mimicry, echoing and enlivening through impersonation are important elements of the local cultural heritage but also re-emphasises the performative dimension of all moral discourse. In other words, in moral discourse it is particularly clear that 'the how is part of the what'. Moral values are expressed not only in concepts but also in the practices of communication themselves. One could go even further by saying that cross-cultural communication about moral issues is possible not because of a core set of values found everywhere but rather on a shared level of meta-communication about moral matters. The shared acceptance of modalities of moral discourse allows us to agree that we disagree and to communicate morality across contexts (Moody-Adams 1997).

The use of moral scenarios or narratives for elicitation is therefore not just another way of 'getting at the data' but seems to tap into a shared repertoire of human interaction. Not all groups may readily accept the narrated scenarios introduced here in the same way as the ≠Akhoe Hai//om do, who themselves tell stories, adapt them and respond to them in their everyday life. However, dealing with moral issues in terms of stories about cases, whether exemplary and idealised or particular and drawn from personal memory, seems to be spread widely enough to make this a productive method for cross-cultural comparison. Methodologically these videotaped semi-structured discussions are halfway between externally controlled elicitation tasks or experiments and the free recording of natural conversation or interaction. This has the great advantage that we can gain results that are equally relevant with regard to both the ethnography of a certain domain (e.g. morality or land) and comparative issues of discourse and cognition. In my examples, the tool has provided insights into key moral issues that today preoccupy the ≠Akhoe Hai//om (e.g. moneylending, dealing with authorities, sharing under conditions of food shortage) but also into issues that preoccupy comparative anthropologists and linguists (e.g. turn-taking, evidentiality, logic of arguments, heterodoxy, context).

Virtuosity and Creativity of Moral Thought

The examples given above underline the creative solutions that ≠Akhoe Hai//om seek when confronted with moral dilemmas or problems. Again, this may be noted in terms of the local cultural style, which puts heavy weight on individual autonomy and ingeniousness and fosters such 'heterodox' solutions and lateral thinking in decision-making and problem-solving. Beyond this case study it is important to note that the low degree of standardization of group discussions as an elicitation tool gives room for this kind of individual inventiveness and provides a means for capturing it. The same holds for the theoretical groundwork that re-emancipates this kind of 'moral spontaneity' in the face of encoded moral knowledge and prescriptions. Looking beyond the ≠Akhoe Hai//om case, this widens the question of what constitutes the domain of 'the moral' in an appropriate way.

The question as to how to recognise morality when it is encountered is a flippant one only to those who think that the phenomenon of morality is exhausted by a description of ethical orthodoxy and of the (self-) imposed codes of conduct that abound. In particular anthropologists working in the field of societies that are not highly stratified and literate have reasons to think that there is more to it. The proclamation of a moral code is only one specific cultural mode of institutionalising norms. Ethical behaviour may only partially overlap with moral intentions or justifications. Situations commonly arise – not only in intercultural communication – in which agents feel that something morally wrong is going on without readily having recourse to a moral norm or code. Moreover, there are also elements of social practice that may be said to be spontaneous and pre-moral but which in turn can trigger moral disagreements and dilemmas. The discrepancies, incongruities and practical dilemmas that result from the complexities of social life and interaction, and not primarily from the complexities of legal or religious codes, are potentially very insightful with regard to the phenomenon of morality. Recording and contrasting the 'streamlined' moral codes in economics, politics and education do not exhaust the sphere of the moral. This is particularly clear in societies such as those of many hunter-gatherers, like the one introduced here, but it also goes beyond the narrow circle of these societies. Comparative research is therefore not limited to that of norms, and individual morality should not be simply considered a derivation or internalisation of such norms. This puts terms such as 'virtue' and 'trust' back on the agenda of comparative research, not as elements of a generalised normative code but as ways to describe the involvement of individuals in their social interaction (Widlok 2004a).

Sovereignty of Moral Phenomena

Compiling a set of scenarios for eliciting moral discourse faces the problem of selecting and thereby declaring situations as morally salient (or morally indifferent) even though this may not match the local perception. As the examples provided here show, even with seemingly clear cases such as that of infanticide, which is in fact part of the local experience and memory, moral reasoning may be transformed into an exercise of problem-solving. At the same time, the phenomenological approach introduced above suggests that there is a basic ethical dimension to all interaction and communication that precedes well-formulated norms and codes. By addressing someone an ethical demand is being created, namely the demand to recognise the address and react to it. There is also a basic act of trust involved in that one trusts that others will recognise the speech act and respond to it. Following Løgstrup (1989, 1997) in this, I have pointed out that, whatever the contents of the communication, the speaker always lays him- or herself open in the hope of a response. Trust and demands of this sort are therefore not constructed by people but they are given by the human condition in a diversity of settings. There is bound to be interactive ethical reasoning, not because there is disagreement in the basic demand made in relationships but because people are positioned differently in the relationships in which they engage. Moreover, since another person who decides to communicate with us is in some sense always in our hand, there is an inbuilt power relationship in interaction and therefore also in ethical reasoning. In other words, independently of whether we (or 'they') categorise an event, a situation or an action as 'morally relevant' or not, there is a sense in which the phenomena themselves carry a moral demand, to which social agents may appeal or respond to in their interaction. However, this does not exclude disagreements and conflicts that arise from the ways in which individuals are positioned in the interaction. The philosophical tradition of moral realism, on which Løgstrup draws, is currently not the majority position in philosophy (although it is probably also not as marginal as its opponents may want to depict it). However, for anthropological research interested in empirical description and comparative analysis, it is not the majority conditions in neighbouring disciplines that are the main criterion for adopting (and adapting) an existing approach but the degree to which it allows us to raise relevant questions that can be answered empirically. As I have tried to show in this contribution, scenarios that relate to the materiality of human interaction, to processes of growth, of life and death, of mutual dependency and of intrinsic power relations have the potential to be productive in comparative settings.

Particularity of Moral Situations

Anthropological contributions to the study of morality, and the contributions of this volume are no exception to this, are predominantly case studies. In my own contribution, I have drawn on one particular ethnographic case (the ≠Akhoe Hai//om) and more precisely on instances of group discussion situations that make up 'the ≠Akhoe case' in my account. While this may be seen as a limitation of anthropological method and theory, I have suggested that giving attention to the particularity of the moral situation should not be discounted as less appropriate than abstract modelling. On the contrary, there is considerable indication for the fact that the moral agents themselves successfully employ the explication of a situation in their attempts to arrive at ethical judgements and behaviour. It is in the nature of the intricate social situations in which humans find themselves that success cannot be guaranteed. For social agents and for researchers alike, it is difficult to judge whether the explication of a situation is deep enough (or too deep, preventing effective action). But it is important to note that the inverse fallacy is no less common: social agents and researchers who too readily abstract from situations may feed into discourses of 'moralism', invoking morality on the grounds of principles that may or may not be moral, and that pose a much greater problem for moral behaviour than explicit amoral or non-moral behaviour, because they are much more difficult to unravel. Considering a completely independent case study may clarify this point (see also Widlok 2004a,b for more details). The divide between 'capitalist' and 'socialist' values was part of the cold war confrontation and continues to inform a considerable part of post-socialist situations, for instance in Germany (Wieschiolek 1999: 220, Stevenson 2002: 131). However, a closer look reveals that in this opposition we are dealing not only (and in some cases not even primarly) with a contrast between two sets of moral values but also with two theoretical positions, namely one that focuses on deontological ethics (oriented towards individual duties) and one that focuses on eudemonistic ethics (oriented towards a good society) or more generally on teleological ethics (oriented towards future goals). These theoretical positions are not mutually exclusive but they are also not arbitrarily and freely chosen since they are cultivated through particular social systems in specific ways, namely a capitalist system that institutionalised individual choice (of profession, place of residence, partners, etc.) and a socialist system that – faced with individual hardships – institutionalised the progress of society (or the party, the state, the international brotherhood). In such a context the challenge for anthropological comparison and for the methods of ethnographic research on which it is based is not simply to identify contrastive systems of values. This task is usually carried out in confrontations between the proponents of each of these moral systems themselves. Rather, it is to identify the positions from which these moral systems are being developed and to which they contribute.

A genuine anthropological perspective focuses on the social positions of agents and how their positioning influences their ethical values and practices. This is akin to the theoretical approach commonly labelled 'ontological ethics' (Løgstrup 1989: 6, 1997: 265), which I have adopted in this contribution. Such an approach is predicated neither on a choice of a set of norms (e.g. socialist or capitalist) nor on a choice between deontological and eudemonistic ethics, but it focuses on ethical demands inherent in social practices and on the given situatedness of moral behaviour. There is then a complementary contribution that an anthropology of moralities can make, and this is to look at disputes, distinctions and oppositions that are framed in moral terms, but to investigate them in terms of the theoretical interests and social positions held by the parties involved in such disputes. In other words anthropology can help to discover when theoretical biases are mistaken for moral biases.

The early anthropology of morality saw it as its foremost task to synthesise the case situations found in the field, to move vertically as it were between the particulars of situations observed and the ethical principles that were often not formulated by the agents themselves. This corresponded to the dominant view on the way in which the ethical judgement and behaviour of individual practice were governed by and derived from the rules and principles formulated by a specialised elite. On the basis of the material presented here I suggest that both perspectives should be revised. The task of anthropology is, above all, to collect information relating to particular situations and then to move horizontally, or laterally, as it were, between these situations. I argue that this also corresponds to the way in which ethics is constituted in practice. As practitioners move laterally from situation to situation they learn to develop their 'ethical skills'. Carrying particular cases of ethical dilemmas into group discussions and carrying the responses of these discussions back into a comparative anthropology of morality thereby become part and parcel of this learning process.

Notes

1. Our temporal and cultural distance from Vedder and his readers allows us to see that his list does in fact not consist of lasting virtues in the philosophical sense (MacIntyre 1981) but rather shallow conventions. Or in Løgstrup's words (1989: 77–8) this list is made up almost entirely of cultural models instead of universal morals, i.e. they follow an appeal limited to certain places and times and not the demand tied to the sovereign expressions of being (*souveräne Daseinsäußerungen*) to be discussed in more detail below.
2. Besides their role in philosophical treatises and Sunday newspapers moral dilemmas also occupy specific niches in events such as court proceedings. Examples of the latter type are court hearings for young men claiming their right of conscientious objection against army service in countries like Germany. The hearings would typically involve 'real life' scenarios such as 'Imagine yourself in a forest with your girlfriend and being attacked by aggressors, what would you do?' The 'right' response to these scenarios was not, or not only, to demonstrate the absence of violent reactions but also the ability to abstract from the situation using ethical rules of behaviour such as the right of self-defence, the duty of assistance, etc. Claimants could be cornered by abstracting from case situations (personal encounters in the forest and national armies facing one another) through generalisation so that an ethical rule could be invoked that would seem to demand the same solution in both cases. I thank Patrice Ladwig for pointing out this facet to me, which I had not thought of initially, even though I had undergone such a court hearing myself many years ago.

Appendice

List of scenarios suggested in the MPI field methods toolkit (Senft 2002). Researchers interested in using these scenarios are requested to contact the Language and Cognition Group at the Max Planck Institute for Psycholinguistics, in particular the author of these scenarios, Gunter Senft.

1. The Abandoned and Re-found Child Scenario

Once upon a time there was an old man and an old woman. Once, on their way to their garden/their field, they heard a child crying. They found this child – it was a small babyboy. The woman picked him up, went back to her village and asked whether anyone knew anything about his mother. But she could not find the mother of this boy. Thus the old woman said that she would take the little boy and treat him like one of her own children, and her husband agreed to this. So the boy stayed with them; the old woman was like his mother, the old man was like his father and they loved him like a child of their own. The boy grew up and worked for the old man and the old woman. He was a very good worker/gardener/hunter/fisherman. One day an old woman came to their place and said:

> This young man is my son. I abandoned him a long time ago in the bush/forest/gardens/fields/desert because I had no food to feed him. There was a famine. I thought he might either die or people might find him and help him. I heard that you found the baby and now I want him to come with me to my village/place and work for me, because I am his real mother.

Now, what are the young man and the old woman and the old man who picked him up as a baby going to do?

2. The Chiefly Authority Scenario

Once upon a time, long ago, the people from the mountains [any location other than the local place] were always fighting with the people from the islands [the local place]. The Highlanders were fierce people, but the Islanders were good people. Once there was a big war. The Highlanders [built canoes and] came to the Islands. The chief (etc.) of the Islanders was thinking very hard and came up with a plan for how they could chase away the Highlanders. He told the people that he himself knew how to win the war, and no one else should do anything on his or her own. He himself would chase away the Highlanders. He will kill any person who acted against this order – and all the people agreed to this. There was one man who heard what the chief had said and thought it was good. He went to the garden (the bush, etc.) to work. In the evening this man saw the canoes of the Highlanders coming close to where his garden was. The Highlanders landed there and slept. This man took the Highlanders' knives, clubs and spears. He then returned to his village, said what he had done and where the Highlanders were sleeping – and the chief and the village people fought them and chased the Highlanders away. This man had actually won the war – but he did not do what the chief had said. Now what is the chief going to do?

3. The Troublesome Partner Scenario

A) Once upon a time there was a man who did not care for his children, did not work in the garden and always slept with other women coming to visit his village. What will his wife do?

B) Once upon a time there was a woman who did not care for her children, did not cook, did not work in the garden and always slept with other men coming to visit her village. What will her husband do?

4. The Cheating Rich Man Scenario

Once upon a time there was a rich man, but all the other people did not have any money whatsoever. Once the poor people from the village came to him and wanted to sell fish (or corn, yams, whatever) to him because they needed the money for a feast. The rich man told them that he would buy lobsters and pay five kina (or whatever) for each lobster. The people went fishing and caught many lobsters, but, when they wanted to sell them to the rich man, he said he would pay them only three kina for one lobster. What will the people do now?

5. The Infanticide Scenario

Once upon a time there was a woman who had given birth to many children already, and she was pregnant again. But she had no food. There was a famine. She gave birth to her child, but the child was very small and weak. She did not want the child because there was no food for all her children, and, if this child stayed alive, all of them would suffer greatly from the famine – the woman, her husband and all their other children. Thus she thought she might kill the newborn child. What do you think the woman will do now?

6. The Lost Son Scenario

Once upon a time there was a chief who had two sons. One of them was a good man. He always did what his father and his mother told him to do. This good man was a good gardener (fisherman, hunter, etc.). But his younger brother was a man with bad manners. He grew up but did not garden (work) for his father and his mother, he went to the Highlands (to another place) and worked there, but he spent all his money on girls. He did not write letters or anything and he did not want to know about his mother, his father and his elder brother. However, this man got very sick, he almost died, and he just had enough money to come back to his village. When he came back and stepped out of his canoe (truck, etc.) his father and his mother were so happy that they killed two pigs, helped him to build a house and gave this bad son money, food, valuables and so on – because they were so happy that he had returned home. But what about his brother, the good man – what do you think he will think and say? And do you think what the father and the mother did was good?

7. The Stealing out of Hunger Scenario

Once upon a time there was a big famine. There was no food, no sweet potatoes, no taro, no coconuts, no pigs (etc.). There was a man who went to another island (place). There he saw a ship (a truck, etc.). He went to it and saw that it was full of food. He was terribly hungry. He saw a stranger who looked as if he were protecting the food. Then this man left (for a swim, a stroll), and no one guarded the ship (truck) full of food. The hungry man wanted to take some food because of the famine and because he was so hungry. He went to the ship (truck), took some food and ate it. Do you think what he did was good, or what?

8. The Food for Life Scenario

Once upon a time there were a man and a woman who loved each other very much. The woman got pregnant and gave birth to a child, but the man said: 'I will not marry her, I am not the father of the child that she has borne'. The woman was very sad and cried; she left this man, she left her village and went to the mountains (to another place). There she worked very hard for her child and for herself. The child grew up, he became a good man and earned much money, gave much to his mother and his mother was now a rich woman. They lived in the mountains. One day the woman read in the papers that there was a severe famine in her old village. Many children had already died and many more people would die if there was no help for them. The woman now went back to her old village and said: If the people would kill the man she loved a long time ago, the father of her child, then she would buy a lot of food, load it into a canoe (a truck) and bring it to the village so that all people would have food to eat. Then there would be no hunger any more. What do you think the villagers will do?

Chapter 3

LIFE HISTORY AND PERSONAL EXPERIENCE: THE MORAL CONCEPTIONS OF A MUSCOVITE MAN

Jarrett Zigon

Wherever one looks these days, morality is showing up in the works of anthropologists. It has been suggested that the use of this concept allows anthropologists to avoid the well-understood difficulties of the traditional anthropological concepts of culture, society and power (Rogers 2004). Morality, so it may be thought, provides a more intimate perspective on the everyday lives of our subjects and interlocutors. While this is certainly commendable, the very concept of morality remains under-theorised by anthropologists. Because of this there is little agreement or coherence among those anthropologists who study moralities about just what it is they are attempting to study and how to do so (Laidlaw, 2002; Robbins in this volume; Zigon 2007, 2008, 2009). This chapter contributes to the current debate over the future framework of a coherent anthropology of moralities. By presenting a moral portrait of Dima, a thirty-six-year-old ex-junkie and current HIV/AIDS activist living in Moscow, I hope to show that life-history methods and hermeneutic analysis of narratives allow for a deep and rich description of individuals' moral conceptions. This is so because they reveal the ways in which personal experiences play a significant role in shaping these conceptions.

Life History and Personal Experience

Recently some anthropologists have argued that stressing the socio-historical-cultural over individual experience often results in a 'distorting simplification of the human condition' and runs the risk of not fully appreciating human ambiguity, creativity and transgression (Crapanzano 2004: 6). Lila Abu-Lughod has argued that because of this anthropologists often engage in the very 'distancing and othering' practices we seek to overcome (Abu-Lughod 1999[1986]: xvii–xviii). The result of such practices, argues James Faubion, is the risk of conceit that comes from anthropologists not always recognising the same individuality in their ethnographic subjects as they recognise in themselves (Faubion 2001a: 32–33). This chapter intends to show that, by acknowledging the personal and individual experience of our ethnographic participants as the starting point for anthropological investigations, we can overcome this divide and in doing so gain a better understanding of the lives of our interlocutors (Bruner 1986: 8–9). In particular, it will argue that it is personal experience that provides a foundation for the moral conceptions of individuals, as well as the feeling that one's moral conceptions are correct, and the motivation to act according to them (Strauss and Quinn 1994: 288). Nevertheless, because the individual is always in the midst of intersubjective social relations, her experiences are always connected to the socio-historical-cultural world in which she lives (Weiner 2001: 80–81). In other words, personal experience is always limited by a range of possibilities found within a particular socio-historical-cultural world. Therefore, experience is always at the same time personal and social.

Recently experience has come into question as a social scientific concept (Throop 2003). Joan Scott, for example, has argued that, because experience is intimately connected with the very socio-historical-cultural processes and structures that give rise to it, experience cannot be an adequate starting point for social scientific analysis (Scott 1992). Desjarlais has similarly argued that a Western notion of experience has been naively adopted by social scientists. He characterises this notion of experience as depth, interiority, coherence and authenticity (Desjarlais 1997). Based on his research among homeless individuals in a Boston shelter, Desjarlais has argued for alternative ways of understanding experience, such as non-reflectivity, episodicity and publicness (Desjarlais 1997: 17–24).

The so-called Western concept of experience, however, has not always been characterised in the way described by Desjarlais. Indeed, experience as a concept has a genealogy of its own, and has only taken the form critiqued by these writers since the eighteenth century. The concept of experience underwent a significant shift in the seventeenth and eighteenth centuries as natural philosophers debated competing methods in the desire to reach conclusions about nature with increased certainty. They turned to mathematics as the only available resource that could provide such certainty. The adoption of this new language of certainty necessitated a shift in method away from the predominant use of the Aristotelian notion of experience to the more narrowly focused practice of experiment. This shift of method, then, led to a shift in the conception of experience from community-based and shared to isolated experiments designed to answer specific questions (Dear 1995: 21). With the further influence of Protestantism, and particularly Methodism (Williams 1983 [1976]: 126), in the nineteenth century and the new psychology that developed at the turn of the twentieth century (Caruth 1996: 61), this notion of the isolated and unique experience was increasingly internalised within individual persons. It is this relatively historically recent notion of experience, then, that critics such as Desjarlais and Scott reject.

I too share many of the concerns of those who critique the concept of experience. But as Geertz has argued, without this concept our 'analyses seem to float several feet above the ground' (Geertz 1986: 374). Therefore, the concept of experience remains central to my work. Nevertheless, what I consider experience is more similar to what Desjarlais calls struggling along than to what he characterises as the Western notion of experience. Rather, and similar to Geertz, by experience I mean that which is derived through processes of memory and recollection, but also of hope, desire and anticipation, and which is in turn attempted to be integrated into one's dispositional way of being in the world. Thus, experience as I use it in this chapter is characterised by interpretive derivation rather than accumulation, attempts to integrate rather than simple aggregation, and publicness rather than interiority (Geertz 1986: 380). Therefore, when I use the concept of personal experience throughout this chapter to show how Dima has crafted his moral conceptions, I do not intend this as simply a subjective process. Rather, and similar to the social memory about which Paxson writes, experience as I have just articulated it is 'filled with various logics, rhymes, and reasons' and can only be understood as meaningful in the context of the particular socio-historical-cultural world in which it is lived out (Paxson 2005: 29).

While it is true that the concept of experience that I have just laid out is not simply subjective, neither is it entirely shared. Therefore, I speak of personal experiences. Personal experiences are the ways in which individuals live in and through a shared socio-historical-cultural world. It is a way of expressing the multiplicity of uniqueness that is always found in shared forms of life. It is these personal experiences that are central in shaping what Rogers calls the 'shades of similarity and difference' between individual conceptions of morality (Rogers 2004: 36). Therefore, while the moral conceptions of Dima may in fact be recognisable, understandable and perhaps even to some extent shared by some other Russians, they remain, to a great extent, fundamentally his own. It is such a notion of morality, then, that will be presented in the rest of this chapter. In particular, and as will soon become clear, Dima's moral conceptions are centred on a well-defined notion of working on himself in order to be the kind of person he hopes to become. Let us turn now to Dima in order to see how this is done.

Dima – A Moral Portrait

Dima is a thirty-six-year-old married, but childless, musician and Programme Officer with an international AIDS prevention programme who has personally benefited from the collapse of the Soviet Union. In the late 1980s during some of the worst years of perestroika, when shop shelves were empty and the hapless economy could no longer be hidden, Dima finished high school and made a decision that would change his life forever. He would forgo the opportunity of attending a university and instead play the guitar in a rock band. This decision was more about choosing to stand outside a social system that he viewed as impeding any opportunity for personal choice in lifestyle and career than it was about choosing to play in a rock group. For Dima, like many others of his and earlier generations (Binyon 1999: 184–87), could have played music and been a student at the same time. By following this less conventional path, Dima exercised what he saw as his right to choose the lifestyle he preferred even if this meant finding himself on the margins of a social order that even in the years of official glasnost had very little tolerance for those who lived in these margins.

For the next five years Dima lived a life on the edge. His band had very little success and brought him no money to speak of. He didn't have any other job. Although Dima supposedly lived at home with his parents, he spent most of his nights out with friends or girlfriends, sleeping wherever he found himself at the time. He had not yet begun to use heroin but was smoking a lot of marijuana and drinking heavily. Because he had no job and his parents were often reluctant to help him financially, Dima began to steal. This soon became a habit, not so much because he needed to steal, he once told me, but because he enjoyed it. Stealing became more of an addiction than the alcohol and marijuana. So too did his penchant for lying. Both of these gave Dima a rush from knowing that, even if just a little, he was standing outside the expected ways of the world. When I met Dima in the autumn of 2002 he told me that he had given up his habit of stealing by the mid-1990s but that he still lied pretty often. He assured me, however, that he never lied to me. One wonders what to make of such an assurance, but as yet I have never caught him in a lie so I personally have never had any reason to distrust him.

In 1994 Dima was walking through central Moscow when he came across a group of Hare Krishnas singing and dancing on the street. Such encounters were not uncommon in the mid-1990s, as the immediate post-Soviet years saw a wave of religious activity hit Russia. Not only did the Russian Orthodox Church experience a major revival in these years, but Russians were also introduced to a wide variety of Protestantisms, non-Western religions, such as the Hare Krishna, and other so-called spirituality cults (Borenstein 1999). Dima stopped and listened, and was immediately captured by the sounds of the Hare Krishna's music. Just as he had once told me that it was the sound of music and not the words that have taught him the most about how to live his life, so too it was in the presence of the sounds of the Hare Krishna that Dima once again chose to radically alter his life by joining this religious group.

In many ways the nearly two years between 1994 and 1996 that Dima belonged to the Hare Krishna have helped him become the person he is today. It was with the Hare Krishna that Dima became a vegetarian, gave up his habit of stealing, because he learned to de-emphasise material possessions, and perhaps most importantly, learned the importance of self-discipline for becoming the kind of person he wants to be. Dima learned much in this period of his life and still points to it as one of the most significant. Although he eventually left the Hare Krishna, he claims to remain today an 'essentially religious person', which means for him someone who respects all life, believes that good will conquer evil and works to better himself and those around him.

One of the reasons Dima left the Hare Krishnas is because it required being very social. Dima is essentially a loner and still to this day prefers to spend most of his time alone. Another reason is that Dima began to use heroin. As he put it to me, 'I did it backwards, most people do the heavy drugs and then join the Hare Krishnas. I left them to start heroin.' This change, however, did not get in the way of some of the most important things he learned with the Hare Krishnas. Rather, he thinks it only added to what he had learned. In fact, Dima attributes many of his most personally cherished characteristics to this period of heavy drug use. But it was not the drugs per se that helped Dima see the world in a different way, but the drug culture, in which he was getting more and more involved. It was in this drug culture of Moscow in the late 1990s that Dima learned the importance of supporting those he loves and having the courage to be himself. It was this experience of being a member of one of the most marginalised groups in Russia (Malinowska-Sempruch et al. 2004), so he told me, that taught him how to be secure in who he is as a person and how to use the strength and courage this brought him to support those around him. It was at this point in his life, while still a junkie that Dima first learned about Doctors Without Borders and their work with drug users in Russia. Dima claims that using heroin may have been the best thing he ever did for himself. For if he had not used heroin, he would never have come into contact with Doctors Without Borders, nor would he have had the courage and self-confidence, so he claims, to join their organisation as a volunteer.

It was this decision to volunteer for Doctors Without Borders that really led to a change in Dima's life. As a friend of his he first met at Doctors Without Borders recently told me:

> When Dima started at Doctors Without Borders he was this skinny little boy riding a bike wearing a green T-shirt that was so big you could fit five Dimas in it, and now he wears a suit and leads these meetings with politicians and businessmen about the HIV crisis in Russia. This is not the little Dima that I remember!

Soon after joining this organisation Dima quit heroin and started working full-time for them. He realised that he could help those junkies who were not as fortunate as himself to have the strength to fight the addiction. Eventually this job led Dima to UNAIDS, where he worked through the ranks to become a Project Manager, the position he held when I first met him. Ever since realising that he was happiest working to help others who have had similar experiences to his own but weren't as lucky as he had been, Dima has worked hard to help fight the spread of HIV/AIDS in Russia by helping to organise needle exchange programmes throughout the country negotiating with the government, NGOs and private business for the legalisation and funding of such programmes, and helping to initiate a legal reform recently passed, which legalized the possession of small amounts of marijuana. This reform led to the release of over 40,000 persons from Russian prisons who had been jailed for the possession of very small amounts of marijuana.

Like other Russians in their thirties, Dima came of age in a time of chaos. This was a time ranging from perestroika through the economic crisis of 1998 when the absurdities, illusions and contradictions of late Soviet/transitional Russia were open for all to see and shaped the lives of an entire generation (Kotkin 2001). The first time I met Dima he revealed how he enjoyed what he called 'the present chaotic state' of Russia. I asked him what he meant by this.

> It was not a comfort feeling [the Soviet illusion of future perfection and the present's necessary path to it], it was not a good feeling. It was boring and grey and – life is still grey in many ways but it is not as grey as it used to be. I don't think chaos is that good. If it goes on for too long it will be counterproductive in the end. We will be totally disoriented and we will lose each and every positive thing we have gained, so that is dangerous. Chaotic times may be good for a while, but not …

And for some reason Dima just stopped talking. I pressed Dima a bit more but he had little more to say on the subject. This is what Dima does. He can talk and talk for what seem like hours straight, but when he decides there is nothing left to say on a subject, he just stops. But, as I have came to know Dima more, I think that perhaps he stopped speaking here because he realised that what he was saying was self-evident, that the story of his own life made this point clear. For in a way, Dima's own life is a story of the gradual movement from chaos to order.

The way Dima spoke in our many conversations and interviews reflects this movement in his life. For, although he continually repeats that we should all be free to do anything we want as long as it doesn't hurt anyone else, at the same time he maintains that there are certain definite ways that we should treat others and work on ourselves to be better. This latter position can be seen in the way Dima spoke about his experience of watching the movie *Lord of the Rings*.

> Dima – Just two days ago I went to see *Lord of the Rings*, because I had two or three hours and I just wanted to see that movie. And I had tears in my eyes, you know. And I was just sitting there crying like a baby. I look at it this way, if I was really a grownup man I would be cynical about all this … it is a great movie, but not great like a David Lynch movie is great. It is great but in a different sense. It's like Good versus Evil. It is difficult to explain, but the way I see it there is a line that goes through the film and, I don't know what happened, but to me it was magic.

Jarrett – Do you remember what in particular brought tears to your eyes?

Dima – There was a scene with the old king and he was possessed. That was the strongest part of the whole film to me, the way Gandalf appeared and he was wearing all white and all that, and he just freed this king. To me that symbolised the power of God, the way that God can liberate people, just very easily, the way that Good defeats Evil. So to me it was a very Christian film, or maybe even bigger than, that a totally religious film. Without all the unnecessaries … I used to be a huge fan of Tolkien when I was a kid, so maybe that is it. But it clearly showed the line between Good and Evil in a beautiful way, and it showed courage and devotion in a very pure way.

Dima, then, is moved by the notion that in the end good conquers evil. So much so, in fact, that he was moved to tears. Dima, the man who describes himself as very cynical – and I can attest that he is – cried 'like a baby' at the sight of good conquering evil. Is it Dima's hope that good will conquer evil that brought him to work for HIV/AIDS prevention institutions and to help injecting drug users organise into unions to protect and educate themselves and to receive clean needles? At some level, whatever drew the tears out of Dima's eyes that evening in the cinema must also play a role in what he has chosen to do with his life and future. But it must also say something about his past. Dima would never describe what he did in the past as evil, but he would describe his present life in better terms than his past. In this sense, then, Dima recognises a progression in his own life towards the better. Thus, while Dima was not the only one of his generation who spoke to me about the freedom of chaos, he is the only one who spoke of it who believes that he can help make his future and the future of Russia a better time.

Several months later, in an interview Dima was telling me about how the drug culture in which he took part during the mid-1990s had a strong influence on him in terms of critiquing mainstream society and coming to understand who he is as a person. It was his experience with this culture, so Dima claims, that solidified his current moral beliefs and ethical practices. Most importantly Dima learned that it is important to have a goal or idea of whom one wants to become. For only with this idea can one begin to work on oneself.

Dima – I left the Hare Krishnas when I started using drugs. The other way around is what happens to most people. And this was very strong in terms of physical emotions and feelings and the reassessment of the world and my place in it. I don't mean just the drugs but the drug culture itself, being different and alternative from the mainstream culture and the mainstream relationships and ways of dealing with people. Of course I very soon grew disappointed but in the beginning it was very strong.

Jarrett – It does get old after a while but at first it is very refreshing because it gives you a chance to step outside.

Dima – Right, and to be yourself also. What I remember clearly was that it was probably not the first time in my life, but I felt very strongly that I had an opportunity to be myself and to express myself. Which is not the same as, I don't know, maybe because drugs are so marginalised in our society, I don't know, but it seems like people who are doing drugs have the courage that other people do not have. The courage and openness and everything that comes with it. And I think that is really true for a lot of people when they first start but when you start on that path it will lead you to who knows where, it all depends on the person. You can use it and then throw it out or else it can throw you out. Drugs are probably one of the most dangerous things, similar to sex, in that it can make you forget about yourself. It can really turn you into a totally, into, I don't know what the word would be. Not that drugs in themselves are bad, but drugs and sex are two very powerful drives that can really drive you and, if you let them drive you, you can really end up in trouble.

Jarrett – I understand how drugs can do this, but how does sex do it?

Dima – There a lot of people who are crazy about sex and when they lose track of it it just kind of ruins their life, they become slaves to it. I don't think, yeah I understand that there are a lot of things connected to our instincts, and if you are unable to control yourself, it doesn't happen to everyone, not everyone has very strong sexual desires, but many people do and when they do it can take them over, but sex as it is is not dangerous at all. But it can be connected to other things that you might not want to do otherwise but you do because of that. A lot of things people do because of sex, and that is what is dangerous about sex. Not sex as it is, of course, because it is beautiful the way it is.

Jarrett – Because it can cause you to forget about other things that are more important to you?

Dima – Right, and instead of being a serious person you would just end up being a junkie, sort of a sex junkie. In the way that a lot of people, I mean, to think of it this is an exaggeration because it is not sex as it is, not in itself, but also connected to many other things. It can happen to you if you, I mean there are other sorts of things, not just drugs and sex. Anything.

Dima seems to be weaving two stories throughout the first part of this narrative. First, he is expressing an admiration for the people he met in the drug culture and the kinds of personal characteristics he thinks distinguishes them from mainstream society. Dima found such characteristics as courage and openness among those who participated in the drug culture of the mid-1990s, and attributes them to the marginalisation of this culture in the greater Russian society. This courage and openness are not only related to the potential dangers of being marginal, but also about expressing oneself. This is the second story Dima is telling. It was during these years participating in the drug culture that Dima finally had the opportunity to be himself and to express himself. Still today, even though he has not done any drugs in over six years, Dima remains a member of this drug culture. Many of his friends are still junkies, counting some of them among his most trusted, and he continues to work with them in trying to establish needle exchange groups throughout the country.

Just as the drug culture allows for individuals to have the courage and openness to be themselves, so too the actual drugs can potentially lead to the forgetting of oneself. This risk, however, is not unique to drugs, but is true of nearly anything that causes one to forget about oneself. Dima mentions sex. Like drugs, sex can activate a powerful 'drive' and cause one to do things that one might not do otherwise. Dima, at this point, seems to backtrack a bit. He does not want to overemphasise the dangers of drugs and sex. As he says, this is an exaggeration and these dangers can ultimately be associated with anything. For Dima, then, the danger he expresses through drugs and sex is not about the substance and act itself, but about how individuals are able to handle it. The point that Dima seems to be making is that no matter what one does, it is important to remember oneself, remember what is important to oneself, and not to let other things get in the way of this.

As I got to know Dima more intimately, it became evident that a central aspect of his ethics is a concern with the consequences of his actions. I asked him once if he now considers consequences more than he used to.

Dima – I think sometimes people can make up an excuse, because in the back of their minds they want to be secure about things. For example, if someone really wants to cheat on their wife, they will do it. These people usually do it. Really that surprises me. Very often people don't think at all and they just do, and then afterwards they start regretting what they did. I'm very happy, I wouldn't like to live without the ability to look at myself from a distance, to be able to look at what I am doing. Sometimes it is the only thing that helps. People get these kinds of ideas pretty often. Like I have decided for myself, OK, what if I do that and then I catch something? What am I going to do? I don't want that. And, however stupid that sounds, it really works for me. I mean, every time I think of something like that, I just, somehow it just pops into my mind, and I'm like, oh, that is really serious. I'm working in the AIDS field, you know ... no I'm not really scared of AIDS, I'm more scared of the smaller sexually transmitted diseases that are quite common here in Russia. If you catch something like that and then you pass it on to your wife, then you can imagine what will happen. On the other hand, I also don't want to cheat on her because I want her to trust me and I wouldn't be able to trust myself if I did that.

Jarrett – So it's not just about consequences but also about being the kind of person you want to be, like being trusted by your wife?

Dima – I think we should always try to look from a longer perspective, this really makes a difference. You have to at least either like what you are doing or train yourself to like it, you know. I don't know, but I think it makes sense to have a habit of analysing the things you do. Of course, you can really become paranoid if you always analyse what you do, but sometimes it doesn't hurt if you do a little of it.

Earlier in this interview Dima had suggested that he chooses particular situations and contexts in which he works on himself. Here Dima gives an example of the kind of situation in which he chooses to work on himself, that of cheating on his wife. In this example it is possible to see how Dima combines the notion of working on himself or developing himself with that of looking towards consequences. Not only is he concerned about what diseases he might catch and pass on to his wife by cheating, but so too is he concerned about her not trusting him. Therefore, it is more than the knowledge of the possible diseases he could contract, a knowledge that comes predominantly through his job, but also his desire to cultivate a trusting and lasting relationship with his wife. Thus, in Dima's consideration of the consequences of adultery, there are multiple factors that go into his decision.

This way of developing himself by means of considering various consequences is what Dima calls looking 'from a longer perspective' or 'at myself from a distance'. These two expressions of distancing himself from himself reveal Dima's conception of self-analysis and self-development. Thus, just as Pesmen has claimed that it is central for many Russians to engage in these practices of analysis and development to maintain a healthy *dusha* (soul) (Pesman 2000: 54n.), for Dima the rhetorical distancing of self-analysis allows him to work on himself to become the kind of person he wants to be. By performing this distance, Dima is able to consider not only the situation and the dilemma it may entail, but, more importantly for him, it allows him to consider himself, it allows him not to forget himself and the things that are truly important to him. Because he is able to perform this distance, Dima can realise that for himself it is more important to maintain a trusting relationship with his wife and remain disease-free than it is to be driven by his sexual instinct. As he put it, he may not like this decision, but in order to be the kind of person he wants to be, he must 'train [himself] to like it'.

A concern for consequences is not the only way Dima spoke about working on himself. During one interview he was telling me about the way in which he sometimes judges other people. This led me to ask if and how he judges himself.

Jarrett – So, if you judge others, do you also judge yourself? For example, if you realise that you have done something that goes against your own standards, what do you do?

Dima – First of all I try to, it's really hard, because people are driven by instincts a lot and I don't like it. I understand that this is how we are built, but still I'm sure there are ways to deal with it. You can teach yourself to do some things and not to do other things, in principle, whatever you choose to be right or wrong for yourself. This is what I mean. So, if I do something wrong from my own point of view or from my inner self point of view, first of all, I don't know, its really painful. It's really painful. And sometimes it gets me really depressed. But I'm kind of helpless about many things. I just do something and then I regret it and then maybe I do it again and then I regret it again and it continues like this until the moment when I can stop doing it. But then maybe something else will come up.

Jarrett – Do you think there is something that you can do to train yourself not to do these things?

Dima – I believe that some people can do that, but not me, not me. I guess that I always wait until the moment that I am conscious about it and then it is usually very easy for me to stop doing something. Like taking drugs or drinking alcohol or a lot of things I used to do in my life that I don't do any more.

Jarrett – You said that a lot of people act on instinct, what do you mean by that?

Dima – I guess that we all tend to act on instinct, I don't know. It is hard to say, but I can give you an example. You know that I have a wife, but I also work in an environment where there are a lot of different girls working in my office. And usually it is OK. But just a few days ago one of them put on a different kind of dress. Usually everyone at this office dresses in a proper way because they have to uphold certain standards. But this time her dress was sort of revealing, a lot, and I caught myself thinking about that for several hours. Really, you know. There is nothing that I could do about it. And I wouldn't go and say that it was wrong and that it is horrible but it is just that I remember that I couldn't help but think about it. So somehow I got aroused by it and that is one of the inexplicable things to me, how things like that happen. And that I believe is proof that we very often get caught by instincts. Although if you start thinking rationally you could of course pretend that everything is all right and that it doesn't exist and that I have a wife and I'm not going to do anything about this anyway. I'm not going to go flirting with girls in my office. But it just sticks somewhere in the back of my mind.

In response to my question Dima wants to begin by telling about the pain he feels when he transgresses. This desire, which is indicated by his parallel use of the phrase 'first of all' to frame both the beginning of his narrative and the beginning of his particular utterance on pain, is interrupted by his setting of the background against which suffering should be understood. As in another interview discussed above, Dima again uses the rhetoric of instincts to characterise individuals who are unable to 'choose' to act in the way that is 'right' for themselves. As he puts it, he understands that 'we are built' with instincts and that if we don't try to overcome them they will control us, but he is 'sure there are ways to deal with it'. He suggests that one is able to 'teach' oneself to do certain things and not others. Once again, then, Dima is emphasising the necessity for people to work on themselves to become the kind of person they want to be, even, as he put it in another interview, if they don't like it.

Dima's attempt to do just that is seen in the example he gives of how instincts can sometimes take over. Dima cannot take his eyes or thoughts off the scantily dressed woman in his office. He doesn't understand why he would do such a thing, it is not what he wants. And yet he looks, he thinks, he desires. These are not wrong, he reassures me. He is not judging himself against some moral standard of what is right and what is wrong. Rather, this is troubling because he 'couldn't help but think about it'. Dima, then, is troubled by this situation because he is unable to control his thoughts about this woman and that is what goes against his own ethical standards. He is unable to be the kind of person he wants to be. He has lost control of himself. The danger, then, is that these uncontrollable thoughts could potentially lead to an act that he definitely does not want to do. Most likely, though, this will not happen. Dima is quite disciplined about this. But he just cannot control his thoughts. He suggests the way, however, that he tries to control them. If 'you start thinking rationally you could of course pretend that everything is alright and that it doesn't exist and that I have a wife and I'm not going to do anything about this anyway'. By thinking 'rationally' Dima suggests he can try to control his unwanted thoughts, his instincts. This rationality, however, leads to delusion. For in thinking rationally he is only pretending that he doesn't have such thoughts. It is through what we might call rational imagination, then, that Dima is able to control his thoughts and not actually physically act out his transgression. Still, this unwanted thought 'sticks somewhere in the back of [his] mind'. In some cases, then, try as he may, Dima cannot entirely be the kind of person he wants.

What I have called rational imagination is not the only way Dima works on himself. For before he gives the example of his reaction to the woman in his office, he talks about the moral suffering he feels when he commits a transgression. Thus, after having established a background understanding for why moral suffering is an appropriate response to transgression, Dima returns to his first words to frame his utterance on suffering. 'First of all, I don't know, it's really painful. It's really painful.' By laying down this background understanding, Dima suggests that his moral suffering is, at least in part, a result of having acted by 'instinct' rather than according to what he chooses to be right for himself. This echoes what he said in an earlier interview about the importance of not forgetting oneself and is shown in the example of his reaction to the woman in his office. When Dima transgresses his own moral expectations, he would say that he has forgotten himself and acted instead according to instinct. The realisation of having done so makes Dima 'really depressed'.

This depression leads Dima to a kind of repetitive state of suffering and a feeling of helplessness that in Dima's case makes it difficult for him to change. 'I'm kind of helpless about many things. I just do something and then I regret it and then maybe I do it again and then I regret it again and it continues like this until the moment when I can stop doing it.' Dima claims to continue to transgress and in this way repeats and prolongs his own suffering. His inability to change and his claim to be 'helpless' seem to articulate his inability to break out of his 'instinctual' being and to remember himself and the way he wants to be. Thus, Dima is unable to stop thinking about the woman in his office and, even after he attempts to rid himself of such thoughts, they linger in the back of his mind. Dima is helpless in the presence of these instinctual thoughts. His suffering and instinctual behaviour continue until he is finally 'conscious' of it. At this point, Dima realises that this is not what he would choose to do and can stop acting that way fairly 'easily'.

Dima emphasises the repetitive nature of his moral suffering in his narrative description of it. This is seen in the last sentence of his initial utterance on suffering: 'But then maybe something else will come up.' In this way Dima further emphasises the repetitive nature of suffering, not only in particular cases of transgression, but also in terms of the never-ending repetition of transgression itself. Because according to Dima humans are a combination of instinct and self-discipline, slippage into instinct as transgression is always possible, and thus so too is moral suffering. Indeed, it may even be necessary if moral suffering, as Pesmen has claimed, is considered an integral aspect of working on oneself (Pesmen 2000: 54–59; see also Ries 1997: 159–160).

How does this repetitive moral suffering help Dima work on himself? When I asked him if he thought there was something he could do to train himself not to transgress, he rejected this notion with some force. This is just the way he rejected my question about having a plan for life in another interview. Dima considered a plan to be too structured for the contingencies of human life, so too is the notion of training oneself. Instead, Dima waits 'until the moment that [he] is conscious' about his suffering and behaviour and it is at that point, so he claims, that he can pretty easily change. This suggests that for Dima moral suffering plays a significant role in his ability to become conscious of his transgressive behaviour. If it were not for his suffering and depression, then of what could he become conscious? Dima, then, articulates suffering as the subjectively felt experience of his transgressions. As such, it is his becoming conscious of this suffering experience that leads him to remember himself and how it is that he wants to be, and, thus, to be able to stop transgressing against himself and, as he put it, not to do it 'any more'. In this way, moral suffering helps Dima to work on himself to become the kind of person he hopes to be.

Conclusion

This notion of working on himself, or developing himself, to be the kind of person he wants to be was common to many of the conversations and interviews that Dima and I had. It is the central focus of Dima's personal ethic. It is not the central focus of any of the other Muscovites with whom I also did life histories in order to collect their moral conceptions and experiences. Thus, through the life-historical method it is possible to see how different individuals have different moral conceptions, how these conceptions are related to the personal experiences of these individuals, and how they are shaped by and shape the practices of theses individuals.

Nevertheless, Dima's focus on working on himself is in no way unique. Ironically, despite his open disdain for all things Soviet, Dima's emphasis on working on himself (*rabota nad soboi*) is reminiscent of the Soviet discourse of creating the New Soviet Man by means of individual self-disciplining (Etkind 1996; Kharkhordin 1999). As Oushakine has pointed out, because many of the disruptions and changes of the post-Soviet years so closely resemble those of the 1920s and 1930s, so too do many of the current rhetorical and disciplinary practices of contemporary Russia resemble those of nearly a century ago (Oushakine 2004: 396). As Kharkhordin has convincingly shown, this early Soviet emphasis on working on the self had its roots in the pre-revolution Russian Orthodox

Church and continued well into the late Soviet years (Kharkhordin 1999). Indeed, these practices continue in the post-Soviet years. Pesmen argues that the tropes of self-analysis and suffering are central to the ways in which her informants spoke of working on themselves, and that they believe such practices are the necessary 'work of *dusha*'. (Pesmen 2000: 54 n.). Similarly, Rivkin-Fish shows that among reproductive health activists in Russia, there is a 'common tendency to construe their work for reproductive health as a mission to promote moral changes in interpersonal relationships and the development of personality (or what might be called "work on the self")' (Rivkin-Fish 2004: 284). As can be seen, then, regardless of Dima's rhetorical attempts to distance himself not only from the Soviet past, but also from many of what he calls his 'mainstream' contemporaries, his emphasis on working on and developing himself has much in common with past and present moral discourse in Russia.

To say that notions of working on the self are common in Russian moral discourse does little to help us comprehend how actual persons experience and understand this for themselves. This chapter has tried to show how the life-historical method and the hermeneutic analysis of the narratives collected through this method can bring to life the moral conceptions and experiences of individuals. They provide a window into the lived experience of individuals living in a social context. In doing so, it is hoped that these moral conceptions and experiences are recognised for the complexity, the intimacy and, indeed, the struggle that they are often felt as by Dima. For, in the end, no matter how shared some moral conceptions may be, they are ultimately enacted and transgressed upon by actual persons in their everyday interactions with other persons.

Acknowledgments

I would like to thank Talal Asad, Gerald Creed, Nancy Ries, and Chris Hann for their help and comments on earlier versions of this article. I would also like to thank Monica Heintz for her editorial guidance in the writing of this article, as well as the comments of the anonymous reviewers. The writing of this chapter was made possible by a Research Fellowship at the Max Planck Institute for Social Anthropology. The research used here was made possible by an SSRC Eurasia Program Graduate Training Fellowship (Title VIII) and a Fulbright-Hays Doctoral Dissertation Research Abroad Fellowship. Parts of this chapter have appeared in an article in Ethos, vol. 37, no.1.

Chapter 4

MORALITY, VALUE AND RADICAL CULTURAL CHANGE

Joel Robbins

The anthropological study of morality is relatively undeveloped. This point is often made and appears to hold as well today as it did forty years ago (e.g. Edel and Edel 1968 [1959]; Howell 1997b; Laidlaw 2002). Many authors concur in pointing to one important reason why the development of an anthropology of morality appears to be almost permanently stunted: the anthropological tendency to treat all of culture or collective life as morally charged leaves morality as a domain of study woefully underspecified. Understood in these terms, to quote Laidlaw (2002: 313), the moral means everything and nothing. It does no distinctive conceptual work and therefore it is not surprising that, despite occasional attempts to arouse some interest in it, it keeps going out of focus and fading away. Laidlaw convincingly traces to Durkheim this tendency to spread morality too thinly over society, making it everywhere present but almost invisible in its role in shaping social life (see also Widlok 2004a). But even Edel and Edel (1968: 7), who do not explicitly engage the Durkheimian tradition, note that anthropology has suffered for rendering 'morality … more a dimension or aspect of living than a separate department with institutions of its own'. When every observance of a collectively held rule of etiquette is as much a moral act as is refraining from killing someone who has injured you, there seems to be little to say about morality beyond obvious nostrums about the force of culture in guiding behaviour. A developing consensus appears to hold that this conflation of morality and culture is not the way forward for an anthropology of morality.

As my reliance on Laidlaw (2002) in the previous paragraph suggests, he has laid out most carefully the difficulties with what we might call the Durkheimian problematic in the study of morality, and his response to these difficulties strikes me as the most cogent yet offered. To counteract the conflation of the moral and the cultural or social, he proposes to recover from Kant an emphasis on freedom and choice as essential criteria for determining what belongs in the moral domain: everything people do is not undertaken as a moral action, but only those things they do with reflective consciousness of having chosen to act in the way they have. Moral dictates possess some 'directive force', as Parish (1994: 287–88) puts it, but not the overwhelming force Durkheim ascribes to them. They are rules 'actors are less obliged than encouraged to realize' and thus ones that provide people with some room for choice (Faubion 2001b: 90). In Laidlaw's scheme, it is precisely in the room cultures leave for reflective choice-making that freedom comes to exist and that the moral domain takes shape.

I have in the past been inclined to accept without explicit modification something like Laidlaw's scheme, and the schemes of others such as Lambek (2000), who draw on Aristotle to oppose moral reasoning as phronesis both to blind, unconsciously driven acts of cultural reproduction and to actions taken in simple pursuit of material self-interest (Robbins 2004b). But I also remain quite attached to models of culture, such as structuralism, that have their roots in the Durkheimian tradition. My initial attraction to anthropology rested in important ways on the extent to which it is has generally been, as Bauman (1988: 4) puts it for sociology, focused on '"unfreedom" rather than freedom' and has thus been in the vanguard of efforts to denaturalise the role notions of individual freedom play in various Western ideologies. Any recourse to freedom within anthropological theory has thus seemed to me to risk falling into the trap of promoting Western common-sense models of social action to the lofty position of universal theories. To be fair, Laidlaw is careful, following Foucault, not to define freedom in naively Western terms – as everywhere consisting, for example, in the liberation of a human nature simply waiting to be set free to follow the path of reason or pursue material self-interest – but rather as something constructed out of the role given to choice in various cultures and in various domains within specific cultures (Laidlaw 2002: 323). I think this is a reasonable solution to the problems we face in safely returning to a concept such as freedom, the rejection of which was constitutive of anthropology and social science more generally. It is reasonable in particular by virtue of the way it continues to give culture a primary role even in moral life, for in this model it is culture itself that defines a space for freedom and for choice. As long as this is kept in mind, the anthropology of morality can contribute to, rather than simply render invisible, the tradition of anthropology that has done so much to move us beyond Western folk models in our understanding of how human life works.

I stress the importance of vigilance here because I think even the most sophisticated discussions of morality in anthropology can, by virtue of emphasising ideas like freedom, choice and creativity, give up on any strong model of culture in the Durkheimian vein. This is how I read Carrithers's (2005: 441ff.) otherwise very stimulating recent article, in which culture comes to be so fluid and ever-changing, so open to the impress of invention and resourceful use, that it seems to cease to have any properties of its own or any power to shape action. Such a move is certainly attractive in the current theoretical climate, where individualist models of culture abound (van der Veer 2000; Robbins 2004b: 330), but I want to strongly resist having to throw out the Durkheimian baby with the bath water of too rigid models of cultural reproduction as the price to be paid for securing an anthropological concept of freedom.

To help fortify the culturally conditioned notion of freedom Laidlaw identifies, I want to suggest a refinement of it that follows from making a theory of value central to our conception of culture. The theory of value I draw on here comes in the first instance from Dumont, but also reads Dumont to some extent through the lens of Weber. My argument is that this theory of value can help us specify why cultures allow choice in particular domains or situations, and how such choices are felt to be moral ones by cultural actors. By doing so, it also allows us to develop analyses of the moral systems of various cultures that also take into account those domains and situations in which the potential for moral choice is not foregrounded and where the moral component of action consists primarily of adherence to norms understood in binding, Durkheimian fashion. We might say that action in these latter circumstances is shaped by a morality of reproduction rather than by the kinds of moralities of choice that are more the focus of the kind of anthropology of morality I have been discussing here.[1]

A second virtue of this theory of culture and value is that it allows us both to say something about the nature of cultural change and to understand something about the role moral discourse tends to play in situations of change. I shall take up this aspect of my argument in the final part of the chapter.

Value, Choice and Morality

My notion of value derives from Dumont (1977, 1980, 1986). Dumont is too rarely read as a theorist, at least in the United States, and thus his understanding of values as an important element of culture, an understanding that shapes all of his work, has largely been forgotten in the midst of polemics focused on the adequacy of his account of Indian culture. I would contend, however, that his analysis of the way values shape cultural structures is his most important contribution to anthropology more generally and deserves to be revisited. In the present context, I want to argue that a clear understanding of how values operate in culture can help us formulate a model of freedom that does not disregard the force of cultural norms and the routines they produce.

In Dumont's scheme, values are determinations of the relative importance of elements of a culture (beliefs, ideas, things etc.) and as such always serve to produce hierarchies of more or less valued elements. The ways elements are arranged in such hierarchies can be further specified by referring to Dumont's idea that the more valued term of a pair encompasses its contrary: that is, in some contexts the more valued term can stand both for itself and for its contrary, as in English the lexeme 'man' can stand for both 'man' and 'woman' or 'goods' can stand for both 'goods" and 'services' (Dumont 1977, 1980). Furthermore, drawing on other parts of Dumont's work, one can suggest that encompassment is just one aspect of the way values organise cultural elements. It is also the case that more valued elements tend to be more elaborately worked out, more rationalised as one might put it in Weberian terms, and to control the rationalisation of less valued ideas such that they can only be worked out to the extent that they do not contradict more valued ones. Finally, it is only in less valued contexts that less valued ideas are able to approach full expression. As an example of these last two aspects of cultural organisation, one can consider how within cultures marked by Western liberalism highly valued ideas of liberty as the right to differ control the rationalisation of less valued ideas of equality, such that ideas concerning equality of opportunity, which support the achievement of individual difference, are fairly well worked out while those of equality of outcome, seen to promote the creation of similarity, are less so. Equality of outcome is in fact only seriously pursued in less valued, private contexts such as the family (where all children, even though their abilities differ from one another, should be fostered, loved and treated equally) (these ideas are more fully developed in Robbins 1994).

One of the great advantages of Dumont's understanding of the way values articulate hierarchical organisation within culture is that he sees value as something internal to culture – not as a matter of subjective appraisal. In a Dumontian framework, one reads values off the organisation of a culture by looking at relations of encompassment and limitation between elements. Where such relations occur, it is clear that there is a value in play. As is the case with linguistic markedness, which clearly served as a model for Dumont's ideas about hierarchy and encompassment, value is understood to be part of the structure, not something people add to structure by virtue of their subjective responses to it (Battistella 1990). Values can be understood, then, as that part of culture that structures the relations between other parts.

Dumont infamously proceeds not only on the assumption that all cultures are structured by values, but also on the further assumption that each culture also possesses a paramount value that ultimately structures the relations between all the other values it contains and hence the overall structure of the culture as a whole. Relations of subordination between values produce the various contexts and levels by means of which Dumont is able to handle apparent contradictions and other complexities that arise between various cultural elements without sacrificing the claim that a single value is also paramount (Barnes et al. 1985). Returning to an example discussed above, the family in Western culture can promote the value of holism, but as such it becomes a subordinated context existing at a lower level of Western ideology, with its values ultimately sacrificed to those of the individualist market when they come into direct conflict (a dynamic that renders incoherent the 'family values' rhetoric of conservative, market-oriented Christian fundamentalists in the United States). This type of analysis tends towards the production of an image of culture as a fully settled hierarchical arrangement of values that structures all relations between cultural elements. It is an image that suggests that cultures are quite stable, with paramountcy settled and all contradictions resolved. In this respect, it tends to treat cultural reproduction as unproblematic, and it is largely silent on issues of morality which, as in the Durkheimian problematic discussed above, are assumed to be taken care of at the level of cultural reproduction itself.

I want to argue here that the sense one often gets in orthodox Dumontian analyses that cultures are stably organised and that those living in them face few pressing moral problems can be challenged without discarding Dumont's insights into the role of values in structuring culture. A productive way to do this is to consider Weber's (1946, 1949) account of value spheres and the relations between them. In Weber's (1946) model, laid out most famously in his essay 'Religious

Rejections of the World and their Directions', he describes cultures as divided between an economic sphere, a political sphere, an aesthetic sphere, an erotic sphere, and an intellectual sphere (which includes religion and science). This particular division is one Weber takes to be particularly modern, and the increasing differentiation of spheres is central to his model of modernisation. But I want to suggest that we can read his discussion of it at a formal level (that is, disregarding for theoretical purposes the substantive content of the various spheres he describes in modernity) as a model of the role of values in all cultures, a model that in many respects parallels Dumont's, while in one important respect diverging from it. Looked at formally, the key to Weber's model is that it assumes that cultures will possess a number of different value spheres and that they will be 'governed by different laws' (1946: 123). Each individual sphere, understood as a cultural phenomenon, is marked by a 'rational consistency' that comes from representing the realisation of its own value in the fullest possible terms, uninhibited by the demands of other values (Weber 1946: 323). Each of these totalising representations is fine within it own sphere, but the fact that in such representations each sphere imagines the ability of its own values to subordinate all others means that in the culture as a whole spheres and their ideal representations are destined to stand in relationships of contradiction to one another. This is why, Weber says, 'the various value spheres of the world stand in irreconcilable conflict with each other' (1946: 147), a point driven home in his famous image of values as the warring gods between whom people must choose. His overall model is thus one of culture as made up of spheres, each governed by a different value and destined as such to enter into relationships of irresolvable contradiction with all other spheres.

Weber shares with Dumont a construal of values as things that possess an ability to consistently ('rationally') organise the elements of culture, and he crucially shares a commitment to looking at culture as structured by values that are themselves part of culture, rather than something brought to culture by individuals with various interests, etc. (see Brubaker 1984).[2] Where Weber differs from Dumont is in his image of cultural values as in constant conflict. He does not rule out the possibility that there might exist a 'standpoint from which the conflicts could … be held to be resolved in a higher synthesis' (Weber 1946: 147), and this is precisely the standpoint Dumont identifies with his notion of a paramount value. But ultimately it is the conflicts Weber sees as more important in shaping cultural life, at least in modernity.

Weber's theme of the conflict between value spheres opens up a way to theorise ethical matters of choice and freedom that is not available in Dumont's model as it stands. As Schroeder (1992: 146) puts it, 'the harmony and conflict between the various spheres imposes various ethical demands on the individual'. Although Schroeder does not go on to make this clear, it is further appropriate to say that harmony and conflict impose different ethical demands. Harmony within and between spheres puts in place a Durkheimian morality of reproduction, where the rules are clear and the compulsion to follow them very strong. Conflict, in contrast, invites, indeed demands, the kinds of reflexive choice that Laidlaw associates with ethical freedom.[3] Weber himself at one point in his methodological essays nearly approaches the way I have shaped the problem up here:

> In almost every important attitude of real human beings, the value-spheres cross and interpenetrate. The shallowness of our routinized daily existence in the most significant sense of the word consists indeed in the fact that the persons who are caught up in it do not become aware ... of this ... motley of irreconcilably antagonistic values.They avoid the choice between 'God' and the 'Devil' and their own ultimate decision as to which of the conflicting values will be dominated by the one, and which the other. The fruit of the tree of knowledge, which is distasteful to the complacent but which is, nonetheless, inescapable, consists in the insight that every single important activity and ultimately life as a whole, if it is not to be permitted to run on as an event in nature but is instead to be consciously guided, is a series of ultimate decisions through which the soul – as in Plato – chooses its own fate, i.e., the meaning of its activity and existence. (Weber 1949: 18)

All that is missing here is an appreciation of the Durkheimian point, maintained in relation to a theory of cultural and value in Dumont, that in fact the unreflective moments of life do not 'run on as an event in nature', but rather unfold within domains of culture in which value hierarchies are stably organised and hence the relations between values well worked out. It is where this is not the case, where conflict between values arises, that a morality of freedom and choice comes into play and people become consciously aware of choosing their own fates. And it is because in such cases people become aware of choosing between values that they come to see their decision-making process as one engaged with moral issues.

The upshot of this argument about how our understanding of morality must be situated within a theory of the way values structure culture is twofold. First, it suggests that a fully rounded anthropology of morality needs to be able to describe and account for those kinds of 'integrated' value complexes that promote Durkheimian moralities of reproduction when and where they occur in a culture. Secondly, we need to be able to understand the nature of value conflicts if we are to further develop our ability to study the kind of moral practice that takes shape through the experience of freedom and the making of choices. It is the second of these tasks I want to take up in what follows.

Value Conflict, Cultural Change, and the Morality of Freedom

If freedom arises most clearly where values are in open conflict, their differences unresolved by the cultural fiat of a settled hierarchical arrangement between them, then the anthropology of morality needs to develop an understanding of the origins and nature of unresolved value conflicts. While there are surely a number of ways to develop such an understanding, I want in this chapter to begin by making a single typological distinction between stable conflicts that are an enduring part of a culture and those conflicts that arise as a result of change.

Stable conflicts are important in many cultures. Laidlaw's (1995) ethnography of the Jains of the city of Jaipur in north-west India, one of the richest ethnographies of morality in the literature, investigates a moral system that arises out of such a stable conflict. In the Jain case, the conflict is between the ascetic values of renouncers who attempt to fully realise the goal of non-violence and the merchant values that govern much of the life of lay Jains, who nonetheless also venerate renouncers and deploy various ritual techniques that allow them to realise some aspects of the rigid ascetic morality that guide the practice of renunciation. It is by living between these two conflicting values that lay Jains find their freedom and come to live lives that are marked by a sense that moral issues are at stake in an unusually extensive range of kinds of action. More generally, all of those cultures shaped by what some, following Jaspers (1953) and, more crucially for our purposes, Eisenstadt (1982), call axial age traditions – that is, those that posit a distinction between this world and a more morally perfect one situated elsewhere in space or time – produce cultures in which people live with a stable awareness of a conflict between their daily actions and those that would be morally ideal. The existence of such cultures marked by stable conflicts raises many theoretical questions, one of the most crucial being why such enduring conflicts have not been worked out by means of the kinds of elaborate arrangements of contexts and levels that are so important to Dumont's theory of culture and which clearly do play an important role in reducing value conflicts in many cultures. For present purposes, however, I simply want to note the existence of such cases and indicate that they do routinely generate a cultural emphasis on issues of freedom, choice and morality.

The second kind of value conflict my minimal typology makes room for is that produced by cultural change. Cultural change itself is not a well-theorised notion in anthropology, and anthropologists tend to be more sophisticated when it comes to ferreting out cultural continuities, even in cases of obvious transformation, than they are at determining when things have actually changed (Robbins 2003). I would argue, however, that one advantage of a theory that sees values as crucial to cultural structure is that it then becomes possible to define cultural change in operational terms as occurring only when key values change. Such change can occur either because new values are introduced or because the hierarchical relations that hold between traditional values have been transformed. When values change in either of these ways, conflicts between them are destined to arise as old values assert their importance in the face of new ones or previously dominant values attempt to hold their position in the face of the growing importance of previously subordinate ones. Over time, new stable structures of the kind described by Dumont may arise, but during the course of change conflict is likely to be the norm. This is why people's sense of the moral weight of their actions is strong during times of change. The rest of this chapter is devoted to fleshing out this model of the way the value conflicts prevalent in the course of change drive moral concern by looking in detail at the single ethnographic case of the Urapmin of Papua New Guinea.

Morality, Values and Change among the Urapmin

The Urapmin are a group of approximately 390 people living in the West Sepik Province of Papua New Guinea (PNG). The Urapmin were colonised only in the late 1940s and never directly missionised by Westerners. They experienced rapid and extensive cultural change in the late 1970s when, in the course of about a year, everyone in the community became caught up in a Christian revival movement sweeping through the highlands of PNG and converted to a charismatic brand of Christianity focused on the availability of the gifts of the Holy Spirit to contemporary believers. When I began fieldwork in Urapmin in early 1991, the Urapmin continued to see themselves as an entirely Christian community. Christianity remained the single most important focus of public life and the struggle to live as a good Christian was the most pressing personal project of everyone with whom I became close. In a pattern that is common in cases of Pentecostal and charismatic conversion in many parts of the world, the beings and ideas of traditional Urapmin religion remained important only as evils whose influence converts need to reject with all their strength (Robbins 2004a). Their continued salience thus does not compromise the claim that in the religious realm the Urapmin have taken on the culture of charismatic Christianity as their own.

The story of how and why the Urapmin converted so quickly and thoroughly to charismatic Christianity is one I have told in detail elsewhere (Robbins 2004b). In the process of telling it, I have been at pains to establish, on the basis of a detailed ethnographic description of everyday and ritual life in Urapmin, the sophistication of Urapmin Christian understanding and the extent to which it demands to be seen as, in important respects, in line with the thinking of Pentecostal and charismatic Christians in many other parts of the world, including the West. One point that follows and that is important for the current discussion is that the Urapmin can fairly be said to have embraced a new culture in the process of conversion. Theirs is not a case of merely adopting a few Christian ideas and symbols and slotting them into old understandings or laying them as a thin veneer over traditional religion. The Urapmin have rather to a large extent come to understand their own lives and the world in new ways.

One of the most notable aspects of Urapmin Christianity is its very strong emphasis on morality. Urapmin define what they call the 'Christian life' (Kristin laip)[4] as one lived in accordance with a wide range of Christian laws (lo, *awem*), which not only prohibit such obvious crimes as murder and theft but also interdict feelings of anger, covetousness and strong desire. More generally, the Urapmin understand Christianity to prohibit all kinds of behaviour in which one imposes one's 'will' (*san*) on others. The ideal Christian possesses a peaceful, gentle 'heart' (*aget*, the seat of all feelings and thoughts) at all times and maintains a quietist remove from the rough and tumble of social life. As the Urapmin see it, they live their lives in constant struggle to make the kinds of choices that will allow them to conform to this model of good behaviour.

By their own account, the Urapmin are willing to work so hard at meeting the rigorous moral standards of their Christianity because they believe that Jesus may return at any moment and that when he does they will face the judgement of God for all time. People regularly worry over the possible coming of the Apocalypse and are always on the lookout for signs of its approach. For the purposes of this chapter, Urapmin apocalypticism is important for the way it renders moral decision-making a matter of private desperation and intense public focus. Individuals constantly review their moral standing in their own thoughts or in conversation with their close relatives, and public discourse is shot through with moral concern. With the Second Coming always at the forefront of people's minds, they are constantly and keenly aware of the stakes involved in their moral choices.

Intense concern with morality is attested to in many aspects of Urapmin life. One place to find it is in the way people talk, both in more formal speech genres and in everyday conversation. Concern with morality is evident, for example, in the moral harangues often given in central village plazas by leaders (*kamok*) as people are waking up in the morning or whenever they have gathered to discuss other matters. Similar moral lectures are a staple of sermons and other speeches given during the church services Urapmin hold at least three times a week and often even more regularly. Urapmin pastors tend to preach not on biblical stories, but on the lists of virtues and vices (the so-called 'moral lists') that make up so much of the New Testament. Taking such texts as their starting points, pastors centre their sermons on the need for people to act morally (for an example, see Robbins 2004b: 226–31). The moralising rhetoric of these public performances finds its way into more private forms of talk as well. People's everyday conversations frequently dwell on their attempts to suppress their own anger and desire or to help others do so in order to prevent their fall into sin, and they often take up the possibility of immorality in all areas of life. Finally, in their confessions to pastors and deacons, a ritual I shall mention again later, people offer detailed accounts of their immoral feelings and behaviours that rely heavily on the moral language that so shapes public rhetoric.

The preoccupation with morality that is so evident in Urapmin ways of speaking also dominates their ritual life. In Urapmin Christianity, rituals are designed either to fortify people so that they can successfully make moral choices, or to help them recuperate from their failure to do so. Church services, the most frequently held rituals, are designed to train people in moral behaviour. They do this explicitly by featuring teaching on the tenets of moral thinking in sermons and other kinds of didactic speech, and more implicitly by the way that success in sitting through a service quietly and attentively is taken as a moral accomplishment because it involves the quieting of wilful desires. Yet, in spite of the constant moral education church services provide, people still regularly find themselves, or feel themselves, to be falling into immorality. It is immorality, or what the Urapmin call 'sin', that motivates the remainder of Urapmin ritual life. Regular confession, delivered to a pastor or deacon, is followed by participation at group possession dances called 'Spirit dances' (Spirit disko). In these dances, people become possessed by the Holy Spirit. As the Spirit fights to throw their sins out of their bodies, their movements become very violent until the Spirit finally triumphs and they collapse on the church floor finally free of sin. Confession and the Spirit dances, along with a variety of healing rituals I shall not describe here that draw on similar ideas about sin and its consequences, provide a ritual technology for overcoming moral fault and returning people to a neutral starting point from which to again begin their project of leading moral Christian lives.[5]

Although the description I have given thus far aims to establish the centrality of morality to Urapmin life in both its everyday and ritual forms, there is one important aspect of their moral system I have yet to discuss in detail. Urapmin moral consciousness is marked not only by its prominence in people's lives, but also by the vast number of domains of Urapmin life in which it asserts its relevance. For the Urapmin, the need to think carefully about the moral outcomes of one's actions is not a matter simply of those areas of life in which they imagine that it is possible to commit 'major' (*dabum*) sins – areas such fighting, theft and adultery. Rather, almost all areas of life, even the most quotidian, are fraught with moral danger. One has to be on guard when going to one's garden, since inordinate desire may lead one to covet others' crops one sees along the way. One also has to be watchful in family life, where anger may lead one to scold or physically punish one's children. Even the realm of commensality and reciprocal giving is not safe, for to take a gift not from the giver's hand but from the ground or floor of the house is also a moral failure (see Robbins 2004b). More generally, since feelings of anger (*aget atul*), shame (*fitom*), and willful desire (*san*) are all immoral in themselves, any situation in which they might arise is one that demands moral vigilance. The very high salience moral issues have in Urapmin life thus follows not only from their apocalyptic sensibilities, but also from the way they have defined morality as relevant to all areas of life.

The goal of this quick sketch of the very broad and prominent role morality plays in contemporary Urapmin religion has been to indicate how fully it makes sense to describe Urapmin people as currently living with a heightened moral consciousness. More than many people, they actually approach Weber's ideal of living life 'consciously' as 'a series of ultimate decisions through which the soul ... chooses its own fate'. Since they treat so many domains of their lives as ones in which they face such ultimate decisions, there is very little room for the kind of smooth morality of reproduction Durkheimian models lead us to imagine as at the centre of social life. Far more often than they experience the moral comforts of adhering to trusted routines, they experience themselves as confronted by the need to make the kinds of free, conscious choices Laidlaw discusses. The question their case raises, then, is that of how they have come to experience their lives in such one-sided terms, terms that leave them perennially fretful about the moral states of their souls and perpetually anxious about the moral demands of even routine, everyday activities.

In answering this question, one temptation is to argue that it comes as no surprise that they see themselves as free, morally responsible individuals because this is the ideology of the kind of charismatic Protestantism to which they have committed themselves. This is no doubt partially true, and I shall develop some thoughts along these lines below when I discuss the values Christianity has introduced in Urapmin. But it cannot be the whole truth, since many other adherents of such individualist, morally strict kinds of Protestantism manage to live lives more neatly balanced between the morality of reproduction and the morality of freedom; they face some areas of their lives, say sexuality or political participation, with a heightened awareness of freedom and its demands, but are happy to treat behaviour in other realms, say in their work, as a matter of adhering to socially acceptable routines. We thus need to find another explanation for the way the morality of freedom has become so dominant in Urapmin. In what follows, I want to suggest that the best explanation turns on their experience of cultural change and the way such change has forced them to live their lives caught between conflicting cultural values.

In order to argue that it is cultural change and its attendant value conflicts that have caused the Urapmin to experience their existence as morally fraught, I need to say a bit more about how cultural change has unfolded in Urapmin. Up to this point, I have emphasised the extent to which charismatic Christianity has come to dominate Urapmin thinking and I have stressed how radical the Urapmin experience of change has been. This account is true in its own terms, but it does leave out one key area in which Urapmin culture has not been so fully transformed. This is the area of what I would call social structure, or cultural ideas about how society is organised and how social relations should be carried out. While Christianity has replaced cultural ideas in many other domains in Urapmin, it has not been able to succeed fully in this regard in the domain of social structure.

There are, I think, two reasons why traditional Urapmin social structure has remained intact in the face of the otherwise radical changes their culture has undergone. First, the kind of charismatic Christianity the Urapmin adhere to is so focused on the individual (see below) that it offers little in the way of models of how to organise social life. In the West, where this kind of Christianity first developed early in the twentieth century, the work of structuring social life was left primarily to the capitalist market. But the Urapmin do not participate in any meaningful way in such a market, and thus it cannot play this role for them. Indeed, the absence of the market in Urapmin points to the second reason why charismatic Christianity has not been able to replace traditional Urapmin models of social structure. Despite all of the cultural changes that have taken place in Urapmin, what we might call their mode of production has remained virtually unchanged. Urapmin are still subsistence gardeners who supplement their diet with meat gained primarily from hunting and very occasionally from domestically raised pigs. Although they desire very much to enter the cash economy, they have as yet succeeded very little in doing so. It is because traditional Urapmin models of social structure are so closely tied to their mode of production that they have not been able to abandon them in favour of other models, including those rather paltry ones that are a part of their Christianity.

Given that Urapmin social structural ideas persist alongside the Christian ideas that have become so important, it is fair to describe the Urapmin situation as one in which two distinct cultural logics are in play. Neither of these logics has succeeded in subordinating the other or in reframing the other in its own terms, and so they remain in struggle with one another as two coherent conceptions of how to live in the world that compete for people's adherence. I have elsewhere tried to theorise the processes of change by which such dual cultural situations come about (Robbins 2004b, 2005). I am more concerned here to demonstrate that living in such a situation leads the Urapmin to experience life as a continual process of choosing between the conflicting values that structure these two logics, and that it is the fact that so many of their choices are ones made between conflicting values that gives their lives such moral intensity.

There is no space here to lay out either traditional Urapmin social structural thinking or their Christian ideas in detail. But my argument only really requires that we realise that these two cultural orders are governed by different values that demand different kinds of moral choices, not that we understand fully the structures such logics put in place. What I want to show, then, is that traditional Urapmin social structural thinking is oriented by the value of relationalism, while their Christian thought is structured by the value of individualism.

Relationalism is a value that defines the creation and maintenance of relationships as paramount. Elements of a culture are judged by their ability to create or maintain relationships, with those that promote relationships accorded more value and those that hinder them accorded less. In developing the notion of relationalism as a value, I have drawn heavily on the work of those such as Wagner (1977, 1981), Gregory (1982) and Strathern (1988) who argue that Melanesian cultures are best seen as centreed around 'gift economies', in which people's primary goals involve the construction and positive transformation of relationships. It is well established that in such cultures there is no notion of the individual outside of relationships or of the social whole that might serve as the focus of values that would compete with relationalism for paramountcy (Robbins 1994, 2004b). This general description of relationalist cultures fits traditional Urapmin ideas about social structure well, and I shall rely on the general image readers have of such cultures to provide a background sense of what Urapmin relationalism is like.

What I want to foreground is how the value of relationalism shapes traditional Urapmin moral thinking. Put most simply, in traditional terms actions that create or enhance relationships are reckoned as moral, while those that prevent relationships from forming or injure those that already exist are immoral. This scheme is fairly straightforward and many kinds of action fall unambiguously on one side or the other of the two possibilities it lays out. Thus, gift giving and other kinds of exchange are reckoned as moral. Eating alone without sharing (*feginin*) is immoral. Cooperating with others in gardening and hunting is moral, while acting alone is suspect, etc. More generally, the Urapmin imagine that people live their life balanced between an impulse to act 'lawfully' (in accordance with *awem*, the law) and one to act 'wilfully' (*futebemin*). In acting lawfully, one honors the demands of already created relationships: one gives gifts to those from whom one has received in the past, one continues to garden with those with whom one has started a garden, etc. In acting wilfully, one asserts oneself in order to start a new relationship by giving a gift to someone with whom one has not previously had a relationship, or by 'pushing' someone to garden or hunt or live with oneself. Such actions are regarded as wilful because they entail a neglect of those with whom one is already in relationship and to whom one could have given the gift or with whom one could have started the garden or gone hunting or built a village. They are also reckoned as wilful because they draw others out of their pre-existing lawful relations and push them to start something new. Thus wilfulness conflicts in important respects with lawfulness, and this conflict is the one that causes the Urapmin the most concern within their traditional moral system.

As difficult as the relationship between wilfulness and lawfulness can become in Urapmin life, however, the traditional moral system does have a way of ameliorating their conflict. It does so by determining the ultimate moral standing of the person on the basis of whether he/she has succeeded in balancing the use of the will to create new relationships with the need to temper it by a lawful respect for the demands of existing relationships. Those who rely too much on the will and race too quickly to make new relations are judged as immorally 'pushy' or 'angry', but those who concentrate only on fulfilling the dictates of the law and do not display enough will in the creation of new relations are judged as weak or disengaged. Unsurprisingly in a culture where the creation and maintenance of relations is the paramount value, it is those who are able to best manage both of these tasks by balancing the expression of lawfulness and wilfulness in their own lives that are deemed the most morally successful. One is judged, in the final analysis, by the quantity and quality of the relationships one has.

In Urapmin Christianity, it is not the creation and maintenance of relationships that is most valued, but rather the creation of an individual self that is worthy of salvation. Because Urapmin recognise that their Christianity holds that it is individuals, not people in relationships, that will be judged in the Second Coming, they have come in many respects to live within the logic of Christian individualism. Once again, I shall forgo detailing all of the individualist aspects of their Christian culture and concentrate only on the way this value has shaped their moral thinking. In Urapmin Christian morality, all wilfulness is deemed immoral in its effects on the self of the person who acts upon it. Feeling anger is the most common sin the Urapmin commit and its regular presence in their hearts stands for them as proof of their sinful nature. Since wilfulness often leads to anger, both in the person who exercises it and in those to whom it is directed, it cannot but be reckoned as immoral. Its relationship-creating abilities do nothing to attenuate this harsh evaluation, because relationships are not themselves of value in the Christian scheme, and thus there are no contexts in which wilfulness might be justified. It is this ban on willfulness that lends Urapmin Christianity its quietist character, and many Urapmin follow out its logic by withdrawing as much as possible from those areas of Urapmin social life where relationship-creating takes place (e.g. marriage negotiations, village formation, etc.).

Just as Urapmin Christian morality makes the wilful creation of relationships dangerous, it also casts doubt on the moral value of even the most lawful kinds of relating that aim simply to reaffirm the value of existing relations. This is so because of what I have called the 'paradox of lawfulness' in Urapmin society (Robbins 2004b). This paradox arises from the fact that in this very small society of 390 people every lawful turning towards someone to whom one already relates is seen by others with whom one has relations as a betrayal of their expectations. Every gift given to a sister could have been given to an affine, just as every hunting trip taken with a father-in-law could have been taken with a brother. From the point of view of those not involved, every lawful gift looks like a wilful act of strengthening one relationship at the expense of others. This leads to a good deal of anger and enviousness, emotions we already know the Urapmin regard in Christian terms as sinful. In their traditional morality, the moral costs such emotions exacted were offset by the more general moral judgement of a person's overall ability to maintain and expand relationships. But, in the Christian system, they are seen as damaging to the person's self, regardless of their outcome in relational terms. As is the case with the will, Christianity thus comes to condemn much lawful relating as well. Its quietism is thus virtually complete and leads many people who regard themselves as morally upright to seek to limit fairly narrowly the range of relationships they maintain.

It is their experience of negotiating between the two would-be paramount values of relationalism and individualism that leads the Urapmin to approach so much of life as a process of moral decision-making. Actions undertaken to realise the values of one system are destined to appear immoral in the other. The relationship-limiting Christian is seen as selfish and as almost a 'rubbish' person (someone without relationships) in the traditional scheme. The traditional type of actor who looks always to maintain lawful relations despite the paradox of lawfulness and to create new relations through acts of wilfulness is judged a sinner in the Christian scheme. Every social act thus becomes a site of moral concern, as people weigh which value to serve in carrying it out. There are few settled routines where the morality of reproduction can hold sway, for the two value systems each aim to govern all of social life and hence come into conflict in all domains. Their war is, as it were, a global one within Urapmin society, and it is this global war that exacts such a heavy moral toll.

If one were to subscribe to a teleological model of cultural change, such that a period of disruption like that caused by having two paramount values in play at the same time was bound to be replaced by a new, settled one in which a single value held sway, it would be appropriate to ask how long the Urapmin will continue to live as they do now. I am not sure that such teleological models, in which cultures are held to tend towards something like equilibrium at the level of values, are really warranted, though a theory like Dumont's would suggest that they are. It is clear in any case that such an equilibrium will not be possible for the Urapmin until they abandon Christianity, find a relational reading of it or learn how to organise their social structure along individualist lines. These solutions, none of which are yet on the horizon, are the ones that would allow them to find what moral comfort that routine reproduction governed by a single paramount value can bring.

Conclusion

This chapter has grown out of an effort to synthesise two often divergent approaches to the anthropology of morality. One approach, inherited from Durkheim, sees all normative social action as having moral content. This leads to a view of moral action as the kind of routine behaviour that reproduces what has come before. A second approach, one that has often been framed in direct contrast to the Durkheimian one, defines the actions people take freely on the basis of conscious choice as those actions to which the notion of morality best applies. My argument has been that both approaches are helpful, albeit in different situations. What is needed, then, is a theory that helps us understand which kinds of situations call for which kind of approach and why they do so. I have suggested that a theory of cultures as organised by values can do this kind of work. Those cultures or cultural domains in which a single value is paramount tend to be structured such that people take moral comfort in reproducing their routines. It is in cultures or domains in which values are in conflict that people become conscious of making choices and feel themselves to possess freedom. It is also in these latter kinds of situations that people are likely to experience a heightened sense of moral concern, a drift towards scrupulosity or fixating on moral debate in everyday life.

On the basis of this approach, I have suggested that situations of cultural change are particularly good ones in which to study the way morality shapes culture and experience. Because situations of change often upend previously stable value hierarchies, they generate the kinds of conflicts that push the morality of choice and freedom to the foreground. Looking at the recent history of the Urapmin people, I have tried to illustrate the worth of this approach by applying it to a case in which moral conflict has been extensive and in which the morality of choice and freedom has almost completely overtaken that of reproduction in the governance of social life. It is my hope that future comparative work can spell out the worth of this kind of approach; one that not only focuses on values but also insists on understanding both the morality of reproduction and that of freedom and choice as valid subjects of investigation by an anthropology of morality.

Notes

*Acknowledgement. A version of this paper has appeared in Ethnos 72(3): 293–314 in 2007 under the title "Between Reproduction and Freedom: Morality, Value, and Radical Cultural Change".

1. Reproduction can, of course, at times be experienced as a choice, but I am referring here to those times when people experience it simply as a matter of doing what is routine or 'natural', without conscious awareness that they might do otherwise.
2. For a brief mention of Weber's Influence on Dumont, see Allen 1998: 3.
3. Sahni (2005: 10) recognises this point when he writes that, for Weber, "conflict is a necessary condition for morality".
4. In this chapter, terms that are underlined are in Tok Pisin, the lingua franca of Papua New Guinea and an important language of Urapmin Christianity. Terms in the Urap language, still the dominant language in Urapmin and the first language of all Urapmin, are given in italics.
5. I have described Urapmin ritual life and its relationship to their ideas about morality much more fully in Robbins 2004b: chapter 7.

Chapter 5

ACCELERATED GLOBALISATION AND THE CONFLICTS OF VALUES SEEN THROUGH THE LENS OF TRANSNATIONAL ADOPTION: A COMPARATIVE PERSPECTIVE

Signe Howell

Children and their well-being became a central public concern during the twentieth century in Western Europe and North America. This ideological focus on the child and the state's commitment to ensure its best interests are thus of recent origin and are linked to changes in the ideology of marriage, procreation and family life more generally. Earlier, one adhered to a moral understanding that adults' needs are paramount, and, according to the influential social historian Ariés (1962), children were perceived as miniature adults with few special needs. This made way during the second half of the nineteenth century for a characterisation of childhood as a particularly vulnerable period during which parents became held responsible for ensuring that children's special needs were met – ranging from nutrition and health to, by the mid-twentieth century, psychological care. This development was accompanied by the notion that the child's needs are paramount, a notion that found its expression in new legislation and guidelines for practice, resulting in Rose's claim that children have become 'the most intensely governed sector of personal existence' (1999: 123). In this chapter I shall explore some ramifications of these historical changes for the value and practice of adoption of the unrelated child. My main focus will be on the recent growth in transnational adoption of children from the poor South and Eastern Europe to the rich North and some implications of the international conventions that were crafted – largely on the initiative of receiving countries – in order to make this transaction a morally acceptable one. Having said that, a question arises: morally acceptable to whom? This question leads to a discussion of values and practices of adoption in countries that today receive and send children in transnational adoption. I shall argue that a paradox has emerged whereby accelerated globalisation creates conflicts of values while, at the same time, the international community is demanding common values. International conventions such as the UN Convention on the Rights of the Child (UNCRC) and The Hague Convention on Inter-country Adoption are expressions of an attempt to formulate universal – or common – values about childhood, parenthood and the state's role in family politics. By examining reactions to these 'common values' of four donor countries – India, China, Ethiopia and Romania – I shall highlight the complexity of the emergent situation. Whether the reaction may be characterised as one of acceptance, modification, resistance or rejection is, in part, dependent upon local values, but, more importantly, it results from the political and economic situation of each country and its relationship with the rich and powerful countries in the North.

Law and Morality

In modern society, perhaps the most explicit formal expression of norms and values is to be found in legislation – not least because laws are made on behalf of society and, from a certain perspective, laws are coterminous with the state. Laws and conventions relating to issues concerning personal behaviour, for example family law, clearly manifest moral concerns about individual and relational rights and duties and lay down premises for action. They may, I suggest, be seen as examples of what Edel and Edel (1968[1959]: 8–11) have characterised as 'ethics narrow', by which only those notions that ought to be, or ought to be realised, come within the scope of morality. The Edels make a distinction between 'ethics wide' and 'ethics narrow'.

The former, they argue, assume that moralities are part and parcel of the whole field of human endeavour and striving, while the latter limit the scope and draw the attention to obligation and duty. The adoption of the unknown child gives rise, I suggest, to precisely a number of 'oughts' and 'ought to be realised' at the same time that the oughts are part and parcel of the wider world view – 'ethics wide'. A temporal and spatial comparative study of adoption practices and legislation therefore provides a vantage point from which one may identify differences in moral perceptions of childhood and, by implication, of parenthood (Howell 2006a).

Legal provisions enable – and enforce – practice to be enacted in line with reigning moral imperatives of the time (and place) and family laws encapsulate a society's embedded values regarding personal relatedness. Moreover, laws form a basis for discursive practices, and hence, family forms today can be said to be crafted through laws (Sterett 2002: 223). Laws are especially interesting in that they reflect contemporary ideas and values while at the same time they seek to modify these in particular directions. Laws are thus descriptive as well as normative and this is particularly apparent in family law. Seen from a different perspective, the law is also a prime technology of government. Legislation on children in general, and adoption in particular, and the establishment of those institutions that ensure the correct application of such laws may be interpreted as examples of what Foucault has termed governmentality. Foucault (1991) argues that the welfare of the population became an increasing concern of the emergent state from the eighteenth century onwards. From that time, good government became not just the exercise of authority over people within the state, or the ability to discipline them, but, more importantly, the fostering of their prosperity and happiness. Or, to put it another way, the state became the moral guardian of its citizens.

According to Miller and Rose, 'Governmentality is a certain mentality that has become the common ground for all forms of modern thought, a way of thinking about the problems that should be addressed by the state and its various authorities' (1990: 76). Governmentality is usually thought of as exercised by national governments, but it may also, I argue, be applied to international organisations such as the UN family. In laws, I suggest, this mentality is articulated and provides premises for action. However, it is, I further suggest, a mentality that pays minimal attention to differences in local (primarily, in the context of this chapter, non-Western) ontologies and moralities. As Western rationality and morality are being globalised along with Western technology and economies, this can lead to what is, in effect, a neo-colonisation through Western moral values of the rest of the world.

As accelerated globalisation has created a demand for common values, it is, as stated above, paradoxical that this demand in itself simultaneously provokes conflicts of values. In order to explore this, my main focus will be on international legislation that is derived from a human rights discourse. In particular, I shall discuss some implicit and explicit notions of two international conventions that deal with the organisation of children in society in general (UN Convention on the Rights of the Child, 1989) and transnational adoption in particular (The Hague Convention of Intercountry Adoption, 1993) and reactions to these by state authorities and professional experts in selected countries that send children for adoption in Western Europe and North America. I shall argue that these conventions reflect moral values of contemporary Western society, that they are perceived as universal values and that they disregard beliefs and practices in many countries in Africa, Asia and elsewhere. I link this hegemony of Western morality to Rose's argument concerning what he calls the growth of a 'psy factor' in the Western approach to personhood and citizenship, which has contributed to the growth of influential expert professions – those who build their expertise upon psychological knowledge (Rose 1999). These experts – educationalists, social workers, therapists – I call psycho-technocrats (Howell 2006a). Partly due to their participation in the shaping of policies concerning children, the discursive practice of transnational adoption is now informed by the concept (or even slogan) of 'the best interest of the child'. While this has become increasingly influential as a moral guideline, no clear definition of what it might mean is provided, an omission that easily gives rise to misunderstandings and resentment amongst bureaucrats and adoption personnel in the countries concerned.

'Childhood' as a Cultural Category with Moral(astic) Overtones

Cultural understanding of adoption necessarily involves cultural understanding of the different parties involved, the so-called adoption triangle made up of the biological and adoptive parents and the adoptees. What meanings and values are attributed to each tell us a lot about the meanings and values of the practice itself and give rise to questions such as: What is the purpose of adoption? Who is thought to be the main beneficiary, and why? What should the role of the various parties be? As the modern nation state has increasingly involved itself with adoption, a fourth party should, I suggest, be added to the triangle, namely the state – making it an adoption nexus. What is, or ought to be, the role of the state in the transaction, becomes pertinent to ask? All these questions have to be considered in connection with the broader issue of the meaning of children, childhood, parenthood and the family. In the case of adoption across national boundaries, the adoption nexus may further be extended to a fifth actor, namely the donor country. In what follows, my main concern is to elicit some areas of disagreements about the understandings of what constitute both an 'ethics narrow' and an 'ethics wide' of children and childhood of the principles of the conventions and the countries that provide children in adoption. I shall briefly consider how different countries handle their disagreement, whether through acceptance, resistance, adaptation or distortion or by just ignoring it.

As stated above, the contemporary Euro-American notion of childhood as a particular stage in life qualitatively different from adulthood is of relatively recent origin. By the end of the nineteenth century, childhood was no longer regarded as a preparation for something else (adulthood), but as a stage in life to be valued in its own right, indeed, not only a separate stage in life but the best of those stages (Cunningham 1995: 61). Under the impact of romanticism, the 'childlike quality of the child' became entrenched, leading to a celebration of innocence and vulnerability. Ariés argues that there is a connection between the idea of childhood and the idea of the family, and that both became imbued with moral significance in France and Western Europe generally. As the family gradually assumed a moral and spiritual function, he claims that 'by today [early 1960s] our world is obsessed by the physical, moral and sexual problems of childhood' (Ariés 1962: 296). Not surprisingly, the twentieth century has been called the century of childhood (Melosh 2002). It was a century that unified new academic disciplines – paediatrics and developmental psychology – into a formidable body of normative expertise whose knowledge spread to other professions – educationalists, lawyers, social workers, therapists – and came to affect the lives of every family in the USA and Northern Europe and, as the century moved on, those in other parts of the world also.

In Europe and North America, the celebration of childhood as a period of innocence and happiness led to a felt need to make arrangements to ensure that this was achieved. According to the modern Western view of a proper childhood, a child should have a carefree, safe, secure and happy existence and be raised by caring and responsible biologically related adults inside a family home (see Panther-Brick 2000). This led to the introduction of children's laws as well as adoption laws in these countries, laws that were adapted throughout the century to both accommodate and shape reigning values. I shall argue that these values were incorporated into international conventions and, increasingly, into national laws in the developing world.

Family laws may be analysed as 'technologies of rule ... technologies imbued with aspirations for the shaping of conduct in the hope of producing certain desired effects and averting certain undesired ones' (Rose 1999: 52). It is in this connection that I find Foucault's concept of governmentality – in the sense of the benevolent but controlling state – to be helpful. I wish to suggest that global governmentality may be discerned in areas of human rights issues – which at a certain level transnational adoption may be classified as – and that in such instances benevolence frequently becomes paternalism (Howell 2003b). Within the legal domain of adoption, one may discern the exercise of three levels of governmentality: first, the national level, where each country codifies basic premises for adoption and issues legally binding directives for the practice; secondly, the global level where legislation on adoption is codified in international treaties or conventions; and thirdly, the introduction of family and adoption laws in a number of developing countries. In this chapter I shall not deal with national legislation (see Howell 2006a, b). I shall argue that a normative project of deliberate globalisation of Western morality and rationality – deriving its legitimacy from human rights discourses – may be observed in the formulation, codification, execution and monitoring of relevant multilateral conventions.

An earlier relaxed attitude to child-adult relationships in Europe and North America was by the end of the nineteenth century replaced by one in which the biological tie between parents and children was made the locus for moral responsibility (Gillis 1996: chapter 8). Due to this increasing association between biology and kinship, abandoned children became, I suggest, dekinned- in effect, denuded of kinship, rendered socially naked and, as such, morally suspect (Howell 2006a). Being outside biologically based kinship, abandoned children became hostages to fortune. This may help account for the rough, often cruel, treatment of them in orphanages that continued in Europe and North America until the late 1950s. While the metaphorical statements 'blood is thicker than water' and 'one's own flesh and blood' continue to constitute a folk understanding (as well as that of the majority of psycho-technocrats) of Euro-American kinship, a parallel discourse that emphasises the constituting significance of the bounded individual is equally dominant. Ever since Kant 'threw new light on the understanding of human nature by insisting on man being autonomous, i.e. self-regulating' (Svendsen

2004: 146), Western philosophical and ideological traditions have maintained the ontological and moral centrality of the autonomous individual. Twentieth-century discourses about identity and personhood occurred within a cultural climate that 'has come to celebrate the values of autonomy and self-realizing' (Rose 1999: xv). Dumont has argued that the flip side of the ideological centrality of the individual is universal man (1979: 792). This means, in effect, that everything social and cultural is rendered epiphenomenal to the existential centrality of the individual. From a normative perspective, kin categories such as mother, father, son, daughter are viewed less as relational and more as statuses. Morality becomes a question of individual rights and obligations vis-à-vis concrete other individuals – and the state- rather than an integral part of being in the world, a constituting consequence of human sociality. The individual emerges as his or her own reference point, the bearer of his or her destiny; rights and responsibilities are anchored in the bounded individual. It is to this understanding that one may trace the discourse of rights that grew up during the second half of the twentieth century and which found its most clear expression in the United Nations Declarations of Human Rights (UNDHR) from 1948 and the subsequent United Nations Convention on the Rights of the Child, as well as The Hague Convention on Inter-country Adoption. It is this insistence on the ontological status of the individual that provokes a strong reaction in many countries in the South.

Governmentality: Local and Global

Justice and fairness are two major principles of European jurisprudence that have accompanied the development of democracy. Interestingly, laws that regulate the private family life of citizens are relatively late arrivals. In particular, laws that regulate the life of children did not appear until the beginning of the twentieth century. From that time onwards, however, childhood has been more and more regulated and increasingly the state has appointed itself as its moral guardian. As the new category of childhood, perceived as qualitatively different from adulthood, became entrenched in people's thinking, children and childhood emerged as prime targets for state intervention. Adoption, a practice that challenges the very foundation of twentieth-century biocentrism of Euro-American kinship, seems to present the state authorities with a practice particularly well suited for the exercise of benevolent control. While the moral principles underpinning recent national adoption laws in Western Europe are in line with an idealistic approach towards governing society in order to achieve the best interest of its subject (see Miller and Rose 1991), they are also normative and universalising.

What we note in adoption laws is a radical shift in the identity of those whose best interest the laws should safeguard; from adults to children; from aiming to satisfy the needs of adoptive parents to favouring the needs of the adoptee (Caiani-Praturlon 1991: 206; Melosh 2002: 52–53). The paramount purpose of adoption became to ensure 'the best interest of the child'. From now on, the state implemented an ideology of civic responsibility for children. These priorities do not correspond to values in the majority of the countries that Western people adopt from. Nevertheless, the shift in ultimate control over children from the family to public authorities that occurred in Northern Europe during the twentieth century is now happening on a global scale. Global laws about children (in the form of international conventions) seek to ensure the 'best interests of the child' by transferring authority not only from the family to the state, but also from the state to the international level. This is very explicit in the case of transnational adoption. The prime aims of Sections 22 and 23 of the UN Convention on the Rights of the Child (UNCRC) and the more specialised Hague Convention on Protection of Children and Cooperation in Respect of Inter-country Adoption (The Hague Convention) are to safeguard the best interests of the child in adoption. In the Preamble to the actual articles of the CRC, we can find some unquestioned assumptions upon which the articles were formulated. Some of the relevant ones in the present context are:

- Recalling that in the Universal Declaration of Human Rights, the UN has proclaimed that childhood is entitled to special care and assistance.

- Convinced that the family, as the fundamental group of society and the natural environment for the growth and well-being of all its members and particularly children …

- Recognising that the child, for a full and harmonious development of his and her personality, should grow up in a family environment …

- Considering that the child should be fully prepared to live an individual life in society.

The diversity of cultural understanding receives a nodding acknowledgement at the end of the Preamble, when it is stated, 'Taking due account of the importance of the traditions and cultural values of each people for the protection and harmonious development of the child.' However, the implications of this are not pursued in the actual articles of the Convention, or in the subsequent monitoring reports. The bounded socially naked individual is made the basic unit at the expense of an analytic understanding that persons are constituted through the particularity of their sociality whose meaning, in each case, is derived from local cultural and social ideas and practices. In this way a conceptual leap is made from the individual to the universal and the global. In effect, humans are desocialised and deculturised. The conventions are based on a morally endorsed Euro-American understanding of the late twentieth-century meaning of the family and of adoption, thereby somehow naturalising them. In order to instil universal ethical values, local understandings about the rights and responsibilities of sociality are ignored. The establishment of a global infrastructure to supervise the implementation of these conventions is the manifest expression of global governmentality, a globalisation of Western rationality and morality (Howell 2003a, 2006a). Accompanying this and legitimising practice are psychologically informed discourses, voiced and managed by the psycho-technocrats who work both nationally and internationally.

There is an intentionality built into the globalisation of (Western) rationality and morality, albeit from the best of motives: a genuine desire on the part of the wealthy nations to safeguard and improve the lives of unprotected children everywhere. However, several assumptions arise from this agenda which remain undebated; e.g. that it is best for children to grow up with their biological parents in a family home; that children are vulnerable and in need of adult protection; that street children and child labour are unacceptable phenomena; that the child of whatever age is an individual with his or her rights; that the child's agency must be encouraged and he or she be empowered to participate actively in shaping their own future.

At the root of the enterprise lies the unquestioned idea of the universal person; a notion that gives rise to the idea that children are culturally neutral. Lopatka, Chairman of the UNCRC drafting committee, has stated, 'The physical and mental nature of a child is identical everywhere ... the process of growth and adolescence takes a similar course in all children. Their physical and mental needs are also similar' (in Burman 1996: 60). This a view reflected in much expert opinion, in which 'culture produces only minor variations' (Penn 2002: 124). Of course, such understandings render the universal implementation of values and procedures unproblematic, and the principle of the 'best interest of the child' need not be debated.

A recent change in global policy about children indicates a change in thinking about moral responsibility. Increasingly, it is argued that to pursue a policy of laying down the law of what is 'best interest' is paternalistic, and that it should be replaced by the principle that children have a right to express their views and to have their wishes taken into account. For example, according to Franklin, the English Children Act 1989 'carefully straddles the divide between protectionist (paternalist) and participatory rights' (Franklin 2002: 4). In recent UNCRC jargon, 'participation is now added to the "two Ps" of protection and provisions' (ibid.: 6). Participation and the related concept of empowerment today dominate child-welfare measures in Europe and are in the process of being exported to the rest of the world. This not withstanding, there is little to indicate that the basic intentions in the Preamble of the two conventions have in any sense been abandoned – at least in the encounter between the adoption authorities of Europe and North America and donor countries (see below). It is clear that the moral values of the conventions do not always find a ready resonance in countries that give children for adoption in the West. Although all contracting states to the UN (with the exception of the USA and Somalia) have signed and ratified the UNCRC, fewer have done so with regard to The Hague Convention. However, signature does not necessarily mean either agreement with the basic tenets or understanding of the constituting values upon which they are formulated..

While the goal of transnational adoption is to bring children to Western couples, state authorities in receiving countries ensure that they control the transaction – although, as will become clear, donor countries have some means at their disposal to assert themselves. An overriding concern of the authorities in receiving countries is to ensure that the best interest of the children is safeguarded, and that the transaction is conducted in a legally and morally acceptable manner – albeit according to the rules that they themselves have made. In order to achieve this, representatives from the Western countries employ a mixture of persuasion and compulsion. They impose conditions before releasing funds or granting legitimacy to local institutions, they monitor practices, they arrange courses and seminars for local staff during which the 'technologies of knowledge' are imparted, they flatter and cajole and invite senior government servants and orphanage personnel to visit (all expenses paid).

I turn next to a consideration of examples of explicit or implicit resistance to the regulations, of feelings of impotence, as well as a lack of understanding of the implications of the conventions. My aim is to highlight the globalisation of Western morality and rationality as well as their ambivalent reception in many non-Western countries.

The African Charter on the Rights and Welfare of the Child

Reservations voiced by some African delegates during the drafting of the UNCRC resulted in a special charter that was intended to give voice to African values and to contrast them to some parts of the UNCRC. The Organisation of African Unity agreed in 1990 on the formulation of the African Charter on the Rights and Welfare of the Child (ACRWC) (see Ojo 1990 for a discussion of the background to the Charter). It is a document that I interpret as an act of resistance on the part of the African states against what they perceive as the attempted imposition of Western values. The ACRWC entered into force in 1999. It starts by affirming its adherence to the UNCRC, but also to The African Charter on Human and People's Rights. The Charter does not diverge from most of the paragraphs of the UNCRC, but makes a strong argument for the need to take account of African practices and values and to regard children as integral members of their communities, not as isolated individuals. Not least, they find fault with 'the Western obsessive concern with the dignity of the individual, his worth, personal autonomy and property' (Leglesse in Van der Waal 1990).

The African objections to the UNCRC, as I read them, are directed at the unquestioned assumption of the Convention that its definitions of what is right and proper are universally applicable. In other words, while the Convention employs the language of universality, the African critics demand that local moral values and practices be granted a voice. In order to balance this trend and to make the provisions more in line with 'African values and practices', the Preamble states: 'Taking into consideration the virtues of their cultural heritage, historical background and the values of the African civilization, which should inspire and characterize their reflection on the concept of the rights and welfare of the child'. And making the point that rights should not be isolated from responsibilities, they continue, 'considering that the promotion and protection of the rights and welfare of the child also implies the performance of duties on the part of everyone.'

The Africans are critical of what they regard as the failure of the UNCRC to perceive children as constituted through their relationship with others: their parents and members of the wider kin group. In other words, an extreme individualistic understanding of personhood referred to above is not accepted by the African delegates. In order to balance the emphasis upon the rights of the child, the Charter places these within a discourse of obligations and duties, putting children and their significant others partners in reciprocal relationships that extend beyond the family to the nation, and even to the African continent. Thus, Article 31, entitled 'Responsibility of the Child', states:

Every child shall have duties towards his family and society, the State and other legally recognized communities and the international community. The child ... shall have the duty:

(a) to work for the cohesion of the family, to respect his parents, superiors and elders at all times and to assist them in case of need;

(b) to serve the national community by placing his physical and intellectual abilities at its service;

(c) to preserve and strengthen social and national solidarity;

(d) to preserve and strengthen their independence and the integrity of his country;

(e) to contribute to the best of his abilities, at all times, and at all levels, to the promotion and achievement of African Unity.

These provisions are indeed different from those contained in both the UNDHR and UNCRC. As such, they demonstrate attempts to resist global enforcement of ideas and values concerning family, kinship and personhood.

Undoubtedly, all the countries that give up abandoned and orphaned children for adoption overseas do so because they are unable, or unwilling, to provide for the children themselves. My argument will be that they all experience an ambivalence regarding the practice. All are aware of the neocolonial overtones as well as the risk of immoral and illegal practices, but the way they choose to deal with these varies from country to country.

Values and Practices in India[1]

Because large sections of the Indian elite are highly ambivalent about their relationship with the West, India is a particularly interesting donor country from the point of view of my study. The 'psy' discourse has been influential, giving rise to the various professions of Indian psycho-technocrats. There is a large body of Indian literature on the psychology of children, and more books on adoption, whether domestic or transnational, have been published in India than in any other donor country. At the same time, there is a noticeable ideological resistance to what is perceived as Western encroachment in Indian intellectual life as well as in its social and economic affairs. Of the four countries to be discussed, India expresses the most clearly formulated anti-transnational adoption sentiments. Senior staff of the national organisation that provides federal guidelines and grants final permission for adoption

(CARA) wish to see the end of transnational adoption and the growth of domestic adoption (Howell 2006a). According to the Guidelines from 1995, the order of priority in allocation of children released for adoption are: 1. Indian families in India. 2. Indian families abroad. 3. One parent of Indian origin. 4. Totally foreign parents. Not more than half adoptees should go to non-Indian parents, a rule the authorities are willing to waive in the case of handicapped or older children, because they know no Indian couple would want them. However, fewer than 4,000 children are adopted legally in India each year, about half of whom go abroad. Given an estimated population of 700,000 children in Indian orphanages, the number represents a drop in the ocean, and many European agencies are frustrated over what they regard as anti-Western attitudes which, they maintain, result in children being the losers.

Undoubtedly, transnational adoption is a sensitive issue in India. Sensational media reports appear from time to time that fuel criticism. However, not all are sceptical of the practice. An article in the influential journal *Economic and Political Weekly* argued strongly that the recent drive to encourage domestic adoption must not become a hindrance for transnational adoption just because this is regarded as politically more correct, and that the current imbalance in the procedure required for the two types of adoption cannot be regarded as being in the 'best interest of the child' (Anand and Chandra 2001: 3892). The authors discuss a recent case of corruption in Hyderabad in connection with transnational adoption, as a result of which several local adoption agencies were closed down, the children seized and a whole group of high-profile individuals were arrested on charges of child trafficking under the guise of transnational adoption. Commenting critically on the case, Anand and Chandra say 'the ones who are really being deprived of childhood, homes, families, future and possibly their lives are the children because the adoption process has come to a grinding halt' (ibid.: 3891).

Values and Practices in Ethiopia

The situation in Ethiopia is very different from that in India. The country has been torn apart by civil wars and famine for several decades. Given these facts, the room for manoeuvre by the state is limited. Most commentators, whether local or foreign, agree that Ethiopia would barely survive as a modern nation state were it not for the foreign aid that the country receives. In recent years, a large portion of the aid has been directed at children and the plight of women. Accompanying the aid are normative values. This renders the country extremely vulnerable, and, in the words of a prominent journalist, 'what poverty does is to discourage debate about Western values being imposed'. Similar sentiments were expressed by a senior officer at the government office handling child care and adoption (MOLSA). He said that most of what he had to handle in his work derived from Western donors' concerns and values. He also said that the Western concern with the value of the individual and the nuclear family in development projects was not very relevant in the Ethiopian context. The fact that both the UNCRC and The Hague Convention base their recommendations upon the centrality of the individual child and the nuclear family makes it difficult for Ethiopians to continue to adhere to traditional values. But he insisted that the underlying premises of the conventions are shared and that the objectives are good. He added that Western targets for development are very idealistic, especially the stress that is continually placed on the best interest of the child, the meaning of which Ethiopians sometimes find difficult to understand. He was not going to disagree, however, since the resources of the Ethiopian government were very limited and, without the assistance they received from the West, the situation in the country would be much worse.

There is little doubt that the idea of the autonomous individual and his or her rights is a major stumbling block for communication and cooperation between receiving and donor countries. In line with the African Charter discussed above, Retta, an Ethiopian lawyer who works for the Juvenile Justice Project Office, considers in a critical article entitled 'On the Rights of the Child' the position of the many street children in Ethiopia and how they may best be helped by the authorities, He poses the question whether the Ethiopians and non-Ethiopians who are engaged in development work in the country share the same understandings when they speak of the rights of children. His answer is that they probably do not, and he insists that the Ethiopians must not allow themselves to be browbeaten into accepting what, after all, are values and notions more suited to the rich countries in Europe and North America. 'Unlike the child in a rich society who undergoes the "luxury of identity crisis", more often than not, whenever an Ethiopian child in a poor family demonstrates delinquent behaviour ... the motive is clear – it is poverty' (Retta 2001: 29). He argues for an acceptance of 'indigenous solutions ... rather than imitate or import prescription' (ibid.). He even questions the relevance of the basic principles and regulations of the UNCRC and other international conventions. To his own question 'are the best interests of the Ethiopian and the British and the American child the same?', he replies that institutions and legal provisions that are designed elsewhere are not necessarily suited for Ethiopia. Whereas Retta is outspoken, others may be more cautious but do not necessarily disagree with his resentment of the rich and powerful nations and organisations which, he says, think that poor nations are 'necessarily backward and inferior [and hence] need to do a lot of "awareness raising" endeavours' (ibid.: 10).

In both India and Ethiopia, intellectuals engage in a critical discourse directed at the perceived globalisation of Western values. Where they differ is in their relative ability to resist. When we turn to two former Communist regimes that are also major actors in transnational adoption, China and Romania, we find that the moral values concerning children and childhood are based upon notions very different from those expressed in the UNCRC. Moreover, they have little sympathy with the latter and little intellectual understanding of their premises. Unless forced (as in the case of Romania), they show little will to adapt.

Values and Practices in China and Romania

The relationship between the Communist regimes of China and Romania and the West was, until recently, highly restricted and marked by mutual suspicion. Only after the fall of the Soviet Union in 1989 did former Soviet bloc countries make it possible for European and North American couples to adopt children, and China soon followed suit. Romania and China emerged during the 1990s as the big new suppliers of children to Western Europe and North America. Institutions for orphans and abandoned children existed, but once Western observers gained access to these, they were shocked to see the conditions under which many children lived. Reports that were often sensational in character appeared in Western media and served as an incentive to organise adoption by Western couples. Despite many differences, the political situation in Romania was in many ways similar to that in China. Both were Communist dictatorships with a highly centralised administration. The prosperity and well-being of the collectivity were prioritised at the expense of the individual. The state in both cases sought to implement its policies through a centralised bureaucracy, a planned economy and a variety of social engineering programmes – accompanied in many instances by repressive measures. The exercise of direct state involvement in the organisation of family life indicated not only that the state knows what is best for its citizens, but, more importantly, that the citizens are responsible for the well-being of the state. The notion of individual rights was irrelevant for good government, and little dialogue was engaged in with the population (Kligman 1998: 6).

Communist state formation does not conform to a standard understanding of governmentality, but I nevertheless wish to keep this concept in mind in my examination of adoption in China and Romania. Neither country took much interest in academic psychology. In Romania the teaching of psychology was stopped in the early 1970s and reintroduced at university level during the 1990s following pressure from abroad. Chinese universities had never taught psychology as a discipline and it is only being introduced selectively today. Training in social work with special reference to children in need is slowly being introduced through financial support from abroad. However, the countries had developed a highly centralised bureaucracy, whose job it was to carry out the state's policies, policies that, ideologically speaking, should ensure the prosperity and happiness of the population – more as collectivities than as individuals.

There are good reasons for the many abandoned children in China and Romania, but they are diametrically different. In China the one-child family policy of 1978 and the strong preference for sons in Chinese families (manifesting a continuation of pre-Revolution cultural values) led to a great number of baby girls being abandoned (Johnson et al. 1998). The politics of demography in Romania, in contrast, was 'pronatalist' (Kligman 1992: 405). During the regime of Ceausescu, the population was encouraged to produce children. Contraception was not available and abortion was allowed only after a woman had successfully given birth to five children (ibid.). Poor people were unable to look after large numbers of children and were forced to abandon them.

Both countries signed and ratified the UNCRC and The Hague Convention early, but questions have been raised as to the extent to which they understood the spirit of them. Both have been on the receiving end of much criticism for their alleged failure to follow the various regulations. The world was alerted to the poor conditions in Chinese orphanages through a TV documentary entitled 'The Dying Room', which led to an investigation by Human Rights Watch in 1996. *Inter alia*, it was claimed that orphanages were instructed to kill orphans as a measure towards population control. The claim was based on official figures that showed that in the early 1990s 'up to half of the children brought into the orphanages died, usually within the first few months after arrival' and that in poorer orphanages the rate was even higher. According to Johnson et al, the high death rate is more due to the poor state of the health of children handed in to orphanages than to any extermination policy. Nevertheless, the example demonstrates a climate of suspicion.

The dichotomy between Western notions about child welfare on the one hand and those of China and Romania on the other is still apparent. Chinese attitudes and practices regarding personhood, family, gender relations and childhood are noticeably different from those of the contemporary West. The state has maintained a strict control over people's lives, emphasising an ideology of community rather than individual growth. Over the past ten years a softening may be observed in some domains, but the state continues to define the common good and exercises control over its implementation. In light of this, it is not surprising that ideas of individual rights, including the idea of the (vulnerable) child's rights recently introduced by the West, did not find a ready response. Although Chinese students increasingly attend universities in Europe and the USA, the majority study the natural sciences, technology and economics. So far, little interest has been shown in the social sciences and the humanities, and any effect of the 'psy' discourse is hardly noticeable.

Hammerstrøm and Wikse[2] noticed that there was minimal discussion about the meaning of the principle 'best interest of the child' in Chinese orphanages. Although treatment of children in care was much better than in Romanian institutions, it was highly regimented. Virtually no concern was shown about the children's emotional needs or the needs of handicapped children or of the slow learner. They were struck by the staff's readyness to characterise some children as pretty or intelligent or ugly, dull or stupid, in front of the children themselves, seemingly unaware of any detrimental effects this might have. The main priorities of personnel in all three orphanages studied were: good health, education and training – in that order. Adoption, whether domestic or transnational, was valued because it would provide improved material conditions for the children. Potential emotional benefits were not mentioned. Although they heard no overt critical comments about the UNCRC, there were sufficient indications from observed attitudes and practices of the personnel to suggest that the focus on individuality and individual needs and rights so strongly apparent in the convention carries little meaning in the Chinese context (Howell 2006a: 213–16).

Western social workers find this Chinese disregard of children's needs particularly provoking. This may be illustrated by the experience of an Englishman who was employed to develop a system of fosterage at a new orphanage near Shanghai. This particular orphanage was built in response to Western criticism of the conditions in Chinese institutions for children, and was meant to be a showcase for the good intentions of Chinese authorities. However, to a Western eye the construction and the facilities were far from child-friendly. The Englishman tried to advise on how to achieve a more 'homely atmosphere', but his advice was not heeded. Whether he and others who advocate Western ideas of 'the best interest of the child' were deliberately ignored by the Chinese as a way of resisting an encroachment of Western concepts and values or whether they just felt that their own notions and practices were better suited for a Chinese reality is not known. What the example does show, however, is that some Chinese authorities are sensitive to Western criticism, that they attempt to take account of it, but that they do so according to their own premises. This may be because they fail to fully understand the Western values or because they place their priorities elsewhere (Howell 2006a).

After the fall of President Ceausescu in 1989, Romania became a major supplier of children to adoptive parents in Western Europe and the USA. In less than two years, the number of children adopted from Romania increased from fewer than thirty recorded instances in 1989 to more than 10,000 in the period from January 1990 to July 1991 (Conley 2000: 77). European media reports, including several heart-rending TV documentaries, described the generally terrible conditions in the state orphanages and this led to 'Romania becoming the adoption hotspot of the year' (Kligman 1992: 410).

Unique in global politics, Romanian treatment of abandoned children was made the acid test for the country's successful application to the European Union[3]. Because of the appalling conditions in Romanian children's homes and the extent of malpractices in transnational adoption, the European Union applied direct and unashamed pressure on the Romanian government to improve the situation. Nowhere has global governmentality been more visible, and nowhere have the expert opinions of foreign psycho-technocrats been voiced more loudly.

Pressure from the EU and UNICEF has led to some new developments in Romania, not least because foreign NGOs organise and pay for many of them, and less due to a change in moral attitude. In its dealings with novel ideas concerning posited children's needs and the ethical considerations of transnational adoption, the post-Communist Romanian state gives a somewhat inflexible impression. It would appear that Romania is not open to new ideas and values about children and childhood emanating from the West. They defend the existing system and only under severe pressure is the state willing to reconsider it (Howell 2006a). However, there are signs that earlier disregard of 'the best interest of the child' is beginning to change. Ulfsnes[4] (in Howell 2006a: 219–21) found that the UNCRC and The Hague Convention are being read more carefully in some circles. Quoting Western social workers and other experts on children, some Romanian officials within the childcare sector are beginning to voice the opinion that it is best for a child to grow up within a family and a home, and the recent introduction of fosterage arrangements, initiated and supported by foreign NGOs, is rapidly gaining ground. By the same token, Chinese authorities appear to be sensitive to criticism from Europe. Changes that are taking place in some orphanages, for example in the Jiangsu province, indicate an intention to improve the conditions of orphanages and childcare. Personnel who have been given the chance to visit European countries that receive Chinese children in adoption return with the desire to implement some of the practices followed there. It remains an open question to what extent they appreciate the philosophical and psychological underpinnings of Western practices.

Conclusion

The examination in this chapter of some values and practices in four very different countries that send children to Europe and North America for adoption demonstrates a wide variety in understandings about children, parents, family and community. It also shows how the dominant values that emanate from the West through the international conventions are perceived as problematic. It is, however, not just a question of difference of values, but a question of relative power. A globalisation – or cultural colonising – of Western ideas and values is discernible within the fields of childcare and adoption in non-Western parts of the world. The mere existence of the UNCRC and The Hague Convention bears ample witness to this. Not only do Western nations get what they want – children for involuntary childless couples in the own countries – but they also, by and large, lay down the rules for how this particular transaction is to be carried out. They do so within a frame of 'ethics narrow', which is universalistic in its premise and normative in its execution. However, against this Western onslaught, the 'weapons of the weak' (Scott 1985) are not without power of their own. An assertion of agency on the part of donor countries is manifest in many ways. Some of the most common are: local regulations concerning the age and civil status of prospective parents; restrictions on the number of children released each year; demands that parents collect their child themselves; specifications as to how long parents are required to stay in the donor country and which procedures they have to undergo while there; criteria for documentation – and payment – required from the receiving country; the length of time taken for handling applications; and other local requirements that the recipient agencies, countries and adoptive parents have to abide by – such as formal renewable agreements with the national authorities, visits of staff or having to provide regular detailed reports on the adoptee's situation for a certain number of years after they have arrived in their new home country.

The 'international community' and Western media have been more directly critical of child policies and provisions of many countries in the South than they have been of other policies that might be regarded as equally worthy of criticism. I suggest this may be explained by the special moral status attributed to children and childhood in Europe and North America. When children are perceived to be neglected, this tends to dominate all other human rights issues, and it gives licence to enforce the prescriptions of the conventions.

The reigning discursive practices of adoption spring out from psychological theories of personhood and identity. As such they may be thought of as 'ethics narrow'. It is a moralising discourse full of 'oughts' and 'ought to be realized' (Edel and Edel 1968[1959]). Further, it is a discourse that is, in effect, closed to debate. One of the most important manifestations of this is the non-negotiable value placed upon the individual and the rights of the individual, expressed in numerous Western European and North American national legislations, and reiterated in the UNCRC and The Hague Convention. To what extent those who drafted the articles and have subsequently sought to implement them are aware of the biased premises on which they are formulated varies widely. It is important to note that transnational adoption is not part of development aid, or of humanitarian aid in the usual sense. It is a rather ambiguous transaction that straddles a number of moral positions. As children and their welfare occupy a very special position in Western social thought, making them part of the field of 'ethics wide', direct interventionist action on the part of foreign institutions and authorities may therefore be deemed acceptable. This is nowhere so stark as in Romania where the EU had no qualms about wielding power in order to ensure the implementation of its own directives.

The history of ideas and values in the West, as elsewhere, has amply shown that ideas know no national boundaries, and that discourses change in response to new impulses as well as in response to changing political and economic situations. As they become codified in law, prescriptions and proscriptions reflect existing values, but also chart out new ones that are deemed desirable. In this sense, laws are normative and, ideally, the values will become internalised by the citizens as right and proper. The influence of Western jurisprudence and cultural and ethical values is observable in recent child and adoption laws in many countries in the South. But it would be simplistic to suggest that these are merely 'imported' laws, having no impact on domestic values. Morality not only influences laws, but is also influenced by them. This may apply even if the laws are 'imported'. Indisputably, a globalisation of Western values is taking place and – albeit to a varying degree – a change in the moral perceptions about the place of children in society and the state's duty towards them is discernible in the four countries discussed above.

Notes

Research on transnational adoption has been supported by the Norwegian Research Council under the project Transnational Flow of Concepts and Substances, the EU-funded project Public Understanding of Genetics and Family in Europe under Framework 5 and the Quality of Life and Management of Living Resources Programme.

1. Much of the information from India and Ethiopia was obtained during short field trips in 2001 (Ethiopia) and 2002 (India).
2. Hammerstrøm and Wikse are two graduate students of Chinese at the University of Oslo who on my behalf undertook one month's fieldwork in three Chinese orphanages in 2002.
3. Romania finally joined the European Union in January 2007. The country's various efforts to improve conditions for abandoned children were closely monitored by the EU.
4. Ulfsnes was for a period my research assistant. She had previous graduate experience from ethnographic fieldwork in Romania and she undertook in 2002, on my behalf, a short period of fieldwork in order to ascertain the situation with regard to childcare and adoption.

Chapter 6

MORALITY, SELF AND POWER: THE IDEA OF THE *MAHALLA* IN UZBEKISTAN

Johan Rasanayagam

This chapter explores the relation between morality and the self. It discusses how we might think about moral selfhood as produced through a creative engagement within a social environment, so that morality is particular and individualised, while at the same time recognising that moral evaluation is made with reference to standards that exist outside the individual. It thus addresses the relationship between the universal and the particular. However, the universal is not a static set of norms or system of values, but is a set of dynamic and flexible moral frames, individually shaped within personal experience while remaining shared moral references.

Attention to the moral dimension of social interaction, moreover, broadens our understanding of the relationship between the state and citizen in authoritarian state contexts beyond the standard analysis of power and resistance. In the context of the Soviet Union, it is commonly argued that the attempts by state authorities to shape the consciousness of citizens caused them to adopt separate public and private lives. In public, people acted as if they believed the ideology of the Communist

Party, while in private they held radically different views (Kotkin 1995: 220f.; Kharkhordin 1999: 270f.). However, a stark dichotomy between public compliance and private resistance or dissimulation focuses solely on the issue of power. It implies that Soviet citizens either adopted state discourses wholesale or more often rejected them in favour of their own alternatives. Alexei Yurchak has criticised this approach, arguing that, despite routinely transgressing officially proclaimed norms, many Soviet citizens remained committed to what they saw as the fundamental values of socialism. Individuals perceived themselves as committed Communists, genuinely engaging in efforts to build a socialist society, while rejecting 'mere formality'. In effect they reinterpreted Communism in their own terms (Yurchak 2003).

Yurchak's analysis hints at how we might progress beyond the linear focus on power and resistance, in that he implies that individuals not only are embedded within relations of power but also make moral judgements (Lambek 2000). In the Soviet Union, official ideological pronouncements and texts did not in and of themselves constitute the core values in reference to which individuals fashioned themselves as committed Communists. Rather, I suggest that socialism is a moral frame within which citizens placed their own particular constructions of ideals such as social justice and equality. Socialism was therefore both individually shaped within particular experience and was a transcendental frame that encompassed a multitude of personal constructions.

The *mahalla* similarly acts as a moral frame in post-Soviet Uzbekistan. On one level this is a territorially defined residential district of a town or village, and it also serves as model for a moral community. In Uzbekistan it is regarded as a historically evolved institution of social organisation that pre-dates Soviet and Russian rule in the area. The *mahalla* as a moral frame incorporates an ideal of mutual aid and communal solidarity among residents, practically realised in the contribution of labour to common projects and the marking of life cycle events, and is overlaid with Muslim religious identity. It has been adopted by the post-independence regime in Uzbekistan as an element within a new national ideology, its own presentation of Uzbekistan's 'spiritual heritage' intended to replace the Marxism-Leninism of the Soviet Union. The regime presents this ideology in moral terms, framing its policies with reference to the region's Islamic history and religious practice and the spiritual values of the Uzbek people. Most citizens recognise the regime's discourse on the *mahalla* as a transparent attempt to legitimate the authoritarian rule of President Islam Karimov. At the same time, however, the moral claims of the regime are not empty window dressing. The *mahalla*, like the idea of socialism, is a moral frame that gathers within itself diverse ideals and practices of individuals. By engaging with the moral frame of the *mahalla* among others, such as Islam, the regime is speaking directly to the subjectivities and 'beliefs' of citizens, who fashion their moral selves with reference to them.

Morality, Self and Power

While it might be tempting to think about morality as the norms and values of a particular society (Edel 1962), this can only produce a static picture of a moral system or structure abstracted from the dynamic interactions and the creative moral reflections of individuals. Rather, a number of anthropologists have suggested that an anthropology of morality should focus on the processes by which individuals make of themselves a certain kind of person though reflection upon the practices and models found in society (Laidlaw 2002). It should explore the dynamic relation between transcendent values and lived practice, and the effects of relations of power in constituting and regulating moral ideals and practices (Howell 1997a). Thus, morality can productively be located in selfhood, in the processes through which individuals fashion moral selves with reference to what they perceive as transcendent ideals. Moreover, this is a creative process. Drawing inspiration from Aristotle's concept of practical reason, Michael Lambek has argued that moral reasoning and virtuous action consist in a person's creative engagement with and manipulation of shared symbols, myths and local histories, and conscious interventions in their societies on the basis of this. Morality consists in the reasoning involved in choosing to contain, exploit or reject the application of power, the practical judgements people make about how to live their lives well, and also virtuous, practical engagement in the form of actions aimed at the general good (Lambek 1996, 2000, 2002).

The intimate interrelation of morality and selfhood has been examined by the philosopher Charles Taylor, who argues that identity is linked to a person's sense of the good:

> My identity is defined by the commitments and identifications which provide the frame or horizon within which I can try to determine from case to case what is good, or valuable, or what ought to be done, or what I endorse or oppose. In other words, it is the horizon within which I am capable of taking a stand. (Taylor 1989: 27)

Taylor argues that moral issues involve 'strong evaluation'. These are 'discriminations of right and wrong, better or worse, higher or lower, which are not rendered valid by our own desires, inclinations, or choices, but rather stand independent of these and offer standards by which they can be judged' (Taylor 1989: 4). Individuals exercise moral evaluation and make sense of their lives with reference to what he calls 'frameworks'. Within a pre-modern 'enchanted' world, Taylor argues, a single overarching framework is unchallenged, whereas, in modern society, no unifying framework can be assumed to be shared by all. This extends Durkheim's opposition between the coercive morality of societies founded on mechanical solidarity, where all members are forced to act within an enveloping system of moral values, and more complex societies in which morality becomes the subject of critical reflection by rational individuals, but where nonetheless members are bound to society though a certain level of shared morality. At a minimum this is a respect for the dignity of the individual. For Taylor, modern society is distinguished by a 'post-Durkheimian' individualism, where the individual no longer conforms to any general societal moral framework, but seeks his or her own spiritual development though personal insight (Taylor 2002: 65f.). However, this modern individual is not an amoral utilitarian, but selfhood continues to be constituted with reference to moral frameworks, albeit personally constituted, within which strong qualitative discrimination is possible. A person with no framework is a damaged, dislocated person.

Following Taylor, I locate morality in selfhood and argue that moral selfhood is constituted through what Taylor calls strong evaluation. However, there is no need to oppose a single shared morality to unconstrained individualism. The moral frames I discuss act in two separate ways. The highly particular values and standards an individual develops in the course of engagement in his or her environment are established as legitimately transcendent and authoritative for that individual by being placed within moral frames. But frames themselves are not the property of the individual. They are shared references which gather a diversity of values as these have significance for individuals. Frames are in this way subjectively recreated within individual experience, while at the same time remaining as 'public symbols' with reference to society as a whole (Obeyesekere 1981). In any society, modern or pre-modern, there are a number of available frames, and individuals might develop their moral selves in relation to a number of them simultaneously. In contemporary Uzbekistan some of these frames are translocal, such as Islam, Christianity and socialism, while others are locally specific, such as the *mahalla*.

A problem with Taylor's construction of frameworks is that it sets up an opposition between a pre-modern mechanical reproduction of tradition and a modern, reflective creativity. Taylor's frameworks are thus either all-encompassing, dictating the values and moral identities of all members of society in a similar way, or are individualised and therefore not shared. However, in any society, pre-modern or otherwise, tradition is never mechanically reproduced from generation to generation but recreated anew (Carrithers 1992: 9). While there may be a greater choice of frames in globalised, complex societies, the creativity inherent in developing moral selves in reference to them is present at all times and in all places. At the same time, while moral frames are creatively recreated by individuals, they continue to act as common references that encompass a number of diverse representations within a single, transcendental moral tradition. Moreover, Taylor's analysis ignores the important dimension of power. The relations of power within which individuals are embedded shape the conditions of possibility within which they can relate to moral frames. The presentation and perception of moral frames, their recreation within subjective experience and the formation of moral selves take place within relations of power. Power and morality mutually constitute each other.

The *Mahalla* as an Institution and an Ideal

There are accounts of a number of different types of social organisation encompassing groups of households in the area of modern-day Uzbekistan, many of which were historically related to regulation of the irrigation infrastructure, cooperation in agricultural work and the marking of life cycle events (Rassudova 1969). In present-day Uzbekistan units of local self-organisation have been formalised by central government as self-governing institutions known as *mahallas*. Residential areas in both rural and urban areas have been divided territorially into *mahallas*, governed by a *mahalla* committee, which is elected by residents. This is headed by a chairman (often known as *oqsoqol* – literally meaning 'white beard'), and includes, among other officers, a secretary, chairman of the women's committee, and a *postbon*. This last is a community policeman who is elected by residents but who works closely with state law enforcement agencies. In some regions the territory of the formally state-recognised *mahalla* is further subdivided into locally organised unofficial *mahallas* with their own *oqsoqol* and locally chosen personnel.

In practice, the extent to which the institution of the *mahalla* is relevant to its residents varies. In many newly urbanised city districts that have no history of *mahalla* organisation, but where it has been imposed recently by central government, the *mahalla* is of minimal social relevance. People turn to it only if they need official documentation such as proof of residence. In other areas, particularly rural districts and the older historical centres of cities such as Samarkand and Bukhara, the social authority accorded to the *mahalla* by residents is greater. Some would also stress the oppressive nature of social control, where people's actions are constantly the subject of gossip, judgement and intervention by the *mahalla* leadership and neighbours.[1] Despite this, the *mahalla* remains a powerful symbol and a model for communal solidarity and virtuous living. The ideal of solidarity and mutual aid within a *mahalla* is available as a model for relations within other social units, such as a household, where the income and labour of household members is pooled and distributed according to perceived need (Rasanayagam 2002).

The post-independence regime in Uzbekistan has attempted to replace the Marxist-Leninist ideology of the Soviet Union with a nationalist discourse founded upon a construction of the 'Golden Heritage' (*oltin meros*) of the Uzbek people. The region's Islamic history, particularly that of Sufism, past literary figures and historical rulers such as Amir Timur constitute this heritage (Schubel 1999; Roy 2000). The moral basis of the new national ideology rests upon an ideal of 'Uzbekness' and the cultural and spiritual values of the Uzbek people. The *mahalla* is central to this and plays a dual role for the regime. On the one hand, the regime uses the ideal of *mahalla* to legitimate the authoritarian rule of the president. The state is presented as a *mahalla* writ large, a family or community where all members perform their allotted duties and look out for each other's well-being.[2] One of the president's often quoted slogans is 'from a strong state to a strong society'. This is used to justify the existence of a strong executive presidency as necessary to protect democratic ideals and individual freedoms. On a more practical level, the institution of the *mahalla* is functionalised as an instrument of surveillance and control over the population (Massicard and Trevisani 2003). Even during the Soviet period state authorities co-opted the *mahalla* as a vehicle for spreading official ideology. During the 1930s the Soviet authorities incorporated the *mahalla* into the state bureaucracy by instituting the *mahalla* committee. The leader of this committee was nominally elected by the local community but in reality the appointment was controlled by the Party organisation. The *mahalla* committees were attached to a Party cell in an educational institution or enterprise and they were responsible for organising ideological campaigns and lectures. They employed personnel (*aktiv*) who devoted their time to this work (Koroteyeva and Makarova 1998; Moryakova 1998).

Since independence the central government has formalised the institution of the *mahalla* and integrated it further into the state administrative system. To this end the network of *mahalla* committees has been expanded. Although these committees are by law self-governing institutions with a locally elected leadership and are outside the state governing structure, in practice they are treated by centrally appointed local governors (*hokim*[3]) as an extension of their own personal authority. For example, they use the *mahalla* to collect payments for utilities such as gas and electricity, to collect taxes, and even to aid in the fulfilment of production targets for industries. *Mahalla* committees are expected to promote regime propaganda through the work of their various sub-committees. They are expected to organise state-sponsored festivals such as Independence Day and Navruz (a festival in spring celebrating the New Year). In addition, the educational programmes undertaken by the *mahalla* committees mirror state priorities, and each year the committee is obliged to present its programme of activities to the office of the district or city governor for approval.

Mahalla leaderships are expected to act as the eyes and ears of the government and to be on the lookout for anti-regime sentiments among their residents. They keep a record of all residents who are working abroad and report this to the district government. After a series of bomb attacks in the capital in 1999, which were attributed to Islamic opposition groups, the president called on *mahalla* leaderships to monitor the populations and mosques in their territories for indications of what the regime considers 'extremist' tendencies.[4] During the period of my field research in the spring of 2004 there was a further spate of bombings and shootings directed against the police, after which *mahalla* chairmen were asked by the state security forces to inform them of any residents who expressed dissatisfaction with the government.

Central government has functionalised the *mahalla* as an element within its legitimating ideology and as a practical extension of its authority and control over the population. At the same time, individuals recreate the ideal of the *mahalla* within their own subjective experience, and constitute their sense of themselves as moral persons. This process is shaped by relations of power, within which access to the repressive capacities of the state play a large part. I explore this through an account of Abdumajid-aka, a person I met on my first day in Samarkand in 2003 and who cooperated with me in much of my fieldwork in that city.[5]

Abdumajid-aka

Abdumajid-aka is in his late fifties. He is a lecturer in mathematics at the University of Samarkand and director of a secondary school. In 2003 he was elected chairman, or *oqsoqol*, of his *mahalla* committee.

Abdumajid-aka is what might be called a social activist. He takes seriously the official legal status of the *mahalla* as a self-governing, institution and believes that the *mahalla* can form the basis for a genuine democratic society in Uzbekistan. He is active in promoting the interests of *mahalla* residents. He does not see himself or his residents in principle as in opposition to the state. On the contrary, he believes in cooperative relations, with residents, the *mahalla* leadership and city officials working towards a common goal. Of course, many local government officials do not share this idealistic view.

Much of his work as *mahalla* chairman is in cooperation with the city government officials or in support of central government policies. For example, he has taken the initiative in working with the public utility providers and local government to find a means to ensure that the gas and electricity bills are paid on time. Abdumajid-aka is not simply concerned that his residents are guaranteed supply. In fact the gas supply to an individual household is rarely cut off because of non-payment. Instead, shortages of gas result in an overall reduction in provision. In the case of electricity, it is common for people to illegally connect themselves directly to overhead power lines, avoiding payment altogether. Abdumajid-aka always has a larger vision of the equitable distribution of resources in the nation as a whole and in the contribution of individuals to the collective good. In the case of natural gas, he believes that it is the property of the people (Russian, *narodnie dostoyanie*) since it is extracted from the ground. He denies that the gas-supplying organisation is in financial crisis, arguing that the cost for gas has increased much faster than salaries and that those who pay are in fact making up for those who do not. As evidence he points to the relatively high salaries of its employees, with their leather coats and mobile phones. The solution he has suggested is to cancel past debts and for the *mahalla* leadership to work in cooperation with local government in collecting payments. In return, the *mahalla* would be allowed to keep a percentage of the revenue in order to aid poorer families.[6]

Abdumajid-aka is widely travelled, having visited Iceland and Israel for academic conferences and courses, and a few years before my field research he had visited the United States on a project promoting the creation of civil society sponsored by the US government. On his return, he founded an association of heads of *mahalla* committees with the aim of protecting their members and increasing awareness of their legal rights and status. To this end his association runs seminars to educate *mahalla* chairmen of their rights vis-à-vis the local state representatives. This is something unprecedented in Uzbekistan and, in the political context in which any hint of activism independent of central government control is regarded as suspect, it is not a little dangerous. What protects Abdumajid-aka and his association is the state discourse itself. It provides space for initiatives such as this as long as they can be presented as fitting within official discourses about the *mahalla* and as being supportive of the regime, or at least not in conflict with it.

This democratic vision of the *mahalla* is exceptional among committee chairmen I came across. Most described the *mahalla* as the lowest layer in the state governing hierarchy, directly under the control of the city or district governors. Some described themselves as 'little *hokims'*, mapping the national structure of executive government on to the *mahalla*. In this structure state power is largely concentrated in the hands of the president, who appoints the provincial governors (*hokims*), who have similar executive authority in their regions. These governors in turn appoint the lower-level district and city *hokims*. Although the *mahalla* leadership is not appointed directly by governors but elected by residents, their appointment must be approved by the district governor.

Even where *mahalla* leaders see themselves as primarily acting in the interests of their residents rather than as mere extensions of the state, they do not perceive this in terms of democracy. They tend to view themselves in paternalistic terms, as acting in the best interests of their communities, upholding and enforcing correct conduct, looking after the economically vulnerable and protecting residents from the excesses of state authorities. To support their authority over residents they use their control over certain resources and functions, such as the issuing of documentation people need to formally obtain exit visas for travel or work abroad, the allocation of state-provided relief for poor families and the issuing of character references for jobs and court cases. They might also organise social boycotts of those they consider are ignoring their authority. Their vision of the *mahalla* and the role of the *oqsoqol* as an authoritarian but benevolent leader mirrors central government discourses. However, since they are not outsiders cynically attempting to instrumentalise the *mahalla* for their own ends, but seek to protect residents from interference from the outside, their self-representations are perhaps more convincing to *mahalla* residents.

Abdumajid-aka's activities have led him into direct confrontation with the city government and the leadership of law enforcement agencies on a number of occasions. One such conflict concerned their efforts to force the *mahalla* chairmen to collect fees from prospective army conscripts for a reduced term of military service. As things stood during the time of my field research, military service was no longer compulsory. However, in order to enter the police force, the SNB (successor of the Soviet KGB) and the public prosecution service (all highly desirable careers, not least because of the opportunities for earning money through bribes), a certificate of completed military service is necessary. People can either serve for a full year or can pay the equivalent of around US$140 to serve for one month. This has led to the unusual situation in which people actually pay a bribe or use personal connections in order to enter military service for the full one-year term as places for this are now limited. There were a large number of people who did not manage to get a place, however, and were signed up for the one-month service but who failed to pay, and the local government was forcing the *mahalla* chairmen to collect this money.

At a meeting organised by the city district authorities to which the *mahalla* chairmen were summoned, the assistant district public prosecutor tried to bully the chairmen into compliance. He referred ominously to certain of them who were refusing to collect this money, claiming that this indicated that they were expressing opposition to the president. When some of the *mahalla* chairmen objected, he dismissed them rudely, telling them to shut up and sit down. Abdumajid-aka and the press secretary of his association decided to publish an article in a national newspaper dedicated to *mahalla* matters about how the assistant public prosecutor was exceeding his authority and failing to treat the *mahalla* chairmen with respect. In a meeting with the head of the provincial branch of the national Mahalla Foundation (a body set up by the government to develop the *mahalla* as an insititution) it was decided that the assistant public prosecutor would be asked for an apology. However, the Mahalla Foundation official refused to allow the article to be published, fearing the image of Samarkand it would create with central government authorities. Determined to publish in any case, Abdumajid-aka and his press secretary did so through the local Uzbek-language newsletter of the Institute for War and Peace Reporting, a British NGO supporting local journalism. As a result of the embarrassment this article caused to the local government officials, showing them to be opposing an institution the president was publicly supporting in his official pronouncements, the assistant public prosecutor was transferred to a position in the provincial administration.

This conflict reveals something about the nature of governance in Uzbekistan, which to a large extent is a legacy of the Soviet period. Formal adherence to the law is not as important as displaying loyalty to the regime. In this situation, state officials themselves can be just as vulnerable to the application of the coercive capacities of the state as citizens within their jurisdictions. It is not simply a matter of state officials having access to state power and directing it at others. Both state officials and non-state actors manipulate presidential pronouncements and publicly stated regime goals to portray themselves as in accordance with them and their opponents as violating them.

Abdumajid-aka is aware that he is treading a dangerous line. He is safe only so long as his actions cannot be portrayed as being in opposition to the regime, and his only protection against such an interpretation is his prominent position within Samarkand society, his reputation for integrity and disinterested public service and the fact that he works closely with local government authorities in forwarding their own work in a number of areas. He does not openly confront the regime but directs his protests at the actions of individual officials, pointing at how their actions are in contravention of presidential pronouncements and the law. He stresses that he is not opposed to payment for the shortened period of military service and considers that the law itself is good since the money that previously went into someone's pocket in the form of a bribe to avoid service now goes to the government. It is the implementation of the law that is the problem. He was not even opposed to being asked to help in the collection of payments, and considered it the duty of the *mahalla* chairmen to cooperate with state authorities wherever possible. What he objected to was the dictatorial manner of government officials. Once the public prosecutor changed his tune in the face of open opposition from the *mahalla* chairmen and asked politely, Abdumajid-aka decided to cooperate and visit those of his residents who had not paid: 'I fulfilled his request, but if he hadn't asked politely, I wouldn't have gone. But I know that the army needs money, needs to protect the borders, fight terrorism. I understand. An educated person should understand, but you have to understand at the level of the subconscious, and not on the level of insult or pressure.'

Abdumajid-aka and the state officials he is criticising are in fact all operating within the same moral frame of the *mahalla* and its presentation within the official pronouncements of the regime, but the meanings they attach to it and the ends to which they direct their actions are very different. State discourse on the *mahalla* emphasises its importance in providing support for residents, socialising and educating young people, and instilling traditional Uzbek 'spiritual' values. It is even described as a primary school in democracy.[7] However, the regime's aim is to instrumentalise the *mahalla* as part of a new national ideology to replace Marxism-Leninism and to legitimate the need for strong executive control. For local governors, the *mahalla* is an extension of their own authority, a tool for monitoring and controlling the population and for fulfilling the directives handed down to them from central government.

Abdumajid-aka views things differently. He translates the ideals and practice of social solidarity and equality within the *mahalla* in the context of the modern nation state as a genuine basis for democracy, taking seriously the regime's own propaganda. He reverses the president's slogan, 'from a strong state to a strong society', to argue instead that in order to have a strong government you need a strong society. In day-to-day interaction he encounters local government officials who have very different ideas of this institution and in struggles, negotiations and cooperation with these officials Abdumajid-aka is attempting to realise his own vision of a moral community and fashioning his moral self in the process.

The Subjective Recreation of Moral Frames

Abdumajid-aka recreates the frame of the *mahalla* within his personal life experiences and this contributes to his vision of a virtuous society. When discussing the *mahalla* he emphasises ideals of mutual assistance and equality, which are universally recognised, if not enacted in practice by everyone to the same extent. In reply to my question as to why wealthy businessmen would want to contribute large sums to *mahalla* projects, Abdumajid-aka replied:

> First of all, the structure of the *mahalla* over the centuries is like a social unity. In the east, in Uzbekistan, Tajikistan and so on, people live within a family. Around each person, the first cover is the family and family property. The second cover is the *mahalla* and the *mahalla* property. When I organise a wedding I use the furniture, necessary things which the *mahalla* has ... I know that is not just the *mahalla*'s, but mine as well. Businessmen who live in the *mahalla* understand this. This is bought with contributions from residents, who donate according to their ability. A businessman wouldn't be comfortable giving only a small amount. Everyone knows he's a businessman, that he has the ability to give 20,000 *sum*. His neighbour is a teacher and gives 500 *sum* ... Businessmen understand this. They are creating the foundations for the future. Where's the guarantee that his own son won't be poor in the future, that his grandchildren will also be rich? If this does happen, then people will say that his father or grandfather was rich but he built houses, a bakery, established electricity or gas for the *mahalla*.

Abdumajid-aka's experience of Islam as well as his Marxist education and life within the Soviet Union also contribute to his vision of a moral community. He claims to believe that one day people will attain what he calls a communist society, where people receive according to their needs and give according to their ability, although he does not think it could have been achieved within the former Soviet socialist system. He also dismisses the current regime's ideology as unconvincing and not reflective of people's lived experience. The ideal society might be arrived at through religious education and upbringing or through ideology.

> I imagine God as complete understanding that has to bring order into our disorder. This may be by the help of different religions, maybe through Islam, Orthodoxy, Judaism or Bahaism ... I think that in the future religion will develop in such a way that it will develop general social principles for conduct in society. Religion first develops for a certain group of people, and then gradually becomes a kind of constitution for all humanity, which people accept in their spirits. It won't be important to pray in a mosque or a church. The principles of behaviour will be important. Religion was a carrier of ideology and in the future this will be the case as well. This ideology will direct people, a general ideology, not like the state ideology which changes. Religion lasts longer than government ideology.

Abdumajid-aka constructs himself as a moral person with reference to multiple moral frames. These include the *mahalla*, Islam, Marxism and democracy. None of these constitute coherent systems of moral norms, or 'blueprints' for moral action. Rather, Abdumajid-aka's particular life trajectory, his educational background, Muslim upbringing, experiences of life and work in the Soviet Union, his foreign travel and engagement with Western development agencies involved in democracy building in Uzbekistan have influenced the way in which he subjectively recreates these frames within his life project. They have shaped his concept of the *mahalla* as an indigenous foundation for democratic governance, and his moral self is created through his efforts aimed at realising this ideal.

At the same time, Abdumajid-aka's freedom to interpret these frames is not unbounded. The form a frame takes, the way it is perceived and how it can be adopted are to a large extent shaped within relations of power. Despite the claims of regime discourses that the *mahalla* is an ancient institution and carrier of Uzbek cultural values, the form the *mahalla* takes today is very different from how it might have existed at any time in the past.[8] During the Soviet period and particularly since independence in 1991, the institution of the *mahalla* has been standardised as a residential unit with a leadership and a set of personnel with defined duties. It has been imposed in areas where it had never had any history before, and variations in local forms of social organisation have been regularised through the now official structures.

Moreover the relationship of the *mahalla* leadership with both state authorities and residents is to a large extent a product of the official duties and practical power bestowed by the state. For example, the official *mahalla* committee is responsible for the distribution of state-funded poverty relief and child benefit, it issues documents and certificates that everyone needs at one time or another, and the state judicial system often refers back to the *mahalla* domestic disputes and other cases that judges consider of minor importance. Thus, the way in which Abdumajid-aka can project on to the *mahalla* his ideals about what constitutes a virtuous society, and so project his moral self into public space, is shaped by relations of power within which state actors play a prominent role. Were Abdumajid-aka to exceed the bounds of expression considered politically acceptable by the regime, he would be forced into the position of political opposition activist with all the dangers and restrictions on personal freedoms that would entail. He would no longer be able to retain a self-representation as a person trying to improve the lot of his residents through cooperative engagement with the state.

Within these limitations, the frame of the *mahalla* is interpreted and enacted in radically different and often opposing ways. However, in order to communicate and present themselves through it, actors do not need to persuade others completely of their own interpretations. The *mahalla* as a moral frame is multivocal. Many members of Abdumajid-aka's association do not share his particular view of the *mahalla* as a democratic institution but rather hold self-representations as benevolent autocrats, enforcing correct forms of behaviour and assisting their more vulnerable residents. They are happy to be active within Abdumajid-aka's association because this helps to protect their *mahallas* against the interference of outsiders. All focus on the *mahalla* as a unit of communal solidarity and mutual support, and on the leadership's duty to protect the interests of residents vis-à-vis outside authorities. Where Abdumajid-aka's concept of democracy encompasses accountability of leaders to the residents who elect them, for many other *mahalla* chairmen, if they think in terms of democracy at all, then it is about guaranteeing the integrity of the *mahalla*, a locally constituted institution, from the illegitimate interference of central government.

When Abdumajid-aka works with city government to forward government policies and programmes, for example, to ensure that state utilities bills are paid, he is acting upon his own ideals of social justice. Abdumajid-aka and the state officials he is working with relate to each other within a conception of the *mahalla* as a microcosm of social solidarity which provides a model for relations within wider society. That this constitutes a genuine value commitment for Abdumajid-aka and that local government officials merely instrumentalise the *mahalla* as an extension of their authority does not prohibit their mutual engagement in these terms. It is only when Abdumajid-aka's vision of ideal relations in society comes into direct conflict with the actions of state officials that problems arise. Even in these conflicts, it is the perception of Abdumajid-aka as an ally of city government in other contexts that helps him to avoid being perceived as in opposition to the regime.

Conclusion

I have discussed how moral selfhood is produced through an individual's creative engagement within his or her social environment, while at the same time recognising that moral evaluation is transcendent, defined with reference to frames that stand outside the individual. Moral frames gather within themselves diverse ideals and practices. They allow communication and productive engagement by individuals with differing, even conflicting objectives and visions of a moral community. Thus, attention to the dimension of morality links the subjective sense of self to a shared culture. It also provides insight into the question of 'belief' by highlighting how moral frames are incorporated within individual selves. In Uzbekistan, the regime's discourses are authoritative because, by engaging with moral frames, they are engaging directly with the beliefs of individuals who develop their own moral selves through subjective recreation of these frames. Regime discourse and practice in Uzbekistan do not crudely produce particular citizen-subjects, and citizens do not simply submit or resist. The regime attempts to fill shared moral frames with a particular content, to fix their interpretation within its construction of Uzbekness. It seeks to persuade others to its vision of society, but mutual communication and interaction do not depend on everyone sharing the same interpretation. The regime's discourse is but one presentation among many, and there is no need for a single hegemonic ideology. When situated within a shared moral frame such as the *mahalla*, the varied and often conflicting visions of different individuals, and even the legitimating discourses of central government, come to constitute a single, shared moral tradition, which can act as a frame for mutual engagement, communication and contestation.

Notes

1. In the context of urban Tajikistan, Collette Harris has described the socially repressive nature of relations within *mahallas*, particularly concerning gender relations (Harris 2004).
2. In official publications, many of which are authored by President Karimov himself, the *mahalla* is characterised in this way (Karimov 1992, 1993, 1995).
3. This term refers to the governors of provinces as well as the heads of city and district administrations.
4. Speech of President Karimov entitled 'Will and Faith: A Test of our Faith', reproduced in *Islom ziyosi ozbekim siyimosida* (The Light of Islam in our Uzbek Form) (Tashkent Islamic University, Tashkent) (2001) 169–82. Human Rights Watch has reported such surveillance activities undertaken by *mahalla* committees (Shields 2004) and some *mahalla* committee chairmen told me that they indeed did this.

5. This chapter is based on material collected during field research in the city of Samarkand between June 2003 and April 2004, although it also refers to previous research in the Fergana Valley, conducted from 1999 to 2000.

6. This is in fact a version of an existing scheme proposed by central government, which has proved unattractive to most *mahalla* committees because to participate they would have been forced to take on responsibility for the considerable debt burdens of the past.

7. *Ideya natsionalnoi nezavisimosti: osnovnie ponyatiya i printsipy* (The Idea of National Independence: Basic Understandings and Principles), pp. 67–68. This is a booklet outlining the new national ideology that President Karimov is promoting.

8. There are accounts of a number of different types of social organisation encompassing groups of households in the area of modern-day Uzbekistan, many of which were historically related to regulation of the irrigation infrastructure (Rassudova 1969; Lobacheva 1989).

Chapter 7

MORALISING FEMALE SEXUALITY: THE INTERSECTIONS BETWEEN MORALITY AND SEXUALITY IN RURAL VIETNAM

Helle Rydstrøm

Introduction

Since the introduction in 1986 of the renovation policy *doi moi*, Vietnamese society has undergone rapid socio-political and economic changes. The dynamic processes of societal transformations in Vietnam pervade all levels of society and have provided the possibilities of reconsidering moral ideas and creating new moral in-between spaces. Especially in urban areas, citizens can highlight their sexuality more explicitly than was possible in pre-*doi moi* Vietnam (Khuat Thu Hong 1998; Truong Trong Hoang 1998; Phan Thi Vang Anh and Pham Thu Thuy 2003; Thang Van Trinh 2003).

However, with a Confucian heritage of comprehensive morals that over the years has merged with communist ideals, even in late-*doi moi* Vietnam *dao duc*, or morality, remains a matter of national and local concern.[1] At national level, the moral concern especially is epitomised by the campaign undertaken by the government to prevent 'social evils' (*te nan xa hoi*) and 'poisonous culture' (*van hoa doc hai*) to overflow into Vietnamese society from the outside world. Because the 'social evils' campaign is imbued with assumptions about moral purity, it attempts to demarcate the boundaries between acceptable, or 'normal' (*binh thuong*), vis-à-vis non-acceptable, or 'abnormal', behaviours (Douglas 1991; Efroymson et. al. 1997; Population Council 1997; Soucy 2000/2001; McNally 2003).

Throughout Vietnamese history, the sexuality of girls and women has been subjected to restrictions, and even the 'social evils' campaign encourages imposed or self-imposed control in regard to female sexuality (Khuat Thu Hong 1998; Mensch et al. 2002; Ngo Thi Ngan Binh 2004).[2] In this chapter, I examine the ways in which rural young women consider the meaning of morality with respect to sexuality, and how such considerations correspond to or conflict with more public expectations concerning appropriate moral behavior in young women in late *doi moi* Vietnam.

In exploring morality, as it intersects with female sexuality, I draw on two periods of fieldwork conducted from 1994 to 1995 and from 2000 to 2001 in a rural commune called Thinh Tri, which is located in the Red River Delta of northern Vietnam.[3] In the local community, morality generally is seen as social practices due to which good relations between people can be facilitated and sustained. Acceptable ways of behaving as a woman, or man, are thus rendered intelligible more by social practices than by a person's moral ideas or emotional mood. If the actions of a person are approved of as morally adequate, she or he is assumed to hold a correct inner state of morality (Potter 1988; Rydstrøm 2001, 2002, 2003).

Over time, women and men successively incorporate the norms and politics of local knowledge, which at the same time inform and shape their practices and choices as gendered, sexed, and bodied persons (Geertz 1973; Bourdieu 1992; Howell 1997b; Butler 2004).[4] In the local community, ideas about the patrilineage and morality are intimately related to one another and frame the upbringing of girls (and boys). Female morality, according to my data, is above all a matter of having a 'feeling' (*tinh cam*) for how to conduct oneself by adjusting one's behaviour in a variety of social situations in daily life (Rydstrøm 2001, 2002, 2003, 2004). Girls' learning of 'good morality' from early childhood, I would suggest, translates into morality for young women, which even encompasses moral considerations regarding female sexuality.[5]

Morality

Morality, according to Emile Durkheim, is a discipline with a double objective, as, on the one hand, it promotes regularity in people's conduct while, at the same time, it provides them with goals that limit their horizons. It 'consists in an infinity of special rules, fixed and specific, which order man's conduct in those different situations in which he finds himself most frequently' (Durkheim 2002 [1961]: 25). Through education morality should be learned, Durkheim argues, as a means to master and restrain oneself. This would be useful not only for the individual but also for society as a collective (Durkheim 2002 [1961]).

Judith Butler (2004), however, is concerned about the limitations of people's horizons through moral restrictions. She agrees with Durkheim that morality holds an important societal function by referring to the aims, aspirations and commonly held presuppositions that orient and direct human action (e.g. the norm of non-violence). But morality, Butler argues by drawing on Michel Foucault, indicates certain ideals that provide coercive criteria for the configuration of, for example, culturally appropriate women or men (Butler 2004; see also Geertz 1973; Howell 1997).

Foucault defines the coercive dimension of morality as manifestations of power. One of the roles of morality and the norms of which it is composed is to signify what is different by identifying social 'abnormities'. Morality supports a continuous process of confirmation and reiteration of what is commonly appreciated as culturally acceptable and thus 'normal' behaviour (Foucault 1978, 1984, 1988; see also Rabinow 1984).[6] Morality and its norms inherently hold the power to normalise and, in doing so, demand self-governing, due to which each person becomes 'the principle of his [or her] own subjection' (Foucault in Butler 1997: 85).

Thus morality can be recognised as a 'normalising' force, in the sense that those who do not regulate their behaviour in commonly approved ways may be condemned and even stigmatised. This is most likely to happen, as Veena Das notes, when one person's crossing of moral boundaries can be registered directly by another in face-to-face interaction (Das 2001).[7] By subscribing to a general cultural fear of challenging the maintenance of a specific cultural universe and its codes, significations of 'abnormal' behaviour are facilitated by estimations of the extent to which a person is able to incorporate and manifest accepted norms, bodily and in speech, when interacting with others (Douglas 1991; Das 2001).

Sexuality is not uncommonly the target of attempts of defining 'normal' vis-à-vis 'abnormal' behaviour (Efroymson et. al. 1997; Khuat

Thu Hong 1998; Cameron and Kulick 2003). According to Gilles Deleuze and Félix Guattari, the immanent multiple energies of sexuality or, rather, the rhizomatic character of sexuality empowers sexuality to transgress established definitions of 'normality'. By drawing on a geographical and even botanical language, Deleuze and Guattari argue that a rhizome is composed of multiple and complex networks, which together configure the topography of numerous plateaus.[8] A rhizome, then, consists of dispersed points of energies that intertwine with other points of energies.[9] Sexuality, I would propose, can be understood as one point of energies that may leave an after-image by blurring and even crossing the boundaries for morally defined acceptable behaviour (Deleuze and Guattari 2002; see also Geertz 1973; Cameron and Kulick 2003).

Studying Morality in Rural Vietnam

Thinh Tri has about 12,000 inhabitants, most of whom are farmers, although many adult household members also have small-scale income jobs.[10] The local People's Committee (*Uy ban nhan dan*) is in charge of political decisions while the Communist Party (*Dang cong san*) is expected to guarantee the ideological line.[11] Together the People's Committee and the Party implement governmental and local politics and hence also the *doi moi* (renovation) policy.[12] Inhabitants usually live in three-generation patrilineally organised households. After marriage, a young woman typically moves from her natal home in order to live together with her husband and her parents-in-law. However, like anywhere else in Vietnam, in Thinh Tri the setting up of nuclear families increasingly obscures the tradition of three-generation households (Rydstrøm 2003, 2004; Ngo Thi Ngan Binh 2004; Werner 2004).

When I conducted my first fieldwork in Thinh Tri from 1994 to 1995 (fourteen months), I went to rural Vietnam to study the ways in which children are taught to become culturally appropriate females or males. In order to do so, I observed continuously the social interaction of five extended or nuclear families. The data collection consisted of intensive observations of all social interaction between the children, their siblings, parents, grandparents, other kin, peers and teachers, as well as of in-depth interviews with all of these groups and, moreover, official representatives. During my fieldwork in Thinh Tri, it became increasingly clear to me that people were highly concerned with the morality of girls and boys (and of women and men). Girls and boys are encouraged to demonstrate morality in highly differentiated ways, as I shall discuss further below, and they bring with them into adolescence different sets of gendered, sexed and bodied moralities (Rydstrøm 2001, 2003, 2004).[13] In order to explore how norms and morals acquired by girls throughout childhood transform into morality in female adolescents, I decided to return to Thinh Tri.

Hence, from 2000 to 2001 (eight months), I carried out yet another period of fieldwork in Thinh Tri, this time focusing on the ways in which young people consider, among other matters, sexuality and morality. I worked together with four extended or nuclear families, three of which had been included in my first period of fieldwork. In-depth interviews were carried out with adolescents, their peers, parents, grandparents, other kin, teachers, and official representatives. In addition, focus group discussions and participant observation were conducted (see Rydstrøm 2002, 2003, 2004).[14] Below, I shall elucidate the morality girls are expected to learn and, in doing so, provide background information for my further discussion of young women's understandings of the connections between morality and sexuality.

Female Morality

As in most of Vietnam, Thinh Tri inhabitants practise patrilineal ancestor worship, and thus celebrate male progeny. Men are understood as inherently superior to women because a son is assumed to be able to reproduce his father's lineage. By mediating physical, symbolic and temporal links across generations, an oldest son is recognised as connecting his patrilineage's deceased and future members. Therefore, a son is rendered intelligible as embodying patrilineal 'honour' (*danh du*), 'reputation' (*tieng*) and ultimately 'morality' (*dao duc*). In this sense a son is not blank, either symbolically or materially, meaning that he cannot lose 'honour', 'reputation' and morality in the most basic sense. Because a son in himself holds respect and esteem, he is defined as representing the 'inside lineage' (*ho noi*) (Tran Dinh Huou 1991; Hue-Tam Ho Tai 2001; Rydstrøm 2001, 2002, 2003, 2004; Bélanger 2003; Carsten 2004;).

In the patrilineal socio-symbolic universe, a daughter's body, on the other hand, emerges as blank as it materialises and symbolises a lack of intergenerational depth. A daughter is not recognised as embodying inborn patrilineal 'honour', 'reputation' and ultimately 'morality'. In this particular sense, a daughter is rendered exterior in the patrilineal kinship organisation and thus literally defined as belonging to the 'outside lineage' (*ho ngoai*). Due to the ways in which sons and daughters are imbued with symbolic and material meaning, daughters must learn to compensate for their deficiency as regards inborn (moral) capacities (Rydstrøm 2001, 2002, 2003, 2004; Carsten 2004;).

One way in which a daughter may compensate for her 'outside' position is by demonstrating and even accumulating 'good morality' through the practice of *tinh cam* (sentiments, emotions, feelings) (Bourdieu 1992; Rydstrøm 2001, 2002, 2003).[15] *Tinh cam* encompasses a number of qualities that together indicate a high moral standard in a girl or woman. A girl or woman is usually acknowledged as demonstrating *tinh cam* if she shows 'respect' (*kinh*), 'self-denial' (*nhuong*) and 'obedience' (*ngoan*) and if she, moreover, has a sense of 'responsibility' (*trach nhiem*) and 'good manners' (*net tot*).

From an early age, Thinh Tri girls are taught about the social capacity of *tinh cam* in order to become appropriate moralised female members of their community. In the spirit of Durkheim, and with the consequences described by Butler and Foucault as subjection, Thinh Tri girls are taught how to restrict their behaviour, in terms of carrying out duties, showing appreciation of seniors' talk, speaking in a gentle manner and avoiding dressing extravagantly, in a sexy manner or indelicately. Living with 'sentiments' means that a girl or woman manifests and even accumulates 'good morality' not only for herself but also for the patrilineage of her father and/or husband (Rydstrøm 2001, 2002, 2003, 2004; see also Carsten 2004).

Whenever adults teach girls how to live with 'good morality', in and through the practice of *tinh cam*, virtually nothing goes unnoticed. Girls' ways of behaving are evaluated continuously in either affirmative or negative ways. For example, if Mai (twelve years old) assists with the cooking, she is 'obedient' (*ngoan*). If Khanh (thirteen years old) gets good marks at school, she is 'smart'/'clever' (*thong minh*). If Nguyet (two years old) puts on a new dress, she is 'beautiful' (*dep*). If Thuan (four years old) assists her grandmother when making brushes from straw, she is 'skilful'/'talented' (*kheo leo*). If Xuan (nine years old) reads aloud from one of her primary school textbooks, she is 'interesting' (*hay*). If Loan (eighteen months old) does not listen to an order, she is 'disrespectful' (*hon hao*). If Hoa (five years old) teases her younger sister, she is 'ugly' (*xau*), and so on. The continuous evaluations teach girls to respond in appreciated ways, something that is taken as proof of a high moral level in a girl (Rydstrøm 2003).

When girls grow up, the guiding moral principles they learn throughout childhood emerge as morality for young women. Holding 'good morality' by practising *tinh cam* means for a young woman that, for instance, she is not of 'easy virtue' (*lang lo*) in terms of engaging in premarital sexual relations, becoming pregnant or having an abortion. Remaining a virgin until marriage and avoiding adultery and divorce are also examples of ways in which a woman can prove her capability of practising *tinh cam* and, in doing so, signalling a high moral standard. Until they are settled in a marriage and have started a family, 'men and women should remain physically distant' (*nam nu tho tho bat than*), as an ancient Confucian precept dictates (Gender Education Group 1996; Population Council 1997; Mensch et al. 2002; Thang Van Trinh 2003).

Family Life

Assumptions about female morality are bound up in ideals concerning family life. Because especially women are expected to practise *tinh cam*, those primarily responsible for establishing and sustaining a happy and harmonious family life are women (Rydstrøm 2003). In official rhetoric, the family is commonly referred to as a basic cell of society that frames the function of biological reproduction and nurturance. The cooperation of members in the family is assumed to entail a unique kind of affection and love governed by emotions and morality, rather than by contracts and law. The predominant ideal for families in late *doi moi* Vietnam is described as happy, progressive, and harmonious families, which are assumed to stabilise and stimulate Vietnam's process of modernisation and development (Marriage and Family Law 2000; see also Collier et al. 1992).

The family ideal in Vietnam reflects recent concerns with morality in the region of South-East Asia. Campaigns to revitalise Confucian family ideals have been undertaken and women have been essentialised and defined as the moral providers of family harmony and happiness in an increasingly global world, which is thought to challenge Asian moral purity (Stivens 2002; see also Douglas 1991). In this vein, the Vietnamese Marriage and Family Law (2000) emphasises the importance of citizens' development and the maintenance of a high moral standard. Article 1 for example, points out that the main objective of the law is:

> [To] [c]ontribute to building, perfecting and protecting the progressive marriage and family regime, formulate legal standards for the conducts of family members; [to] protect the legitimate rights and interests of family members; [to] inherit and promote the fine ethical traditions of the Vietnamese families in order to build prosperous, equal, progressive, happy and lasting families. (Marriage and Family Law 2000: 31).

Happy and lasting, morally sound families are officially, and widely in Vietnamese society understood as heterosexual families. In the former

Law on Marriage of 1986, homosexuality was not explicitly prohibited, although it was not legally accepted either. However, in the Marriage and Family Law of 2000, the focus is clearly on heterosexuality. In article 8 (paragraph 2) the law, for example, reads, 'getting married is an act whereby a man and a woman establish the husband and wife relation'. The heterosexual point is repeated when the law emphasises, 'marriage means the relationship between husband and wife after getting married' (article 8, paragraph 6).[16]

In this heteronormative spirit, women are assumed to hold a moral obligation with respect to the building of families. By subsuming female sexuality to ideals about family life, female sexuality not only becomes highly moralised but also desexualised (Yuval-Davis 1997). For example, in the national discourse, women are approved of as having a 'Heavenly mandate' (*Thien chuc*) owing to their 'physiology, especially the ability to bear children and breast-feed them' (Franklin 2000: 46).[17] Women, furthermore, are expected to 'maintain ... the race" (Mai Thuc 1997: 311) because of their "glorious function' (Le Thi Nham Tuyet 1999:177), that is, 'the function of becoming pregnant and giving birth' (Tran Thi Que 1999: 16). Nguyen Thi Binh, who is affiliated to the national Women's Union, summarises these ideas by saying that it is imperative always to remember that women, as mothers, have a significant role regarding the nurturance of the family and the teaching of Vietnamese morality to children. Such an ideal mother is even expected to prevent her children from becoming involved in deviant activities (see also Thi Ninh Xuan 1997; Stivens 2002).

Corrupting Forces

The official concern about 'social evils' (*te nan xa hoi*) and 'poisonous culture' (*van hoa doc hai*) shows how more conservative forces in Vietnamese society have succeeded in challenging the reform policy of *doi moi* and Vietnam's increased integration into the global world by denouncing globalisation as fuelling the rise of 'poisonous culture' and 'social evils' (Rosen and Marr 1999; McNally 2003).[18] In 1993, a representative of the national Women's Union, for example, commented: 'It is our view that we need to do much more to strengthen the traditional values in the family relations and increase the role of the community in the monitoring and surveillance of ethical actions of each individual'. (Le Thi Quy, quoted in McNally 2003: 114).

The 'social evil' campaign intends to eliminate any 'aspects of society considered unhealthy and thought to contribute to harmful and anti-social practices' (McNelly 2003: 114).[19] In attempting to do so, a whole range of activities, such as premarital and extramarital sex, homosexuality, pornography, prostitution, drug and alcohol addiction, gambling, theft, abuse and violence, as well as paintings (e.g. pin-up calendars), music videos and music referring to sex, are condemned by the campaign. Sexual activities included in the category of 'social evils' are those corresponding to official definitions of 'dirty' (*ban*) behaviour. Premarital and extramarital sex, pornography and prostitution are associated with HIV and AIDS and thus labelled as manifestations of 'dirty' behaviour (Marr 1997; Population Council 1997; Truong Trong Hoang 1998; Soucy 2000/2001; McNally 2003).[20]

Hence, since its introduction in 1995, the 'social evils' campaign has attempted to counteract any behaviour defined as impure. A representative from the Social Evils Prevention Department, for example, describes the problem regarding 'dirty' influences from the global world in terms of clean and polluted water: 'When we open the doors of our society, the water flows in, the clean along with the dirty. Our duty is to screen it, and to help people recognize and protect themselves from bad influences' (BBC 1999; see also McNally 2003). In this spirit, in 1995, the Vietnamese government carried out a campaign that focused mainly on houses of prostitution, karaoke bars, video shops, massage parlours and advertising signs of foreign origin. Semi-nude or nude pictures, such as wall calendars with Western models, were confiscated from shops because the material was deemed to represent 'social evils' that were able to undermine a high moral standard (Marr 1997).

According to official statements, families and especially the youngest generation should remain 'pure' by not being influenced by 'social evils' (Do Thi Ninh Xuan 1997). The General Secretary of the Central Committee of the Communist Party of Vietnam, Le Kha Phieu, for instance, points out that by protecting young people from 'social evils' the future decision-makers of Vietnamese society will remain 'non-polluted' (Le Kha Phieu 2001).[21] If adolescents were to be influenced by foreign morally 'dirty' forces, the future of Vietnam would be jeopardised (Marr 1997; Rosen and Marr 1999). With respect to the moral purity of young people, female prostitution and the ways in which it manifests female sexuality are matters of particular concern. For example, in 1996, a writer of a public security news article noted that 'social evils' in the form of 'whorehouses in disguise and sex tours pos[e] extreme dangers to the health of our race, and destroy the moral foundation of our nation through the scourge of AIDS, and the bad influence on the lifestyle of our youth, especially those of the feminine sex' (Nguyen-vo Thu-huong 1998: 113; see also Douglas 1991).

By demarcating a thin line between 'clean' and 'dirty' behaviours, the governmental campaign to combat 'social evils' facilitates restrictions on, or in the words of Foucault and Butler self-governing in, citizens in general and young women in particular (i.e. 'the feminine sex'). Hence, the 'social evils' campaign inevitably stimulates identifications of 'normal' vis-à-vis 'abnormal', or non-acceptable, behaviours. In the local community of Thinh Tri, young women are aware of the public discourse on morality and sexuality, which provide a resource when they themselves construct moral guidelines regarding female sexuality. Below I shall, by drawing on Butler, illuminate the ways in which morality is rendered meaningful in gendered, sexed and bodied terms in the local Vietnamese setting.

Sexual Order

In urban Vietnam, premarital sexual relations tend to be romanticised by young people as they are seen as an outburst of love that 'carries one away', rather than as expressions of moral decline (Bélanger and Khuat Thu Hong 1996; Truong Trong Hoang 1998; Gammeltoft and Nguyen Minh Thang 2000; Phan Thi Vang Anh and Pham Thu Thuy 2003). In rural areas, assumptions about sexuality are in contrast to urban ways of romanticising sexual relations because here female sexuality is circumscribed by ideas of female morality. Thinh Tri young women, for example, frequently repeat the ancient Confucian precept of 'females and males should keep a distance' as a guiding principle for appropriate behaviour in young women (Population Council 1997; Quan Le Nga 2000; Rydstrøm 2003, 2004; Thang Van Trinh 2003).

Some young women even note that sexuality should not be a topic of conversation at all. Talking about 'this problem'[22] (*van de nay*) means that someone may overhear the conversation and condemn the interlocutors as suffering from lack of morality, in terms of not having a 'sense' (*tinh cam*) for how to display appropriate female morality. By resembling national moral discourses, Thinh Tri young women suggest that sexuality should be reserved for the building of a family. When one has got a husband, a sexual relation should be established between the couple, and a family be started. Sexuality as regards married life, however, should be treated with secrecy and thus not be a topic of conversation. In the words of eighteen-year-old Van Anh, 'the [sexual] relation between a husband and wife should be secret [*giu kin*] [because], for example, if the children accidentally overheard their parents' talk [about sexuality] it would not be good because the children could get bad ideas'.

The word for sexuality in Vietnamese is *tinh duc,* which literally means sexual desires, but Thinh Tri female adolescents nevertheless matter-of-factly define sexuality as a 'relation between a girl/female and boy/male [*quan he con trai/nam gai/nu*]', because, 'like animals, male and female have intercourse [*giao phoi*] in order to continue the race'. Clearly, sexuality is not recognised by Thinh Tri young women as an expression of desires or pleasures. Rather, sexuality is rendered meaningful as a functional kind of female-to-male interaction which is considered to be imperative for human reproduction and the continuation of a patrilineage (Efroymson et. al. 1997; Gammeltoft and Nguyen Minh Thang 2000; Bélanger et al. 2003; Rydstrøm 2004). Due to the ways in which ideas about marriage, sexuality and morality are enmeshed with one another, Thinh Tri female adolescents voice a heterosexual preference, not uncommon in Vietnamese society.[23] On a sunny spring day in Thinh Tri, in the living room of the family of Nguyet (eighteen years old), the young woman addresses the connections between morality and sexuality by invoking the heterosexual norm:

> Sexuality is a relation of the flesh [*quan he xac thit*] between two persons of different sex. I think sexuality is one of today's most important problems. On the television I have seen that there is much display of sexuality. Because of the open door policy; [i.e. *doi moi*], people develop a very loose morality. There are many problems because of the [societal] changes and it is necessary to understand the relationship [between females and males] and also to keep a distance from boys. It [i.e. sexuality] is a delicate [*te nhi*] matter but actually we should talk more about this in order for everybody to understand about this most important problem. Everybody would like to know and understand clearly [about sexuality].

As is clear, Nguyet reiterates official rhetoric regarding ideas of 'dirty' moral influences from the outside world and their negative impact on the moral standard in Vietnamese citizens. The focus on sexuality in media and broadcasts worries Nguyet, because she thinks it may compromise the moral standard in young people. Due to worries about a decline in the level of morality in Vietnamese society, young women wish to learn more about sexuality. Van Anh (eighteen years old), who is also present, agrees with Nguyet, saying, 'If anybody thinks I am too young to learn about sexuality, I don't agree. I need to know about health and sexuality, what it is, and how it might be harmful [*tac hai*; harmful both to one's health and reputation].' Female adolescents thus fear a moral decline, which they assume more open and globalised attitudes to sexuality may provoke. However, they would like to be well informed.

Moralising Sexuality

Thinh Tri young women generally interpret sexual relations prior to marriage as expressions of 'social evils' that violate governmental recommendations and rules. On an early spring day in the household of Xuan (eighteen years old), Xuan and her friends are sitting on a big mat on the floor sipping tea and listening to Linh (seventeen years old) who says: 'My mother and sister told me that it is illegal to have sex before marriage.' Linh's comment reflects the conclusion of a Population Council report, which registers a widespread concern in Vietnamese society 'about increasing "social evils" which include [...], premarital and extramarital sex, pornography, and a variety of other social practices' (Population Council 1997: 9; see also Thang Van Trinh 2003).

Sexual relations prior to marriage should be avoided, Xuan explains, because 'for a Vietnamese woman it is important to be a virgin [*trinh tiet*] [upon marriage]'. If a young woman has a relationship with a man – even though it may not include a sexual relation – it would easily give her a reputation as being 'careless' (*boi*) and of 'easy virtue' (*lang lo*). Such a girl signals that she does not know how to demonstrate *tinh cam* and hence appropriate female morality. In other words, she may be one of those who, in a Deleuzian sense, are carried away by the uncontrollable energies of sexuality. While urban young women may romanticise the more uncontrollable forces of sexuality, young rural women foreground the fact that being carried away by one's spontaneous desires by having sex with a man would be most likely to result in condemnation and maybe even stigmatisation. If carried away by uncontrollable sexual desires, the morality, 'reputation' and 'honour' not only of a young woman would be damaged, but also of her entire patrilineage. Lan (eighteen years old) considers why it is crucial for a young woman to pay attention to the demonstration of 'good morality':

> Because of an old and feudal opinion, old people do not accept if two friends [i.e. a female and male] hold hands when walking in the streets. Surely, old people would think that those two have a relationship [i.e. including a sexual relation]. If people think so about us [i.e. females], we will get a bad reputation [*bi mang tieng*] even though those who hold hands might only be friends. Old people will think we are *xau* [i.e. have bad morality] and therefore they will try to ruin the relationship.

Other young women, though, challenge the more puritanical sides of national and local moral discourses by stressing that it could, or rather should, be considered 'normal' to hold hands with a boyfriend. Doing so should not cause any problems as long as the couple does not 'go too far' (*di qua xa*), in terms of having sex. Hence holding hands should not give one a reputation of being 'careless', improper and non-decent. At the same time, young Thinh Tri women, however, repeat that it is important not to be 'careless' when interacting with men. A young woman should always sense and obey the 'limit' (*gioi han*), thereby verifying that she lives with *tinh cam* and thus is able to conduct herself in morally appropriate ways. Minh (sixteen years old) summarises the moral dangers of becoming sexually involved with a man: 'One should be careful [*giu gin*] in a relation with a boy because a girl could become pregnant, and everybody would think that the girl is frivolous and immoral/improper [*khong dung dan*].' Minh and her young female peers emphasise that a young woman should not be 'too involved' with her boyfriend. After all, it is preferable that a young woman remains focused on getting a good education, as this will enable her to increase her chances of getting good marks and a well-paid job in the future. And most Thinh Tri female adolescents do demonstrate 'good morality' by practising *tinh cam*. They stay at home, conduct household chores and prepare their homework. However, some young women are passionate and do get carried away, according to inhabitants' gossip. Such young women do not know when it is time to draw a moral line by controlling the subversive forces of sexual desires.

Blurring Moral Boundaries

Even though some young women do ignore predominating moral guidelines regarding how female morality should be demonstrated in and through the practice of *tinh cam*, 'going too far', in terms of having premarital sex, means problems. If a young woman has a relationship with a young man and it results in a premarital pregnancy, the situation is delicate – especially for the young woman, as her life will become very difficult, I was told. One of the teachers from the primary school in Thinh Tri explains how she attempts to handle female students who are involved in a premarital sexual relation:

> If a girl, for example, in grade nine has problems because of a sexual relation with a male, I insist on talking about it, for instance, by telling her: 'Nobody can correct your mistake. The Vietnamese always tend to forgive a boy [engaged in a premarital sexual relation] more easily than a girl.'... Girls always have to pay more attention to morality [than boys] in order to remain virgins [upon marriage]. But they can't always control their desire to be together with a boy and might be so attracted that they do something [i.e. have sex].

Occasionally young women cross the moral boundaries by giving birth to a child out of wedlock. This was the case with the Thinh Tri couple that 'loved one another and had a baby six months before they got married'. Young women who are not married but, however, become pregnant usually have an abortion at the provincial or district Health Care Clinic. The abortion will be hidden from others and kept secret. At the Thinh Tri Health Care Clinic, the male medical doctor describes the policy of the clinic with respect to unmarried, pregnant young women:

> If a girl gets pregnant and if she and her boyfriend still go to school, are eighteen years old and love one another, then a wedding should be arranged. If they are too young for marriage, the girl should have an abortion ... If girls have an abortion they keep it a secret and don't talk with anybody about the implications of the abortion. If a girl is sixteen or seventeen years old, she hasn't reached the age to have a child or the age for getting married.

According to the Thinh Tri medical doctor, young women below the age of eighteen who become pregnant prior to marriage do not need to be involved concerning how to handle an unexpected pregnancy. Such statements illuminate how a young woman who is associated with a low moral standard may be excluded from deciding as to whether to continue or terminate her unexpected pregnancy. Female adolescents, however, shed light on the medical doctor's statement by explaining that the crossing of moral boundaries, in terms of having a child out of wedlock, will have devastating consequences for a young woman and even for her family. Such a young woman would bring shame upon herself and her family and, moreover, she would most likely be socially isolated because people would avoid having contact with a girl with 'bad morality'.

On a rainy and grey winter day, I visit Phuong (seventeen years old), and meet those of her female friends who have come to Phuong's household to address the matter of sexuality. Phuong considers the problems encountered by a woman who does not practise *tinh cam* and thus 'good morality': 'Having a child before marriage is not good. I would get a bad reputation. I would not fit in, would become isolated, and I even would have lost my virginity. Some [girls] are of easy virtue [*lang lo*] and don't know how to take care of their virginity by restricting themselves.' Within other rural communities, young women are similarly worried about being stigmatised as immoral persons if engaging in a sexual relation and/or becoming pregnant prior to marriage. A female adolescent from another community once had an abortion, and she continues to worry as to whether she might be condemned by others if the secret about her abortion is revealed: 'I am very afraid that people will find out about this [i.e. the abortion] and talk badly about [me] and offend me. So I have not told anyone about it, except [for] my boyfriend' (Gammeltoft and Nguyen Minh Thang 2000: 115; see also Truong Trong Hoang 1998; Quan Le Nga 2000; Soucy 2000/2001).

Having a child out of wedlock is usually connected with harsh moral disqualification and even stigmatisation. An abortion may not only lead to guilt, sorrow, pain and worries about possible physical consequences but also to fear about whether anybody might discover and even reveal the secret (Gammeltoft and Nguyen Minh Thang 2000; Thang Van Trinh 2003). However, not all young women who have a child prior to marriage should be judged too harshly, Binh (seventeen years) argues: 'Girls who cannot control themselves [i.e. have sex] and give birth to a child should not be blamed because they were weak and did not know how to avoid having a baby. But those who know about sexuality, and have sex, and a child before marriage they have bad morality.' According to Binh, a young woman with a 'weak character' who has a child prior to marriage should be treated with forbearance. It is another matter altogether with those young women who are well informed about sexuality and thus assumed to be able to handle their sexual desires in rational ways. Such well-informed young women, Binh indicates, should be condemned because they ought to know better than giving in to their sexual desires.

Conclusion

By referring to general aspirations, morality generates ideals for human behaviour while it at the same time holds the power to condemn any behaviour that challenges the limits for accepted ways of conducting oneself, as Butler and Foucault argue. The study of morality, as I have shown in this chapter, calls for an analysis of national and local discourses in particular cultural settings. By doing so, studies of morality can augment our knowledge about the processes through which morality takes shape over time as norms that encourage and direct 'normal' behaviour in women and men. With respect to the local Vietnamese community of Thinh Tri, the intersections between the practice of *tinh cam* and appropriate female morality are intimate and epitomise the ways in which morality, in the spirit of Butler, becomes gendered, sexed and bodied. A daughter who does not demonstrate that she holds 'good morality' by practising *tinh cam* is susceptible to moral disqualification in ways that sons are not.

In Vietnamese society, women's sexuality has been, and remains, subjected to imposed and/or self-imposed control. Girls and women continuously need to practise *tinh cam* in order to prove that they keep a high moral standard. This is illuminated by Thinh Tri young women's understandings of sexuality and, furthermore, is amplified by the 'social evils' campaigns, as the campaign indicates a need for control of female sexual energies. As Deleuze and Guattari point out (2002), sexual energies hold subversive powers to transgress the boundaries of a moral order and, in doing so, sexuality emerges as necessary to govern. Premarital sex, becoming pregnant and having an abortion are all actions that symbolise dispersed sexual energies, which may leave an after-image in terms of disrupting a predominant moral order that values the reservation of female sexuality for the building of morally sound families (Yuval-Davis 1997).

In conclusion, I would suggest that studying morality means attempting to unfold coexisting and/or contesting norms that guide and restrict human behaviour, appreciations, considerations, decisions, agreements, disagreements and so on as manifested in local and national discourses and practices. Because of the differentiated and multiple ways in which moralities are configured and lived by in various places, such as Thinh Tri, the study of morality invites examinations of the complexities, ambivalences and ambiguities contained in particular moralities, as they become gendered, sexed and bodied in local contexts (see Geertz 1973; Howell 1997b).

Notes

This research was generously funded, partly by the Swedish Department for Research Cooperation (SAREC) of the Swedish International Development Corporation Agency (SIDA) and partly by the Bank of Sweden Tercentenary Foundation (*Riksbankens Jubileumsfond*). The Center for East and Southeast Asian Studies, in addition, has supported my research. I am grateful for the comments provided by Nguyen-vo Thu-huong on an earlier version of the text and for discussions on the topic of the chapter with Thomas Achen, Lisa Drummond, Don Kulick, and Angie Ngoc Tran. I greatly appreciate my communication with Jean La Fontaine on anthropology and morality. Many thanks to Monica Heintz and Johan Rasanayagam for inviting me to present a previous version of this chapter at the workshop 'Rethinking Morality in Anthropology' at the Max Planck Institute of Social Anthropology in Leipzig. Similarly, the chapter has benefited from workshop participants' useful comments. I am grateful for the support of the Institute of Educational Science in Hanoi and for the valuable help offered by *em* Huong. My deep gratitude goes to the persons and families in Thinh Tri with whom I worked, for their kindness and support. Fragments of this chapter have previously appeared in the *Journal of Gender, Place, and Culture*, 13 (3): 283–303.

1. For a discussion of the ways in which Confucian and communist ideals have merged with one another, see Nguyen Khac Vien (1975).
2. For an introduction to Confucianism in Vietnam, see David Marr (1981). For a discussion of Confucian moral guidelines for women in Vietnam, see Ngo Thi Ngan Binh (2004).
3. The name of the commune and any names of persons referred to in this chapter are pseudonyms.
4. Rather than employing the concept of gender, I refer to the gendered, sexed, and bodied ways in which females and males are rendered meaningful morally. See Helle Rydstrøm (2002, 2003).
5. According to Vietnamese understandings of *dao duc* (translated into morality, virtues, or ethics), someone's morality can be good or bad, while, in a Western context, people would rather be considered as being immoral than as having bad morality. The expression for 'bad morality' in Vietnamese is *dao duc xau*, with *xau* meaning 'ugly' or 'bad'.
6. The normative, and serialised, order is 'an essential component of the regime of bio-power. Such a power has to qualify, measure, appraise, and hierarchize, rather than display itself in its murderous splendor it effects distributions around the norm' (Rabinow 1984: 20).
7. On stigma and stigmatisation, see Erwing Goffman (1963).
8. Plateaus are the circumstances that bring an activity to a pitch of intensity without, however, leading to a culmination point, thereby referring to 'the heightening of energies [that is] sustained long enough to leave a kind of afterimage of its dynamism that can be reactivated or injected into other activities, creating a fabric of intensive states between which any number of connecting routes could exist' (Massumi 2002: xiv).
9. Rhizome is a network that 'connects any point to any other point, and its traits are not necessarily linked to traits of the same nature; it brings into play very different regimes of signs, and even nonsign states' (Deleuze and Guattari 2002: 21).
10. [NB: Majucule] Inhabitants are *Kinh*, i.e. the majority group of the Vietnamese population.
11. Like any other Vietnamese commune, Thinh Tri has 'Mass Unions' (*hoi*) such as the Youth Union (*Hoi thanh nien*) and the Women's Union (*Hoi phu nu*).
12. In December 1986, the policy of *doi moi* was introduced at the Sixth National Congress of the Communist Party of Vietnam. The *doi moi* policy aims at maintaining socialism in Vietnam but in a market oriented economy and has led to new forms of management and ownership, including a resurgent private market and sector. With the introduction of the *doi moi* policy, Vietnam entered a new era of rapid socio-economic change (Ljunggren 1997).
13. The data resulted in more than sixty-four hours of recording (i.e. more than forty-nine hours of cassette tapes and fifteen hours of videotapes), all of which have been transcribed in Vietnamese. During both of the periods of fieldwork, a young woman assisted me while collecting data, albeit a different woman for each period of fieldwork. The support of my two female co-workers has been invaluable. (Like anyone participating in my research, even my co-workers have been guaranteed anonymity).
14. My data from this fieldwork resulted in forty hours of tape recording, which have been transcribed in Vietnamese. In addition, each of about forty seventh grade female and male students wrote an essay for me on how they consider the past and future.
15. Drawing on Pierre Bourdieu (1992), *tinh cam* can be recognised as symbolic capital, which can be accumulated and even lost.

16. Homosexuality is treated with much secrecy in present-day Vietnam and homosexuals, as current research indicates, tend to engage in a heterosexual relationship in which children are produced (Aronsson 1999; Colby 2001; Khuat Thu Hong 1998; Truong Trong Hoang 1998).

17. For a definition of discourse, see Michel Foucault (1978).

18. In December 1995, Vietnam's Prime Minister Vo Van Kiet launched the campaign to combat 'social evils' and 'poisonous culture' (Marr 1997; Rosen and Marr 1999).

19. David Marr (1997) argues that the 'social evils' campaign was originally a response to a general public anxiety in Vietnamese society about the perceived explosion in violence, social vices, crime and cultural depravities, which was supported by media stories on killing, rape and crime. Vietnamese media reported about widespread consumption of pornographic and violent videos, drunkenness (especially among young men), drug addiction, young men's sexual harassment of young women, homosexuality, gambling and loss of respect for authorities and seniors, all of which were associated with the country's increased integration into the global world.

20. Recently the National Vietnamese AIDS Committee identified alarming high numbers of young people in Vietnam infected with HIV. People below the age of thirty are estimated to account for about fifty per cent of the HIV/AIDS-infected persons in Vietnam (Quan Le Nga 2000; Colby 2001; Thang Van Trinh. 2003).

21. Le Kha Phieu emphasises: 'The family is the foundation of society, the natural environment for the development and happiness of all members, especially children. For this reason, we must highlight even more the role of the family, cause each family to realize that the family is the first body to be responsible for the bringing up of children into good citizens' (Le Kha Phieu 2001: 59).

22. Due to its morally sensitive character, Thinh Tri adolescents would not uncommonly use a euphemism when referring to sexuality. Thus an abstraction such as 'this problem', 'it' or 'this' might be used for sexuality to indicate a distance from a morally troubled phenomenon and topic of conversation. The ways in which young people living in Asia region may attempt to deal with the morality of sexuality by using euphemisms even has been described elsewhere, for instance, in a number of the articles included in Manderson and Liamputtong Rice (2001).

23. This does not mean that homosexuality may not be practised in the local community (Truong Trong Hoang 1998; Aronsson 1999; Quan Le Nga 2000; Colby 2001).

Chapter 8

NARRATIVE ETHICS: THE EXCESS OF GIVING AND MORAL AMBIGUITY IN THE LAO VESSANTARA-JATAKA

Patrice Ladwig

The road to excess leads to the palace of wisdom. (William Blake – 'The Marriage of Heaven and Hell', 1975)

All that I give comes from without, and this does not satisfy me; I wish to give something of my very own. If one should ask my heart, I would cut open my breast, and tear it out, and give it; if one ask my eyes, I would pluck out my eyes and give them; if one should ask my flesh, I would cut off all the flesh of my body and give it. (Jataka 486 (Maha-Ukkusa-Jataka))

Introduction

Stories of exemplary donors who give away huge amounts of wealth, body parts or even their own life are not uncommon in Buddhism. The most famous of these, *The Perfect Generosity of Prince Vessantara*, in which the protagonist loses his right to inherit the throne because of his excessive giving, is expelled from the kingdom and finally gives away his children and wife, is perhaps better known in Laos than the biography of the Buddha himself. Whilst in the field surrounded by monks with an often profound knowledge of and love for traditional literature and participating in hour-long recitations of this and other stories, Martha Nussbaum's (2001) idea that narrative poses and attempts to answer questions about how best to live in the world evolved in an almost natural way into a starting point for my enquiry into Lao notions of ethics. The more explicit treatments of ethics and morality in doctrinal Buddhist texts commonly used by scholars as material to analyse ethics may somehow inform the tales, but are ultimately of limited use for anthropological analysis: the refinements and subtleties of the Buddhist canon are of little interest to the average Lao monk and more often than not remain completely obscure for the lay Buddhist. In contrast to that, folk narratives, often performed by monks in a dramatic, hyperbolic and witty way, constitute a body of knowledge that is used by laypeople and monks to discuss ethics, models of the good and virtuous life, matters of law and sometimes also problematisations of these latter that reach beyond simple didacticism.

Although there has been a tendency to move away from a mainly philological approach to Buddhist ethics, the conceptualisation of ethics as being encoded in text and simultaneously affecting people's praxis and their way of actually reflecting on ethics has only been marginally investigated for the case of Buddhism. Hallisey and Hansen (1996) have applied some theories of narrative ethics to Buddhist texts and I think reading texts not only as pure ethical instructions but as potential areas of reflection with a multiplicity of voices in the text is an approach worth expanding upon. This chapter will therefore explore to what extent some works in literary studies that in different ways emphasise the moral aspects of narratives and the encounter between reader/listener and narrative can be used to rethink some aspects of the study of ethics and its didactics. One of the aims is thus to root ethics in narrative practice and to move to a 'performative' approach (Tambiah 1985) that allows for analysis of the conditions of perpetuation and transformation of ethical understandings, including the expression of moral ambiguities and paradoxes in ethics. When taking ritual recitations as a starting point to think about ethics, it is vital to point out that in Laos these are didactic (the monk instructs a layperson), but that they also leave space for one's own reflections on the topic and even stimulate them. The reception by the audience is not simply passive and not a reproduction of an ethical homeostasis; through their hyperbolic and emotionally loaded aesthetics, ritual and narrative also create a field of discourse that articulates and dramatises conflicts and ethical dilemmas and are therefore places of dialogical exchanges between an idealised moral system and the requirements of the quotidian. The latter point is of particular importance for religions like

Buddhism or Jainism as the translation of the somewhat extreme ascetic system of values and practices into an ethics that is applicable to the lives of laypeople and sufficiently coherent in relation to its ascetic propagators.

After a brief presentation of the story of Vessantara and the context of its ritual performance, I shall first discuss the didactic relationship between monk and lay Buddhist and the position of ethics in that. In the third part, I shall set out to discuss the question of how narrative works on people's understanding of ethics. Following Heim's (2003) idea about the significance of emotions in South Asian Buddhism, I shall primarily focus here on the role of emotions and their importance in Lao Buddhist conceptions of sermon-making and performances of narratives. The recurring themes of pity, fear, strangeness and failure in these stories will play a central role here. The forth part will relate to concepts of responsibility and sovereignty as topics in the story and discuss Steven Collins's (1998) reading of the story. Here the different voices in the text, the ethical dilemmas of the protagonist and the diverging understandings of some of my informants will serve as examples for a short discussion of Derrida's ideas on responsibility with respect to a Lao Marxist critique of Buddhist kingship. In the same part, the partial moral defeat of the protagonist of the story due to his excessive giving and subsequent interpretations in Buddhist discourse will serve as an example for the potential functions of conflicts in ethical reasoning and the ethical value of failure.[1]

The Story and Performance

The Vessantara-Jataka (hereafter VJ) is the most important and final 'birth story' (*jataka*)[2] in a series of 547 tales that describe the various rebirths of the entity that later became the Buddha.[3] In a so-to-speak aeon-stretching ethical bricolage including rebirths as matter, animal, woman and men, he finally succeeds in achieving the perfections (*pharami*).[4] The last ten lives of the Buddha-to-be are related to an enumeration of the 10 essential perfections and are the most widely known in Theravada-Buddhism and Laos. Each story represents the perfection of one virtue, with giving (*dana*) being the paramount one.[5] The story of Vessantara and his concluding act of renunciation through giving away his possessions, children and wife are the telos of this process of ethical self-perfection and will lead to Vessantara's rebirth as a Buddha, his enlightenment and the proclamation of Buddhist teachings (*dhamma*).

Researchers like Tambiah (1970: 180), Spiro (1971: 108) and Formoso (1992: 233) agree that the VJ is one of the most-well known stories in Buddhist South-East Asia. Cone and Gombrich (1977: XV) state that people in Sri Lanka know it as well as the biography of the Buddha. In Laos, as in Thailand, Burma and Cambodia, there is a yearly Vessantara festival and during the ritual the full story is recited in the vernacular language by monks without intermission in a performance lasting between twelve and eighteen hours, with monks and laypeople from other temples being invited and treated as guests. The temple is decorated imitating the forest in which Vessantara retreats with his family after being exiled, and some scenes are acted out in theatrical performances by laypeople one day before the festival, a practice which is now often relinquished. Each monk is assigned in advance to a specific part of the text and the recitation is an explicit chanting competition, with a judging audience of laypeople that have heard the story dozens of times and are capable of detailed aesthetic evaluations concerning voice modulation, the expression of emotional, dramatic moments and clarity of recitation. The use of amplifiers and huge speaker systems today facilitates the acoustic irradiation of the whole village area. The audience rewards a good performance with special gifts, the striking of gongs and enthusiastic applause. Because the ritual takes place on different days in each temple, some people may hear the story several times a year. Pictorial expressions of the story feature prominently in temples – around 80 per cent of all graphical depictions in Lao temples are related to that story, usually giving the full story and key scenes arranged in the order of the thirteen chapters. In Thailand the VJ is screened on television, and there are comics and other forms of modern artistic adaptations that sometimes make their way to Laos.

Synopsis of the Story[6]

In his final reincarnation, the Lord Buddha is born as Vessantara, Prince of the Sivirat Kingdom. His mother, Queen Bhudsai, radiates sympathy and charity towards other people while pregnant, and astrologers predict that a Bodhisattava, who has the meritorious *dana-parami* (perfection of generosity), is going to be born. Directly after he is born, Vessantara asks his mother for alms he wants to distribute to poor people. As a child he repeatedly takes off his precious ornaments and other trinkets and gives them away. One day after Vessantara's birth, a magic white elephant is born that becomes Vessantara's riding elephant and protects the kingdom, and wherever it lives there is rain. When Vessantara is sixteen years old, he gets married to Princess Mati and they have two children together, a boy named

Sali and a girl called Kanha. As a grown-up prince, he continues to gives alms regularly in order to complete his moral perfection of generosity. One day, Brahmins from the Kingdom of Galinkarat come to Sivirat and report that there is a horrible drought in their country and ask Vessantara for the magic white elephant. After brief reflection, he gives them the elephant. The people of the kingdom are enraged and are afraid that the loss of the elephant will bring drought, poverty and chaos to their kingdom. They laud his compassion and generosity, but say that he is not an appropriate heir to the throne. It is decided that Vessantara is to be temporarily exiled from the kingdom. His wife and children decide to come with him into exile, but before that he makes the 'gift of the 700' [700 horses, 700 carriages, etc.] and gives away all his wealth. Together they wander the forest where Vessantara and Mati take up a life of hermitage and chastity by keeping the ten precepts. One night Mati has a horrible dream and when she tells it to her husband, he knows that somebody is going to come and ask for his two children. He doesn't tell his wife and sends her back to sleep and the next day Mati leaves for the forest to collect food. Vessantara, alone with the two children, is visited by Jujaka, an ugly old Brahmin who is in need of slaves to work in his house and has heard that Vessantara gives away everything he is asked for. Vessantara sees the chance to make a 'gift of the body', but hesitates a moment. Jujaka teases him and ridicules him until he agrees to give away the children. Sali and Kanha run away and hide, but finally after protesting Jujaka receives his gift. He binds them together with a vine and lashes the children until blood oozes out of their skin. The children urge the father to wait until the mother comes back, but Jujaka leaves with the children. The great gift makes the earth shake and the gods in heaven become downhearted and take pity on the children while others silently support Vessantara's decision. When Mati comes back and receives the news, she faints. The god Indra, watching the gift of the children from heaven, transforms himself into an old man and descends to earth in order to ask for Vessantara's wife. Once received, the supplicant exposes himself as Indra and gives Mati back to her husband. Meanwhile Jujaka on his way back home passes through the Sivirat kingdom where Vessantara once was prince. His father, the king, recognizes the children and asks the ugly Brahmin to be his guest and finally manages to buy the children back. Upon hearing the story, some of the nobles of the Sivirat Kingdom blame Vessantara again and say that he is hard-hearted and has no responsibility. But the King manages to convince the nobles and the people to ask Vessantara to come back to the kingdom and a great procession is prepared. The magic white elephant is also returned as the drought in the neighbouring kingdom is over. After the messengers that have been sent to Vessantara's hermitage tell him about the King's decision, he at first refuses to return because he suspects the people of the kingdom are still angry about his actions, but he is finally convinced. While returning to the city, Jujaka, who is still a guest in the Sivirat kingdom, dies because he eats too much while being a guest of the king. Finally, Vessantara and his family are united and he becomes heir to the throne of the kingdom and the country is prosperous because he rules righteously.

Layperson and Monk:
Sermon-making as Ethical Didactics

Although there are many areas of Lao society in which ethics are perpetuated, transmitted and negotiated (family, school, etc.), the relationship between monk and householder is also constitutive for a specific ethical field. The clergy can be seen as an interface mediating between the ethical demands of the quotidian and rather abstract soteriological Buddhist teachings. Monks visit local schools and talk about virtuous behaviour, family values and current topics, like drug addiction (Ladwig 2008). Apart from these more visible and 'official' missions, monks are considered to be advisers, and individuals and families consult them for advice and blessings. The interaction between monk and layperson very often takes on characteristics of sermon-making and preaching. Indeed, the words spoken by a monk even in everyday conversations very often have (in their style of speech and reception by laypeople) features of sermons, which may, depending on context, be properly ritualised or in a one-to-one situation rather less regulated. Whether in a more official ritual sermon or in a sort of counselling situation, every sermon and preaching of the Buddha's teachings is considered a 'gift of the *dhamma*' (*dhammadana*), and actually the preaching and exegesis of the *dhamma*, 'giving' moral precepts and explaining virtuous models of behaviour, is considered one of the main tasks of a Buddhist monk.

An important part of sermon-making is its performance and aesthetics. Preaching in specialised and vernacular language and more specifically chanting are major arts a monk has to master, and the ability to build one's reputation as a monk is very much dependent on being a good speaker, advising people in appropriate language and also being capable of entertaining them and expressing the beauty of language through chanting. The bodily postures a layperson assumes when listening to ritualised preaching like the VJ indicate the respect due to monks as well as the special position they occupy in society. The layperson should ideally kneel in a lower position than the monk, with hands folded continuously. Some people keep this posture up for hours while listening to the recitation and approaching a monk in the temple hall can often only be done by crawling on one's knees. For special occasions like the VJ festival, a sort of pulpit is used on which the monk sits, holding a palm-leaf manuscript from which the text is read out or on which his improvisation is built. The holding of the palm-leaf document[7] in a monk's hands is comparable to the position occupied by the Greek *skeptron*, which signifies a position of authority and clearly imbues the speaker's ritual discourse with symbolic capital (Bourdieu

1991: 109). The words of monks and their effect on the listener are also clearly distinguished from the everyday efficacy of words, even when not always understood semantically (Tambiah 1985).[8] Listening to a sermon is in itself an ethical and meritorious activity that works positively on one's karma and contributes to the cultivation of wisdom; in Lao the term *thammasavannahmay* signifies 'merit received by hearing a sermon'.

Official readings of narratives in the temple are in that sense a form of moral education through the medium of literature. Almost every temple in central Vientiane has readings of a variety of stories during the three months rain retreat. Each evening, twenty to forty people gather in the main hall of the temple and monks read out different stories (often *jatakas*) to the audience. Difficult passages are explained by monks and also discussions about the stories come up and interpretations are put forward. The educational flavour of this textual exegesis is obvious, and discussions about appropriate ethics, values and morality are prominent subjects. Monks can even indulge in spicy commentary, usually not appropriate for them but nonetheless appreciated by the audience.[9]

Because the story is taught in schools, theatre groups play scenes of it and people know it from many other sources, the VJ occupies an important position in the public imaginary throughout Buddhist South- East Asia. The range of topics it touches on and its loaded aesthetics involving hyperbolism, tragedy and even comical elements, and it is one of the crucial narratives that serve as a means of reflecting on a variety of moral, political and even feminist issues. On a popular and also more intellectual level, the VJ has been a yearlong subject of discussions by Thai feminists, reflecting on role models, and competing interpretations of more conservative and reform Buddhists in neighbouring Thailand (Gabaude 1991). Community peasant leaders have often chosen Vessantara as a sort of role model for community mobilisation (Cohen 1983: 105). The more or less detailed knowledge of the story on the part of most Lao is also reflected in sayings and expressions and its significance for other, extra-ritual areas of discourse. If you generously give something away, a friend might say you are *'cai phavet'* ('heart of Vessantara') instead of using the word generous, or a good wife that follows her husband without hesitation is said 'to behave like Vessantara's wife'. Children that listen to their parents and follow their orders are equated with Vessantara's two children that are given away by him. These are the more traditional interpretations that are also elaborated in some Lao commentaries of the story (Vessantarasadok 1972: 2). The story serves as a model for the confirmation of traditional roles, family models and discourses such as that of respect for the head of the family and it is in that sense very didactic. Monks like to employ it in order to point out the meritorious character of giving, refer to the great rewards Vessantara received through his generosity and motivate the laypeople to follow his example on a more moderate level and make regular donations to the temple. However, there are also critical potentials in the text that move beyond a call for emulation. For example, certain Lao government-inspired interpretations have used the story to reflect on the inadequacy of Buddhist kingship and argue for a more Marxist and 'democratic' point of view, to which we shall return.

Listening to sermons like the VJ is alongside gift-giving (*dana*), meditation (*bhavana*) and the keeping of precepts/moral training (*silatam*), another method that enables the individual to gain merit and cultivate wisdom and virtuous behaviour. Listening to and reflecting on stories is often slotted into the category of 'moral practice'. It is one of the various strategies Lao society offers the individual to actively shape his ethical subjectivity. These technologies or practices of the self (Foucault 1997: 225; 263) are linked to didactics and pedagogies taken care of by the temple qua institution, with monks as specialists who define a specific 'regime of truth' (Foucault 1980: 131) and practise an exegesis of ethical standards. The interpretations put forward by monks in, for example, the case of the VJ partially serve as the reproduction of role models and values (practices of generosity, obedience of wife and children, etc.) and often aim at an ethical homeostasis. However, the story itself and discourse surrounding it are much more controversial and mixed than might at first sight be visible. Suggested meanings can be appropriated, interpreted and transformed by the individual as a form of autopoietic practice,[10] and, as will be discussed in the next part, the performance of the VJ also entails sequences that actually open up the text and expose the listener to ruptures and fissures that give room for ambiguities and contrarious interpretations. I shall largely focus on the critical understandings that facilitate a diversity of readings and defy a purely didactic interpretation of the story.

Excess, Emotions and Hyperbolism

Some Lao and Western interpretations of the VJ postulate that the heroic act of excessive giving is just an exaggeration that in a hyperbolic way reflects the virtue of giving and should inspire laypeople to imitate – on a less drastic level – the exemplary figure's actions. Spiro (1971: 108), for the case of Burma, argues that the story's 'sacrificial idiom provides the charter for and reinforces the Burmese belief in the religious efficacy of giving' and furthermore sees his excessive giving as a sort of narcissist drive typical of stories of Buddhist monastics (ibid.: 337). Many monks I have asked in Laos about the meaning of the VJ have given similar answers and referred to the exemplary character of Vessantara, but insisted that he was a special case, which should nevertheless make laypeople think about the high value of generosity for self-cultivation. In contrast to these opinions, Egge (2002: 103) poses a legitimate question in relation to the VJ: 'One may ask, however, why stories of what may seem like immoral and insane acts committed against self and family appeal to Theravadin audiences.' In a similar manner, Gombrich (1995: 321) tells of two Sri Lankan monks who say that Vessantara acted in an egoistic way and who think the act morally wrong. So the intuitive response can in many cases be more than simple praise of the acts. Despite Vessantara being an 'exemplary donor' worthy of admiration due to his selflessness, his acts in themselves and their consequences carry an ethical ambivalence with them that is reflected in Buddhist commentary and the statements of Lao laypeople and monks. Why then does the VJ work with such drastic, excessive means, and what role does this hyperbolism have for the listeners' potential ethical readings of the story?

Stories with excessive giving like the VJ actually constitute a subgenre in Buddhist scriptures. Heroic and transgressive acts of giving, and especially 'gifts of the body' (*dehadana*), are themes often used (see Ohnuma 1997). In a *jataka* story when the Buddha is born as King Sibi (see Kharoche 1989), we witness a donation of eyes: here the Buddha-to-be pulls out his eyes and donates them to a blind Brahmin, and in another narrative he roasts his own body, which he then donates as food (Auer-Falk 1990). The VJ deals with donation in a less graphic and drastic way, but the depiction of the dramatic moment of giving is nevertheless a similar stylistic device: the giving away of children (in the Lao story also classified as an inner-body-object donation – *thaannaygay*; they are the 'fruit of his loins') is the climax of the story. In the VJ and many other stories the protagonists' acts are often quite transgressive and as with Vessantara's gift, they are clearly beyond the call for equanimity and modesty so often associated with Buddhism. These acts are not invariably applauded by the witnesses and some stories report of a more ambivalent, even disgusted audience response to these acts (e.g. Heim 2003: 538).

The gift of the magic white elephant, the giving away of the children into slavery to an evil Brahmin and the gift of his wife are the climax of the story and the acts that are most frequently evoked when discussing the story with laypeople and monks. On the one hand,

Vessantara is praised for this final act of renunciation, but his behaviour is also highly questionable. How can the act of giving away one's family, an obvious transgression of moral values, be seen as a meritorious act? In the famous Buddhist commentary, *The Questions of King Milinda* (Dilemma seventy first [1890]),[11] Vessantara's gift is described as just that – excessive and transgressing the moral order:

> A hard thing, Nâgasena, was it that the Bodisat carried out, in that he gave away his own children, his only ones, dearly beloved, into slavery to the Brahman. And this second action was harder still, that he bound his own children, his only ones, and dearly beloved, young and tender though they were, with the jungle rope, and then, when he saw them being dragged along by the Brahman – their hands bruised by the creeper – yet could look on at the sight. And this third action was even harder still, that when his boy ran back to him, after loosing the bonds by his own exertion, then he bound him again with the jungle rope and again gave him away. And this fourth action was even harder still, that when the children, weeping, cried: 'Father dear, this ogre is leading us away to eat us!' he should have appeased them by saying: 'Don't be afraid.' And this fifth action was even harder still, that when the prince, *Gâli*, [Vessantara's son] fell weeping at his feet, and besought him, saying: 'Be satisfied, father dear, only keep Kanhâginâ [his little sister]. I will go away with the ogre. Let him eat me!' – that even then he would not yield. And this sixth action was even harder still, that when the boy *Gâli*, lamenting, exclaimed: 'Have you a heart of stone then, father, that you can look upon us, miserable, being led away by the ogre into the dense and haunted jungle, and not call us back?' – that he still had no pity. And this seventh action was even harder still, that when his children were thus led away to nameless horrors until they passed gradually to their bitter fate out of sight – that then his heart did not break, utterly break! What, pray, has the man who seeks to gain merit to do with bringing sorrow on others! ... And excessive giving is held by the wise in the world held worthy of censure and of blame ... And as king Vessantara's gift was excessive no good result could be expected from it. (Book IV, chapter 9, pp. 114–15)

Although this commentary does not belong in the standard repertoire of the Lao Buddhist, the opinions of some laypeople and monks address similar questions when discussing the story. In some way, Milinda's question is from a moral perspective 'only natural' – how can irresponsible and transgressive behaviour like this be the final and supreme act of renunciation? A friend of mine, a high-ranking monk with an administrative position in the upper echelons of the Lao Buddhist Fellowship Organisation, wrote a 'critique' of the story pointing out the failures to adhere to values linked to Vessantara's responsibilities at the level of the state (the gift of the elephant) and particular family values (gift of the children and wife). Although the

story has a clear happy ending, the sequence of dramatic gifts also leads
laypeople to the opinion that, at least in these instances, Vessantara acts
in a selfish way. A well-educated elderly man I interviewed during a
festival in a Vientiane temple told me:

> When he gives away his personal wealth [the gifts of the 700], this is a
> skilful act of generosity and renunciation. But the more he gives away, the
> more problematic and egoistic his generosity becomes. His drive for giving
> becomes a burden for other people and it produces considerable suffering.
> His excessive generosity is almost comparable to a kind of illness. Only in
> the end are people able to understand it.

When one employs some sort of 'emotional Geiger counter' and
carefully observes the reactions of the audience during the
performance, it becomes clear that the intensification and production
of certain emotional states is indeed a main feature of VJ recitations,
and both the chanting education of monks and the reactions of the
audience confirm that. The invocation and intensification of emotions
such as horror, pain, grief as intended reactions towards these ethically
ambivalent acts are an essential part of the VJ. In the 1972 Lao edition
of the VJ the author of the preface invites the audience to 'share the
sensations of the difficulty of Vessantara's sacrifice and take pity on
him, his children and wife' (Vessantarasadok 1972: 2). A teacher at the
Buddhist College in Vientiane, has been running a course specifically
designed for chanting training for the VJ. In his work, Boundteun
(2003, 2004: 4) gives explicit instructions as to how the chanters
should use voice-modulation techniques to make the audience
cultivate [feelings of] the heart and sensations which are depicted in
the story' and then he lists 'domains of emotions', which include
admiration, awe, love, fear, calm, grief, suffering, pity and, most
interesting for the analysis here, an emotion that is said 'to make the
heart feel *phalaad*'. *Phalaad* translates as strange, bizarre, abnormal,
extraordinary (Reinhorn 2001: 1336, 1394). When I asked about the
latter emotion, he stated that the recitation should inspire awe and
admiration for Vessantara's acts, but also a feeling that provokes
perplexity and confusion. This strangeness and bizarreness that in the
case of inner-body-object donation stories are likely to occur are an
important component of the VJ and other Buddhist narratives. Maria
Heim (2003: 538), also referring to Nussbaum's work on ethics, has
skilfully suggested that in South Asian Buddhist literature these
rhetorical devices of 'horripilation' are based on concepts of emotions
and aesthetics that move emotions into the centre of processes of
accessing and interpreting the story. For her, this particular view of

emotions in Buddhist narrative confirms 'that such terrible events invoke emotional experience but also that such events are morally ambiguous in themselves; the texts lead us – through emotion – to a place of moral bewilderment' (Heim 2003: 545). In current Lao Buddhism we seem to encounter a similar idea: the audience of the VJ is both with the protagonist and against him – it admires his generosity and is filled with awe for his heroic renunciation of family life (trying to approach 'selflessness'), but also shocked by the excess that is a result of his selfish striving for perfection.[12]

The reactions of the audience during the recitation are at times quite emotional: the chanting of the monks is accompanied by a steady appreciation of the scenes depicted. When arriving at a particular dramatic or intense passage of the story, an enthusiastic audience moans, groans, sighs, applauds, strikes gongs and throws rice about. At the climax of the story, which illustrates the essential acts of giving away children and wife, women sometimes start weeping and run out of the temple hall.[13] The scene of the excessive gift reflects the difficulty of the decision and the ambivalence of the situation:

> Vessantara's eyes were filled with tears, as Jujaka pulled his children away and lashed their tiny bodies repeatedly with the rough and tough vine. While they left whimpering tearfully, he was heartbroken, as the moon was moved into the mouth of Rahu. He went to his cottage and muttered: 'My children will confront a violent fate. No one will take care of them ... Their tiny legs, feet and soles which are used to stepping along a short way and on smooth ground, will walk a distant way and rough ground; they will swell, blister and be bruised painfully. This old man is cruel, I have given him my children; I have not hindered him from taking them away, and they have agreed to go with him without resistance ... Why do I not untie the knot that I have knotted myself? I should pick up my sword, bow and arrows, and force him to give back my children. No, I won't do that. I will continue to do what I have done in order to gain meritorious perfection, to reach nirvana – for my children, my family, and myself'. ('Luang Phavetsandoon' 2002: 46)

One woman whom I asked in a temple in Luang Phrabang why she started crying explained:

> It is like I can't stand the suffering of the father, mother and children. When Jujok [the evil Brahmin] starts hitting the children and they are tied together with a jungle rope, it breaks my heart and I have to cry. Otherwise it would drive me crazy. Giving away your own children and seeing them mistreated – this must be one of the most horrible things that can happen.

The reactions of the audience and the feelings of the protagonist are embedded in ambivalence. The heroic act of giving away the children is by no means a firm decision without thought for the suffering of the children and the harshness of the decision. In the end, the quest for moral perfection in order to reach nirvana is stronger, but is taken only after considering the use of weapons to get the children back. Vessantara here seems to be momentarily estranged from his usual rational calculation,[14] a point to which I shall return in the next part.

Martha Nussbaum has dealt with situations similar to that of Vessantara in Greek tragedy, which she calls 'tragic conflicts'. In these situations 'we see wrong action without any direct compulsion and in full knowledge of its nature, by a person whose ethical character or commitments would otherwise dispose him to reject it. The constraint comes from the presence of circumstances that prevent the adequate fulfilment of two valid ethical claims' (Nussbaum 2001: 25).[15] These dilemmas can be stylistic means to evoke certain feelings in the audience. Although a comparison between Buddhist notions of narrative and ancient Greek ones might seem a bit far fetched, the feelings of pity and fear play an important part both in Aristotle's *Poetics* (see part XI), with its fundamentally ethical approach to narrative, and in the VJ. In Aristotle's philosophy of virtue ethics, emotions are closely connected to judgement and belief and their cultivation is an important part of moral education. Nussbaum, referring to Aristotle's treatment of emotions and ethics, supports the view that 'emotions become intelligent parts of the moral personality, which can be cultivated through a process of moral education. Such a process will aim at producing adults who not only control their anger and fear, but experience anger and fear appropriately, towards the appropriate objects at the appropriate time in the appropriate degree' (Nussbaum 1998). In this view, the invocation and experiencing of emotion are thus a didactic practice that can contribute to the cultivation of virtuous behaviour, or, as Geertz (2005: 83) has put it for the Balinese cockfight, 'a kind of sentimental education'.[16]

In addition to the emotional and ethical didactics that can be ascribed to literature and narratives like the VJ, I think Lao or Buddhist understanding reaches beyond Nussbaum's thesis. The VJ here exposes a conflict that is quite common in cultures divided between a professional ascetic ethics designed for monks and renouncers and the values of the householder with obligations towards wife and children. For the Buddhologist Steven Collins, the VJ is one of Buddhism's most compelling stories when it comes to presenting the 'subtle, but rueful and triumphalist acceptance of the disparities between temporal power, in every sense of the word, and the ascetic quest for the timelessness'

(Collins 1998: 445). Thus it is not only about appropriate moments and spaces in which emotions can be articulated and thereby be an element of ethical didactics, but also about conflicts of value systems, in which feelings are not just easily 'worked off' in mimetic experience. The question of whether the conflict is finally resolved in the story is a vital one. Is there a cathartic effect involved in which the audience, led at first through feelings of pity, fear and strangeness, is finally relieved? Aristotle's claim (*Poetics*, IV) that the audience is purified in catharsis 'through pity and fear effecting the proper purgation of these emotions', is, in my opinion, only partially true for the VJ. The story has a happy ending and ultimately all Vessantara's sacrifices materialise in his ethical perfection, but the act of giving nonetheless remains essentially both cruel and egoistic and heroic and selfless. Only a stringently consequentialist interpretation ('the positive outcome legitimising the means') could classify his behaviour as ethically appropriate.

The question here is whether narrative, in order to be ethically efficacious, has to offer solutions to conflicts in order to give guidance to the reader/listener. Hegel, dealing with Greek tragedy and dilemmas similar to that of Vessantara, claims that the 'true course of dramatic development consists in the annulment of contradictions viewed as such, in the reconciliation of the forces of human action' (cited in Bradley 1950: 71), through a sort of dialectics of conflict resolution. I think approaches like that would fail to consider the effect the recitation of VJ is meant to have on the audience. In the end the VJ does not offer an exemplary world in which ambiguity is eliminated. The recitation of the story is not a constant process of affirming how the world should be ideally, but it deals with the confrontation of an excessiveness that exposes and points to ethical rifts primarily through the evocation of certain emotional states of bizarreness and bewilderment. The exposition of a dilemma in which none of the options can be correct is an essential feature of how narrative can address problems and conflicts of spheres of value. In some readings of the VJ, there is no 'point of closure' in the narrative, no catharsis that purges the dilemma. Instead, there is an intentionally and emotionally augmented rupture that exposes the listener to an ethical dilemma. In conceptualising the ethical efficacy of narrative, Gibson (1999: 8) proposes that 'the point is not to purge a paradox, either by reining back one's sceptical critique, or by leaping into some magic sublation beyond antagonism of suspicion and affirmation, but rather to find productive ways of living and thinking within and through paradox'. In that perspective, the ethical efficacy of narratives like the VJ is partially based on the fact that the listener is emotionally conducted into an ambiguous emotional state where ethical judgements are destabilised or temporarily suspended.[17] This 'non-response' (Ricoeur 1991: 283)[18] adds new elements to the process of a potential ethical autopoiesis.

Sovereignty, Responsibility and Failure

The feelings of pity and fear provoked by the performance of the VJ have their roots in the failure of the protagonist to find a medium path between the quest for salvation and its absolute demands and on the other hand the burdens of the social world, in which one has a family, children and even a political position.[19] In the VJ, the evaluation of generosity, as a paramount value in Buddhism, goes through a gradual transformation with changes in intensity. Vessantara's acts of generosity become increasingly alienating for the other characters in the story (and the listener). From simple acts of lauded generosity when he is still a king, we move on to the realm of Buddhist kingship and politics (the magic white elephant and Vessantara's exclusion from society) and finally to the sphere of family and body-object donation. By following this linear ascension of excessive generosity, Vessantara himself gets closer to a realm that, one could say, is ethically pure because it is beyond the ethics of the quotidian.

Interestingly, Vessantara's excess has some strong Nietzschean connotations. He appears as a sort of Buddhist *Übermensch* who increasingly moves away from the 'justice of commoners', which according to Nietzsche (1994: 49) is based on the principle of reciprocity. For Vessantara there is no reciprocity in the immediate social realm; he gives everything without hesitation and increasingly becomes a parasite of the social domain.[20] What he gets from his acts of gift-giving are the 'transcendent' rewards that will enable him to become the future Buddha. He is, though, still caught between the two realms and, as can be seen in his reaction to giving away the children, there is still doubt and guilt. His free gifts make enemies and he is expelled from his own kingdom because of giving away something of which he was not sole proprietor. He is a lawbreaker in that sense, someone 'who has broken his contract and his word to the whole' (Nietzsche 1994: 50), and is consequently exiled. In a sort of Bataillean economy of excess, he increasingly alienates himself from Nietzsche's slave economy, which is grounded in the law of equal returns, and enters what Schrift (2001: 116) calls a 'higher, noble economy'. The depiction of the basic attitude of this excess fits the VJ quite well: '[It] is the feeling of fullness, of power that seeks to overflow, the happiness of high tension, the consciousness of wealth that would give and bestow: the noble human being, too, helps the unfortunate, not, or almost not, from pity, but prompted more by an urge begotten by an excess of power' (Nietzsche 1994: 166). In the VJ, Nietzsche's ideas of master and slave morality clash. Vessantara creates and represents new values, transgresses traditional values and arouses fear and insecurity among his subjects, and receives his punishment for that.

This excess and this 'reckless' striving for sovereignty beyond the social world also have some political implications regarding responsibility and ethics. In Vientiane I met a few very well-trained monks and laypeople who used the VJ as a field of reflection on the vanished institution of Buddhist kingship.[21] These were mostly members of the Communist Party's mass organisation and trained in Marxism-Leninism, but also fervent Buddhists, who used stories such as the VJ for reflecting on contemporary society. A friend of mine, who had been a monk for seventeen years and then disrobed and was given the opportunity to study literature in Vietnam, gave me a good summary of this view of responsibility in Buddhist kingship and the way the VJ problematises this:

> I think there is nothing wrong with generosity and it's important in our culture. But it depends what one gives and in what context. As a king, Vessantara has responsibility for the kingdom and all the people living in it. They pay taxes, are his subjects and the kingdom flourishes until he gives away the magic white elephant. Although the elephant was born on the same day as Vessantara, it's strictly speaking not his personal property. It is the *ming-khwan* [magic symbol; essence] of the kingdom and it is necessary to protect it and make the rice fields fertile. The elephant is the property of the people. Vessantara knows that, but still gives it away without any conditions when the Brahmins from the other kingdom beg for it. The people are right to demand his dethronement, because he has acted in a highly irresponsible manner. A king cannot simply do what he wants to do, he has to care for the people and listen to them. That is sometimes the problem with kingship.

What at first sight might be seen as a crude Marxist interpretation of a story, with an argument drawing on property relations and the 'voice of the people', is actually a well-informed opinion, equally present in Buddhist literature, but here presented in novel guise. As Collins (1998: 414f.) has shown, the relationship between worldly responsibility/power and an ascetic Buddhist philosophy is not an unproblematic one, although they draw power from each other and are symbiotic. The responsibilities of a king always involve a partial violation of moral precepts: one has to punish delinquents, make war, extract taxes and do all sorts of other morally reprehensible things when confronted with the social world. The monk and the ascetic, outside society, are often not exposed to these problems. It is easy to locate Theravada-Buddhist texts from all periods and regions that take a very critical stance on kingship and compare kings to thieves and other phenomena that can bring danger and ruin, contrasting this with the pure lifestyle of the monk and renouncer (Collins 1998: 423).[22]

Thus, to complete his perfection, Vessantara has to move out of the sphere of normal morality and move into a realm where he, with the help of excessive giving, becomes a perfected sovereign, not bound to society by the responsibilities of kingship or family ties, but now capable of being reborn as the Buddha, who will declare the *dhamma*. For that, however, he has to leave the rules of the social world behind him, and transgress, or betray, the ethics of kingship and the household. The possibility of becoming the most ethically perfected being is bound up with the ethics of betrayal, a sort of 'possible-impossible aporia'. Similar to Derrida's reading of Kierkegaard's treatment of the story of the son sacrifice demanded of Abraham[23], the absolute call for ethical perfection (or in Abraham's case the absolute duty towards God and the simulation of an ultimate sacrificial test) makes Vessantara move beyond rational calculation and planning into a moment of 'madness' (Derrida 1992: 26, 1996: 65) inherent in the decision and beyond the possibility of acting fully responsibly:

> In both general and abstract terms, the absoluteness of duty, of responsibility, and of obligation certainly demands that one transgress ethical duty, although in betraying it one belongs to it and at the same time recognizes it … duty demands that one behave in an irresponsible manner (by means of treachery and betrayal) while still recognising, conforming, and reaffirming the very thing one sacrifices, namely the order of human ethics and responsibility … I am responsible to any one (that is to say to any other) only by failing in my responsibility to all others, to the ethical or political generality. (Derrida 1996: 66, 70)

This moment of madness or, less drastically, the opaqueness of the subject's decision to himself is triumph and failure at the same time. This failure is a result of a collision with a value regime in a social world that demands responsibility for one's family and kingdom; nevertheless, in the sense of fulfilling an ascetic ideal, Vessantara becomes an actor of truth, renouncing everything he has. How do less Marxist-inspired Lao Buddhists view this problem? People were here often distinguishing between the positive long-term effects of Vessantara's excessiveness and the immediate moment of the giving. The story has a happy ending and all of Vessantara's sacrifices ultimately lead to his ethical purity and his achievement of the perfections. His children are liberated, the evil Brahmin dies, the people love him again and he rules the kingdom with the righteousness of the *dhamma*. Still, the moment of decision is seen as an unavoidable failure by many Lao. During one of the recitations a man told me:

> If you think about the difficulty of his decision, what options did he have? He also loves his wife and children, but he also wants to attain enlightenment. He acts incorrectly in some sense in order to advance on the path of enlightenment. I pity him for that, but through this big sacrifice he becomes the Buddha and will be able to show humanity the way out of suffering. And in the end, when he was Vessantara, he was a being with much merit, but still a human, and as humans we sometimes fail.

In some sense the pity and compassion the audience shows for the protagonist during the performance is also an approval of his failure. The feeling of 'strangeness' discussed in the previous section is also accompanied by pity and compassion, and people in the audience repeatedly referred to the immense difficulty of Vessantara's decision. Instead of having a perfect and flawless exemplary figure in the story, the audience is confronted with a doubting protagonist who through his excessive acts exposes himself, puts himself at risk. Is there a moral lesson to be learnt from this exposure and the partial failure of the protagonist in the story? At first, a protagonist that has an absolute clear and calculable subjectivity with the capacity to judge everything in an appropriate way would perhaps be too tedious. Furthermore, though, witnessing the failure of others in narrative (or real life) and understanding the difficulty of some decisions, or the sheer impossibility of making a just decision in certain situations, also allow the option of recognising one's own opacity and thereby cultivating patience and compassion. Even when there is no option of eliminating my own emotional ambivalence, which is eventually involved in judging the actions of the other, there is nevertheless the possibility of recognising that 'I am exposed to the other, whom I cannot completely predict or control' and seeing this 'exposure as a sign of a shared violability' (Butler 2003: 95). An exemplary figure that is human in the sense that it fails to accomplish perfection without producing suffering and carrying out acts that are at least ambivalent is probably more accessible for the listener than a completely perfected being. The sharing of the suffering resulting from failure in narrative and the pitying of the protagonist is therefore ethically relevant for the listener.

Conclusion

By participating in ritual recitations like the VJ, the listener is exposed through the rhetoric and aesthetics of chanting to a range of emotional states. The situations the listener is led through touch on basic values, such as generosity, responsibility and failure, and comfort the audience. In the VJ and other Buddhist narratives, the role of emotions such as pity, fear and bizarreness is didactic in the sense that they are invoked and augmented. The story and the performers not only teach the listener through the generation of particular emotional states what is an appropriate experience and the ethical evaluation of an action, but moreover expose the listener to radical situations without necessarily pointing to an ethical model. This differentiates the role of emotions in narrative from a pure emotivist[24] approach to ethics. Instead, narrative here opens up a gap of strangeness and bizarreness in which conflicting regimes of values can be thought through and reflected upon; narrative understanding enables us to deal with complexity in that sense (Carrithers 1992: 91). Emotions that are invoked in the VJ are not only a posteriori expressions of ethical reasoning and do not merely sustain them, but are also intentionally employed to destabilise the listener and decentre his basis of ethical judgement. In contrast, the position of emotions in the ethics of Western moral philosophy (especially deontological traditions)[25] has been partially one that is considered to be 'potentially destructive of moral rationality and consistency' (Williams 1973: 207). Indeed, it is just this aspect of emotions that in the case of the VJ recitation is used as an instrument for enhancing ethical reflection on conflicting regimes of value.

Buddhist stories and their recitations, which involve excessive dramatic giving or gifts of the body and make use of 'horripilation', bear some resemblance to Antonin Artaud's concept of the 'theatre of cruelty' (1988). Artaud intended to remove the spectator from the everyday and use symbolic objects to work with the emotions of the audience, attack the audience's senses through an array of technical methods and acting so that the audience would be brought out of their desensitisation and forced to confront themselves. The use of the grotesque, the ugly and pain in this form of 1930s French avant-garde theatre might be driven by other motives, but it shares the strategy of destabilisation and the undermining of the audience's sense of security through the invocation of strangeness and bizarreness. This invocation opens up space for what Ricoeur (1988: 120f.) calls the reconfiguration of the listener/reader through narrative and the option of designing one's own views about specific topics (ibid.: 127). This also postulates a certain 'porousness of the reading [listening] subject' (Gibson 1999:

183). Hence, when looking at the ethical contents of narrative recitations like the VJ, they also have the potential to become a vehicle for reflecting on the nature of responsibility concerning the political sphere and family values in contemporary society.

Talking about the didactic effect the recitation of the VJ is intended to have on the audience, there is also the element of ambiguity that facilitates a decentred reading, as mentioned above, a visible striving for ethical homeostasis. More conservative readings of the narrative insist on the fact that the obedience of wife and children is exemplary behaviour despite the protagonist's failures. Here Vessantara's transgression is framed in terms of excessive, but still skilful selflessness in the quest for an ascetic life. The emphasis here is more on Vessantara as an exemplary figure whose acts are extraordinary and inspire awe but can also perhaps be taken as an ethical model for a Buddhist's behaviour in social life, though in less intense form and transformed into generosity towards Buddhist institutions. As Lambek (2000: 317) puts it for religion and ritual in general, 'religion at its best attempts to provide a space and direction for moral practice, to enlarge opportunity and access; at its most limited, it aims to make a virtue out of constraints.' In some cases the narrative can also inspire practices that are quite mimetic in their relation to the exemplary figure. The donation of body objects, which in the VJ is only indirectly dealt with (the children as a part of Vessantara's body), has in the other *jataka* story mentioned (King Sibi's eye donation) more direct effects in real life, as for example documented for Sri Lanka, where monks recite the story on festival days in order to motivate laypeople to donate their eyes or bodies for organ transplantations or medical research (Simpson 2004: 847).[26]

Hallisey (1996: 37) has suggested that the search for a unitary theory of ethics in Buddhism is a task that many have focused on, but which cannot be accomplished 'simply because Buddhists availed themselves of and argued over a variety of models'. He instead pleads for an 'ethical particularism'. When moving away from strictly canonical text material and if one includes a broader range of narratives in the analysis, stories like the VJ can reveal a complex moral universe with all its situations, paradoxes and contingencies. Important here, however, is that the use of the text in performance and the didactics and pedagogies involved are taken into account: which institutions, places and occasions are chosen and to what extent they prescribe a moral understanding (rules, duties, etc.) and at the same time leave space for ethical autopoiesis. As discussed, Buddhist monks, qua respected authorities and performers, 'instruct' laypeople through the recitation of narratives, and their performance and the subsequent commentary can aim at a reproduction of values and actions by, for example, pointing to exemplary figures like Vessantara. However, the openness of both text and the listening/reading subject and a space of emotional indeterminacy create the basis for a dialogical relationship. In a performative manner, the relationship between the idealised moral system of the text and ethical reasoning is negotiated and concatenated. Vessantara's narrative about the achievement of perfection on the road of excess therefore simultaneously contains elements of an ethical homeostasis and the potential for an ethical reconfiguration.

Notes

Fieldwork was carried out in Vientiane, the capital of Laos, from September 2003 to June 2005. The financial assistance of the University of Cambridge and the German Academic Exchange Service (DAAD) is gratefully acknowledged. I am indebted to all Lao monks and laypeople who welcomed me in their temples and houses and shared their thoughts and lives with me. I also thank the Religious Section of the Lao National Front for Reconstruction and the Ecole Française d'Extrême Orient in Vientiane for their generous help. An earlier draft was presented in the PhD writing-up seminar in the Department of Social Anthropology, University of Cambridge. I have greatly benefited from comments on earlier drafts by Matthew Carey, Jacob Copeman, Bernhard Krieger, James Laidlaw and Michael Carrithers.

1. Instead of giving a 'complete' interpretation of the story, I have largely followed my Lao informants in identifying central themes of the story (generosity, responsibility, failure, emotions, etc.) and discussed key scenes with them, focusing on the acts of giving that constitute the various climaxes of the story. Obviously, a number of different readings are possible, and my intention is not to give a thorough philological account of the story, but rather to see what potential ethical claims and problematisations the story of Vessantara might contain. I also emphasise alternative interpretations that go beyond the pure mimetic understanding of the story (see the third part for further details).
2. I have transliterated Pali and Lao terms.
3. For a translation of the oldest remaining Pali version from Sri Lanka, see Gombrich and Cone (1977). Oskar von Hinueber (1998) has written an excellent philological discussion of the origins and form of *jatakas* as a part of Buddhist literature. The significance of *jatakas* in 'modernised' versions seems to have undergone some crucial changes as, for example, attested for Thailand. Patrick Jory (2002: 892) speaks of 'the jatakas' marginalization in Thai Buddhism'. He traces the significant shifts of their position and interpretation under the reign of King Chulalongkorn and Thailand's encounter with modernity and orientalist scholarship in the nineteenth century.
4. In Pali the word *parami* (perfection) literally signifies 'having reached the other shore' (Kawamura 2004), but in Lao it is also used in the sense of 'charisma'.
5. In the list of the ten perfections and other enumerations of virtues, *dana* (giving, generosity) is usually stressed as the most important one. This does not come as a surprise as the order of monks is largely dependent on donations of laypeople and the very existence of Buddhism has been dependent upon the gift, ranging from daily alms-giving to large-scale donations of plots of land and incredible amounts of

wealth. On a general level, the giving of gifts (*dana*) and the practice of generosity constitute, along with *sila* ('moral undertaking', 'keeping precepts') and *bhavana* (exercise of contemplation/meditation), one of the three elementary meritorious acts in Theravada Buddhism that lead to a gradual approximation of the soteriological goal of nirvana and better rebirths (Rajavaramuni 1990: 48). Giving in its different forms is a way of renouncing the material world. Hibbets (2000: 30) therefore concludes that the gift is often 'described as primarily an ethical category', but one probably has to distinguish different kinds of gifts and rewards. Ohnuma (2005) postulates that in doctrinal Buddhism the gift of, for example, alms to monks is not directly reciprocated, but only in the form of 'transcendent' karmic rewards. In practice, however, laypeople often expect a direct return and an effect in this life. Egge (2002: 3) insists that giving in Buddhism is not only the practice of generosity, but also an act of worship directed towards the recipient. Vessantara's gifts and the cases of 'gifts of the body' (*dehadana*, i.e. donating one's limbs, eyes and other body parts) are again of another kind, and extreme acts of heroic giving are described in many *jatakas* (Ohnuma 1997). What is interesting here is that givers like Vessantara – living in a time before the clergy was established – often do not take into account the status of the receiver (*supatra*, 'worthy vessel'), as later became common in Buddhism. The practice of giving remains a prominent focus of discussions about what defines 'proper' Buddhism. For *dana* practice in contemporary Thailand and a criticism thereof as being based on materialism, see Gabaude (2003).

6. Although the story is part of the Buddhist canon, it occupies an interesting middle position between canonical text and folk narrative (Ohnuma 2004). It is usually adapted to the local context and there are multifarious vernacular forms to be found in Laos that are connected to different chanting styles. The basic story outline is kept in each of them, but the extensive depictions of nature in it are variations and one also finds references to local customs (like specific Lao rituals) in the text that distinguish it from the original Pali version (A. Boundteun, personal communication, December 2004). I here use an unpublished Lao–English prose version adapted from a version from Luang Phrabang in the north of Laos by an anonymous author ('Luang Phavetsandoon' 2002).

7. The physical form of the text preached is also significant: palm-leaf manuscripts are written in a special script (*dtoo tham*), which has a greater number of letters than normal Lao script. Although the words used in the chanting and writing are mostly normal Lao with a higher frequency of technical Pali terms, most people are convinced that only monks and very learned people can master the script. Palm-leaf manuscripts are in themselves containers of merit and auspiciousness and always have to be placed higher than other objects. The chanting of monks based on these manuscripts is believed to have a direct, 'physical' effect on the listener, increase his positive karma and protect him. This belief might derive from the fact that in a form of esoteric Buddhism the human body itself is made up of different constitutive letters that all together make up the Buddhist *dhamma*. The correct pronunciation of the syllables of a text can in some schools of Theravada Buddhism be a means of salvation and purification. (Bizot and Lagirarde 1996), or in less ambitious understandings be a source of blessing and protection. The knowledge kept in palm-leaf manuscripts can almost be appropriated by being able to pronounce the letters, even when they are not understood semantically. In recent years more and more books have been used for chanting the VJ, and monks in the provinces have been quite upset to discover that in the capital palm-leaf manuscripts are now rarely used. Hence there are now differing and competing notions of textuality.

8. The extent to which the texts and the recitation of the VJ are really understood in this context is debatable. The holiness of the words that give access to a source of

merit beyond semantics has led some observers to doubt the scrutiny with which people listen (Koret 1996: 113; 121–122), but this may also depend on how fervently or seriously one takes one's belief. The VJ is highly poetic in style and has a lot of special Pali vocabulary that makes it hard for the average educated Lao to grasp everything. According to my experience, people attending the ritual understand between 50 and per cent of the chanting. However, everybody knows the story and the visual depictions in the temple, the more prosaic forms of it taught at school and its screenings on Thai TV ensure that most people know it by heart.

9. Since the economic liberalisation of the mid-90s, however, other leisure-time options (like watching Thai TV) have taken over much of Lao people's evening entertainment and most temples in the centre have abolished these evening sermons. The further one goes into the suburbs of Vientiane, the more widespread the practice still is. On Thai television and on the rarely watched Lao television there are also some programmes that feature Buddhist sermons and preaching, as on the radio.

10. Here I largely follow Faubion's (2001b: 89f.) discussion of Foucault's technologies of the self as an interplay between institutions (or, in general, the environment) that represent certain values and truths and the appropriation and transformations of these meanings through a sort of autopoietic practice. The latter term is used by Faubion (ibid.: 100) in the sense of Luhmann's (1990: 9–10) system theory and gives rise to change in the system through the appropriation and inclusion of new elements beyond pure reproduction; i.e. the subject not only blindly follows the practices that society offers, but also uses them to attain certain states of freedom and wisdom and to form its own ethical subjectivity. On the latter point and its use for anthropology see also Laidlaw (2002).

11. *The Questions of King Milinda* is a long conversation between the Greek King Milinda, who rules parts of northern India, and the Buddhist monk Nagasena about the essentials and problems of Buddhism. In Laos it is known under the name *Milinda Panha*. Many of the questions posed by Milinda can be seen as representative of the interrogation of difficulties with some Buddhist teachings. Nagasena, as a monk, defends the *dhamma*, but has some difficulty in answering the question and replies that Vessantara certainly loved his wife and children, but that he loved enlightenment more. Furthermore, Nagasena replies that there is nothing negative about excessiveness in general and refers to the excessive hardness of diamonds which is a sign of high quality.

12. There is an interesting interplay between selflessness and selfishness at work here. In order to practise selflessness, i.e. giving away and renouncing, Vessantara has to be selfish. The action itself is therefore caught up in contradiction.

13. This is an audience at its best, however. Depending on the location, the skills of the monk and the appreciation of the audience, one might also witness rather unspectacular performances with a present but inattentive audience more involved in chatting and other distracting activities.

14. In other scenes Vessantara is rather instrumental and just waits for an occasion to give away his children. When his wife has a dream the night before the children are given away, he knows that the Brahmin will come to ask for the children and immediately sees that as a chance to perform a body-object donation. He does not tell his wife, though, and just says that she should forget the dream.

15. One could argue that Vessantara's dilemma is not the one of Greek tragedy because there is still a choice he can make and escape in the dilemma, namely just not giving away his children and wife and not attaining perfection. But the fact that he has waited for aeons to realise the ten perfections and that this is the ideal occasion

almost puts him under a form of pressure that moves his decision-making into a similar domain.

16. Geertz also draws a nice parallel between theatrical performance and emotions:

    'If, to quote Northrop Frye again, we go to see Macbeth to learn what a man feels like after he has gained a kingdom and lost his soul, Balinese go to cockfights to find out what a man, usually composed, aloof, almost obsessively self-absorbed, a kind of moral autocosm, feels like when, attacked, tormented, challenged, insulted, and driven in result to the extremes of fury, he has totally triumphed or been brought totally low.' (Geertz 2005: 86).

17. Asking Buddhist laypeople whether Vessantara's behaviour is correct from a moral point of view was mostly answered with responses of the nature 'Yes, but…' Most informants admitted that an ethical evaluation of his action is very hard to accomplish, and some monks answered that his actions cannot be evaluated at all.

18. Arguing in the context of the larger historical approach, Ricoeur states: 'The non-answering to the moral problems of an epoch is perhaps the most powerful weapon which literature has in order to influence morality and change practice' (1991: 283).

19. Indeed, 'abandoning' one's family was one of the first things the abbot of the monastery where I was ordained explained to me.

    'Monks don't have families in the sense others have it. I still have a father and a mother and we see each other now and then. But they can never really comfort you or embrace you. In the ordination ceremony you have left your family behind; the circle we closed around you when the ceremony was at its end represents that. You have entered the monk's homelessness, and you are not a householder any more'.

    Vessantara does not become a monk in the story, but a hermit who lives according to similar standards. Although he takes his wife with him, they live in chastity according to the monastic rules – an arrangement that is prone to give rise to conflicts. The failure of Vessantara is therefore also rooted in the fact that he sets out to live in both orders, a liminal state.

20. By using others as gifts to achieve his own ends and not only giving his personal belongings, the VJ also portrays a sort of parasitic relationship of unequal exchange. The excess has to be paid with gifts extracted from domains that are beyond the property of the giver. Serres (1982: 35f.) has argued that the parasite is a catalyst for complexity, because it interrupts the normal flow of things and introduces a break into the system, which can then lead to transformations. In that sense, the achievement of Buddhahood entails a parasitic component. See also Brown (2002: 15–17) for an exegesis of Serres's idea of the parasite and exchange.

21. Laos was a kingdom for more than 600 years and Buddhism and kingship were from the beginning intricately intertwined, with the king usually supporting the clergy and vice versa. This configuration of power has been labelled the 'two wheels of the *dhamma*' (Tambiah 1977; Smith 1978). Buddhism is indeed imbued with ideas of kingship and the Buddha was a prince himself, who abandoned the luxuries of his palace and his family after seeing the suffering in the world. In the case of Laos it does not come as a surprise, then, that the disappearance of kingship after the socialist revolution of 1975 (the king was arrested, sent to a 're-education camp' and died there) brought some problems of political legitimisation (Evans 1998) and stimulates discourses like the one inspired by the VJ.

22. Other birth stories of the Buddha take a much more explicit stance than the VJ; in the 'Birth story of the dumb cripple' (*Muggapakkha/Temiya Jataka*), still very popular in Sri Lanka, the Buddha is born as a king again, but tries to escape kingship. He

reflects: 'I was a king here for twenty years, and as a result cooked for eighty thousand years in hell, now I have been born again in this criminal house'. Then a deity comes to give him advice and says: 'Dear Temiya, don't be afraid. If you want to escape from here, act as if you can't walk properly, even though you can; act as if you are deaf and dumb, even though you are not' (Collins 1998: 425f.). In order to escape his responsibility, he fakes being handicapped and unable to rule. Not all stories contrast the strict ethics of the ascetic with that of the more worldly householder or king like this, but there is often a certain ironic critique involved.

23. The case of Abraham, on which Derrida builds his argument, is in some respects, however, fundamentally different from that of Vessantara. Abraham follows his duty towards a monotheistic God ('the wholly Other') and the sacrificial lamb could be put to death. Vessantara does not follow God (who is absent in Buddhism), but only a personal striving for self-perfection, and his gifts are in that sense not put to death, but just given away or enslaved. One could therefore speculate that Vessantara has a different kind of freedom of choice from Abraham.

24. Emotivism denies that moral judgements can be true or false, maintaining that they merely express an attitude or an emotional response. I think Nussbaum's idea is different from that, as there is a basis for ethical judgement (Aristotle's virtues, or *eudaemonia*) and emotions are constitutive of that.

25. Although Kant gives emotion a certain place in his idea of virtue, he rejects, for example, pity as a morally significant emotion. His 'sympathy with joy and sadness' (*sympathia moralis*) (Kant 1971: 6: 456) is an inborn capacity that cannot enhance correct decision-making. For him, with an apprehension of duty that is based in rationality and rational decision-making, emotions are secondary products of ethical reasoning.

26. For the case of autopsy-body donation in Thailand, Wongthes (2000: 8) even finds that there is even a problem of an oversupply of bodies. In Laos, where hospitals are chronically underfunded and even quite simple operations often cannot be carried out, this topic has as yet no real significance. In the past, however, people donated their bodies as meditation objects to the local monastery where monks than sat around the decomposing body in order to meditate and realise suffering and the perishability of life. This was abolished in Laos after the revolution in 1975, but continues in Thailand (Klima 2002).

Chapter 9

ADOPTING AN OBLIGATION: MORAL REASONING ABOUT BOUGAINVILLEAN CHILDREN'S ACCESS TO SOCIAL SERVICES IN NEW IRELAND

Karen Sykes

This chapter elaborates a case study in the various negotiations over the moral value of obligation, whereby people justify and challenge the state's responsibility to provide social services for children in Papua New Guinea (PNG) after a decade of violent political conflict within Bougainville Island. Just as Gluckman (1955, 1963) used the ethnographic case study to illuminate how a person's actions could seem unreasonable in the eyes of state courts but be reasonable within the detailed description of the paradoxes of their specific situation, I use this case study to show that apparently difficult reasoning about obligations is actually sensible when the PNG state meets responsibilities to citizens. Gluckman demonstrated the universal presence of the 'reasonable man' in his careful ethnography, thereby toppling assumptions about the impossibility of self-government in the post-colonial nation. Like Gluckman, I argue that the moral value of obligation for the 'reasonable man' is grounded in neither cultural Western rationality, but firmly situated in detailed ethnographic description that describes how that value informs the social actions of reasonable people.

As a subject of enquiry, the moral obligation is not new. This contemporary case study elucidates a single instance of the more general theory of obligation, which early anthropologists at the start of the twentieth century had advocated for the political issues of their own times. Durkheim and Mauss had argued that obligation, rather than need or utility, should be a value by which the state delivered social services to its citizenry (Durkheim 1973; Ganes 1992; Fournier 2005). The two social scientists recognised very well that the impetus to meet moral obligations was embedded in social life, so they proposed to consider the value of obligation to social relations with the state in some depth. Durkheim argued that the cultivation of a sense of obligation was a cornerstone of modern education, as it was in socialisation processes in many other societies. Mauss aimed to make a general theory of obligation pertinent to France in his day, by comparing specific cases of gift exchange across cultures.[1] Fournier (2005) discusses how Durkheim and Mauss advocated the value of meeting obligations against the abstract concept of rights in the utilitarian trends of their day, as exemplified by the thought of Leon Bourgeois, the Nobel economist distinguished for his theory of social democracy, which awarded social services on the basis of human need. Gane (1992) argued that their theory of morality based in obligations enabled, rather than disenabled social democratic policies of the French state at the turn of the century. This is not news to many anthropologists: Mauss argued against the concept of 'need' as a social value, as readers of the *The Gift* (1990 [1925]) recall of Mauss's discussion of the state and moral obligation in its last chapter.

My aim for this chapter about obligation as a moral value in the Islands Region of PNG is very modest, and simply accepts the insight of Mauss's splendid general comparative theory that people feel obliged to reciprocate out of interest in their common good (see Godelier 1999). I share Mauss's critical project by showing that obligation is one possible moral value amongst others. He interrogated the utilitarian motivation underlying the contemporary French state's work in providing services by elaborating the different cases in which obligation was a moral value. I propose, by way of interrogation of a specific case in which some Papua New Guineans debate the delivery of social services, that Durkheim's and Mauss's concept of moral obligation aids anthropological understanding of lived experience in its totality in contemporary PNG post-colonial politics, where the negotiation of obligation is as much in the midst of villager lives as it is in the centre of state politics. The contemporary liberal era differs in so far as states are charged to show their viability and legitimacy by putting the responsibility to provide social services into the hands of private business; meanwhile, international regulatory organisations, groups such as the ILO, Amnesty International and Transparency International, appeal to the new international social mores to monitor the provision.[2]

There is a more provocative aim in treating obligation as a moral value in a liberal democratic state, namely that it contrasts with human rights as a moral value. In the first section of this chapter, I describe how obligation contrasts with rights as a moral value in an unusual grass-roots attempt to access social services on behalf of children caught in the peace processes following the crisis of civil war in Bougainville. I discuss the detailed example of New Irelanders' successful inter-provincial legal adoption of Bougainvillean children in the aftermath of civil war in the North Solomons as a specific social action in the progress towards peace, which they perceived to be part of the wider effort to ameliorate the delivery of social services to citizens in Bougainville and to establish a new morality of obligation to inform and shape Bougainville and PNG politics. My analysis of inter-provincial adoptions, as a way of negotiating access to social services in the aftermath of civil strife in Bougainville,[3] demonstrates the potential for Mauss's study of obligation in the contemporary concerns raised by indigenous sovereign states or Fourth World political constituencies.[4] I show that moral obligation is known best through negotiations of social action whether in Mauss's analysis of tribal or state life. In the present case, negotiations of the value of obligation become an instrumental step towards peace, a means to nurture the future of PNG citizens and a collective claim on the PNG State to provide social services for children across the country.

The Bougainvillean Case: From Right to Obligation as a Moral Value

This case study from the equatorial Islands Region of PNG[5] demonstrates how people kept obligations to provide children access to social services by making inter-provincial legal adoption[6] and thereby exposed the possibility of charging the state with its obligation to provide services of health care and education for its citizens. I shall examine here how some Bougainvillean children were surrendered for adoption from a crisis-torn province of the North Solomons and legally adopted by a number of New Ireland matrilineal clans in PNG throughout the late 1990s during the political crisis in the region. It is not clear at first glance why clans and individuals legally adopt refugee children, while fostering relations would provide them with the same access to service. However, I show through a detailed case study that reasonable judgement about social service provision is underpinned by 'obligation' to care for others as a moral value. By interrogating how different clans and the state in the wider Islands Region of PNG legally adopt children in order to rescue them from the conflict and provide them with social services, I show how this legal action is reasonable on the basis of obligation as a moral value, which people also expect of the state.

The case shows that New Irelanders decided consciously to meet the obligation to provide access to education and health services for Bougainvillean children, and thus they precipitated discussions of the obligations of the state. The Islands Region first intitiated direct action for children's access to state services as a form of protest, then as part of a means to secure peace and finally as an instrument of establishing rights of citizens in the long-term process of social reconstruction. The PNG customary adoption process, working with national laws, was predisposed to encompass the changes to the delivery of education and health services precipitated by the Bougainville crisis.

It should be noted that New Irelanders did not petition the state to confer abstract rights for children, the usual rights of citizens. But in pegging obligation as a moral value they succeeded in turning a bad into a good situation.[7] Access to social services emerged as a central concern of the Bougainvillean crisis, and international attention was drawn to watch over the management of the crisis. International delegations enquired into the claims that Bougainvilleans suffered abuses of civil rights to access health care and education and asked for the reinstatement of these in 1994. In the process towards accomplishing peaceful social order, the government aimed to prove its legitimacy by fulfilling its duty to provide health and education for all citizens, and yet it faltered. In its wake, citizens from elsewhere in the New Guinea Islands Region took control. The case is exemplary for current concerns: children's vulnerabilities in the restructuring of global capital that precipitates shifts of social milieux in the post-colony when changes in socialisation entail changing social needs for children of transnational communities (Appadurai 1996, Ong 1997; Comaroff and Comaroff 1999). The United Nations Convention on the Rights of the Child (UNCRC) (1989) had asked governments and non-government organisations to demonstrate protection of children's human rights. Ethnographers have asked if this a matter of a universal humanitarian principle (Sargent and Scheper-Hughes 1998). Or should the UNCRC result in better international law (Stephens 1995)? As I show, New Irelanders and Bougainvilleans were concerned with state obligations, rather than statements of children's rights or international recognition of human rights.

It is clear, despite the contemporary concern with state obligations, that a history of international concern for Bougainvilleans' rights can be understood as a background to the present effort to call upon the state to meet its responsibility. The story begins before the world's attention turned to Bougainville Island, of North Solomons Province (NSP), after the Bougainvilleans' call for international assistance in confronting the PNG Defense Force, which the PNG state had sent to quell a local movement for compensation and autonomy when it exploded in 1989. For over twenty years before, Bougainvilleans had sought compensation from Bougainvillean Copper (a subsidiary of the British-based multinational company, Rio-Tinto), which operated one of the world's largest open-pit copper mines in the southern region of their province, for damages to society, land and environment caused by the operations. They also called for compensation from the PNG government, an investment partner in the mine, because it had used mining profits to support the independent state. The situation came to crisis point when the company shut down its operation after Bougainvilleans destroyed mining machinery. In what appeared to be punitive actions, the PNG state embargoed trade and withdrew education and health services from residents.

Amnesty International had petitioned the PNG government about NSP citizens' rights to social services. Health care and education were partly restored with the help of PNG teachers, nurses, doctors, and clergy from other Islands Region provinces. In particular, people from nearby New Ireland had come to Bougainvillle as government employees and as volunteers to make the peace[8], along with a small international corps of unarmed peace monitors overseeing the delivery of social services.[9] When the PNG government failed to pay wages to the government employees (which was an indirect result of the period of capital restructuring in the 1990s) the peace workers from across PNG came to depend upon the people of South Bougainville to feed and house them. The real work of restoring infrastructure was impeded while PNG workers depended upon the South Bougainvillean population. Nevertheless, new relationships of mutual trust and interdependence grew between Bougainvilleans and New Irelanders as they struggled to find ways to give children access to modern services. They found an unusual solution by considering the complex web of obligations that could be woven in social actions in which obligation was valued.

Bougainvillean clans chose to use innovative PNG adoption laws, which allowed another clan within PNG to adopt their children within a wider understanding of obligation to care for others' children. In PNG, post-colonial legal adoptions are new, in so far as the legal paperwork for such arrangements had not been a part of village life until the 1990s, some twenty years after the possibility existed in the nation's constitution. Notably, Luluaki (1990) asks that PNG law must also address the transformation of kinship values as part of adoption processes if it is to aspire to be fair-minded in the work of jurisprudence. In the case of the legal agreements between New Ireland clans and Bougainvillean clans, which I shall describe here, the legal adoption does not negate the claims of natal clans but affirms a complex web of connections across the provinces that obligated all three clans involved in the act: the birth clan, the adoptive mother's clan and the adoptive father's clan. Clans in Bougainville arranged to send their children out of the province for adoption, with the help of Bougainvillean lawyers who were resident across the Islands Region. Children found homes with the Islands Region men and women who had come to restore social services to Bougainville. Bougainvilleans reasoned that away from NSP the children would have access to health care, which they would not have in the event of illness in their home province.[10]

In cases I have studied from New Ireland, a man footed the legal bill as an adoptive father. His financial support will make the Bougainvillean child a member of his New Ireland wife's matrilineal clan (rather than a child of a nuclear family). New Irelanders and North Solomons people recognised that formal adoption was an opportunity to use legal adoption to open pathways of kinship in claiming rights as citizens in relation to the state, the clan and their children.[11] At the same time, by using legal adoption, PNG Islanders protected children's well being, not through establishing children's rights as abstract concepts, but by enjoining each party in mutual obligations of the state and respective clans to protect the child's well-being.[12] Lawyers' many reports to me on the adoption process confirmed that courts normally approved the adoption of Bougainvillean children by New Irelanders because the children were surrendered by caring clans, who could not provide health and education because the PNG state had prevented them from doing so during and after the embargo on these social services. Further, the court recorded the Bougainville clans' surrender to the New Ireland adoptive clans, and thereby established the whereabouts of the children and their social identity in New Ireland so that they would never lose their Bougainvillean identity. Moral reasoning about obligation had a very social and human face, which did not reside in the abstractions of legal rights.

Legal decisions of this kind were possible because in the New Guinea Islands Region clanship and citizenship are not conceptualised by people at the grass roots as oppositional forms of society with divergent conflictive rights, but as complementary and related forms of social life

(Clark 1997; Sykes 2001; Foster 2002). Clanship, with its associated notions of moral obligation and responsibility, is articulated though idioms of nurturance and mutuality transcending generations and is also a key modality through which citizenship is accessed.[13] This was particularly the case in the context of trans-provincial adoption, whereby those communities excluded from full participation in state-defined citizenship utilised the institution of clanship to access what they saw as their children's rights to an education as citizens of the PNG state. In New Ireland, especially where moieties structured daily interactions, fathers met their obligations across clans.[14] The adoptive clan exercised their moral and legal authority over children and adopted children became the responsibility not of their adoptive parents but of their adoptive clan.

The case of New Irelanders' adoption of Bougainvillean children presents a chance to examine how changing family and kin relationships make citizens who are prepared to fulfil their obligations to their kin, as an aspect of a critically engaged citizenship. At the same time, New Irelanders' efforts to re-establish social services for Bougainvilleans at the grass roots clarified at least one demand: namely, that the State fulfil its obligations to provide these. Obligation as a felt moral value was an aspect of the complexity of social life and open to negotiation. In the rest of this chapter I describe the negotiation of divergent obligations to the peace process, to nurture young citizens and to restore social services.

Adopting an Obligation as a Moral Value in the Bougainvillean Peace

Before I discuss how New Ireland fathers reasoned about their obligations to adopt Bougainvillean children, it helps to know a little about the fluidity of the adoption process involved in these cases. Legal adoptions of Bougainvillean children involved three 'groups': the Bougainvillean child's matrilineal clan (the birth mother's clan), the New Ireland mother's matrilineal clan (the adoptive mother's clan), and the New Ireland father's matrilineal clan (the adoptive father's clan). I am most able to speak about the eight adoptions that I observed of the nearly fifty that I know of directly and indirectly amongst the 5,000 Mandak speakers in central New Ireland. It is claimed that several hundred Bougainvillean children and young people live in the New Guinea Islands Region as if they were the children of other clans there. Such numbers are hard to confirm as not all legal adoptions are completed for public record, and those who are not relatives find adoption court records difficult to access. Thus, my knowledge of adoption is most full with regard to the New Ireland clans I know best. I have personal accounts from New Ireland clans about how they were given children by the Bougainvillean clans, but I did not witness how children left the North Solomons province after negotiations made on Bougainvillean soil.

Adoption was an extremely familiar customary practice in New Ireland and contemporary legal adoption entrenched the customary adoption, which had always been a three-party affair in New Ireland from the earliest memories of the residents there. Both processes of adoption included the matrilineal clans of both the adoptive father and mother with the matrilineal clan of the adopted child as well. In peaceful times, people also use fosterage for the process of transferring responsibilities for children between adults, as when a child would choose to live with a mother's sister or a father's brother just because the child and adult liked each other. The reasons for adoption are several. Most usually adoptions are made because children desire the recognition as child of a clan, rather than cousin or even niece or nephew. At other times it is done to nurture the membership of a dwindling clan or to mark peace between clans after periods of violent conflict.

Child-rearing so often includes care for the children in permanent adoption and long-term fosterage that it is usual to care for children born to other clans. Parents aim to expose children to the many clans who participate in the person's social life, and socialisation entails teaching the child to recognise his different kin by connecting him or her into the everyday transactions in which they meet the obligations of social life. At the very least, the child learns to address his different kin by names that acknowledge his connection to them – as his father's or mother's clansmen, or even his mother's father's clansmen. Adoption in the Islands Region reorders these relatives so that the names are re-identified and adopted children will remember the alternative kin terms they might use to address the same people.

Now, consider the examples of the adoption of Bougainvillean children by New Irelanders during that period of conflict. The local head teacher, a middle-aged man whose work has taken him around the Islands Region, said the arrival of the Bougainvillean newcomers had been a widespread and well-known development in village life. Like many 'new' children who lived in the village with matrilineal clan relatives,[15] the Bougainvillean children were adopted into the matrilineal clan of the adoptive mother. For example, Roland, a Bougainvillean boy of ten had been born after the embargo of 1988. People reported the story that his devout Protestant mother had said many times in Bougainville that he had survived 'through divine providence'. When I knew him, he lived with the minister in charge of the smaller area of central New Ireland, known as the Kimidan Circuit of the United Church. The minister had brought him back from Bougainville, at the request of the child's parents. They said that the crisis restricted the boy's access to schools and hospitals and stopped him from learning his responsibilities both as a citizen and as a clansperson in his home village. The minister paid the solicitor's fees for the adoption of the boy into his wife's clan, taking him away from his Bougainvillean parents, who could not provide for him in their home province during the military occupation. Also the minister customarily adopted the boy with a number of small gifts, and began to nurture him into recognising adult responsibilities.

Bougainvillean children quickly became clan relatives with New Irelanders because they normally integrated newcomers immediately into the clan system, making them kin. They were addressed as relatives in order to make them into relatives because 'that is the way to make social relations work'.[16] As Larson, who cares for a Bougainvillean child in his home, said, 'He is my child. He calls me father, and I call him child. I clothe and feed him, and pay for his education.' Significantly Larson's speech did not effectively create comparisons or analogies for his relationship to the child. He did not say that he treated him 'as if' he were his own child because, as far as Larson and the boy are concerned, he became the father, claiming the responsibility to act as one.[17] Fatherly actions should express care and nurture, (especially when addressing the child as a person of a different clan). Larson assured me that his wife's and her clan's concern for the Bougainvillean children matched his own affection and care for the child. Larson's wife's matrilineage adopted the child, as one of its own members, seeking to formalise the adoption via state law when it was already a social fact.

As matrilineages affiliated individual Bougainvillean children into them, New Ireland men became active fathers to the adoptive children's entire matrlineage, simply by showing their care for the children. The father's care created the agency of the child's matrilineal clan, rather than of the individual child. This is true within the acts of normal child-rearing, as well as the exceptional circumstances of the adoption of children in the Bougainvillean crisis. A father makes the capacity of his children's clan into a social agent in contemporary matters. Melanesians claimed that the man aims to make the clan effective, not only the child of the clan. The gift made to the child's clan had to be acknowledged by the clan, but only at the time of the man's death. Then, the clan of the child would enhance the man's renown at the time of his funeral feast, and enable him to find prestige, fame and, more importantly, respect. Ironically, in the funeral feast the man's individual agency found public expression, entirely through the largesse of the clan of his children. By making the clan the collective agency, a father won back his own agency. His children's clan can proclaimed his prestige after his death.

In the exceptional times of crisis, a New Ireland man, Loren, married to a Bougainvillean woman, Ellen, undertook to protect and enable the best interests of his wife's Bougainvillean matrilineal clan, opening the door for himself to future recognition from the Bougainvilleans. Loren and Ellen kept contact with Ellen's clansmen in Bougainville, and chose to care for two of her junior clansmen. In this case, there was no need for adoption as the children already belonged to her clan. By ensuring that the Bougainvillean children reached adulthood, the New Ireland couple believed they acted to enable the best interests of the wife's clan and of Bougainvilleans more generally. In addition to this considerable accomplishment, Loren enabled the social agency of the children's matrilineal clan, and he provided reason for them later to reflect on his own efficacious role in fostering their agency. Other villagers acknowledged that his actions might contribute to future prestige and honour at the time of his funeral, as the father of a distant Bougainvillean clan and a virtuous and generous man of New Ireland.

Some New Ireland fathers and matrilineal clans nurtured Bougainvillean children into readiness 'to make a new Bougainville'. Their vision for a Bougainville in the future was sometimes expressed in accounts about the possible connections that might have existed in the past. At times, New Irelanders spoke of how they imagined an early history of trade and migration throughout the region, and said that they had the same 'grandfathers' as the Bougainvilleans. A few insisted that the new independent state, as well as the colonial state, acted to undermine and restrict the historical relations between the New Ireland and Bougainvillean clans. Others argued that, whatever their past or present problems, the inter-provincial adoptions of children made Bougainvilleans kin, with whom they would rebuild it as a new country.

Other New Ireland villagers had more modest aims to simply recruit members to matrilineal clans in their province. They adopted Bougainvilleans into the obligations of the kinship system and the work of customary life, as well as into state-sponsored education and health care services. The New Ireland adoptive fathers took responsibility for accessing education and health services on behalf of the Bougainvillean child by legally adopting them, and thereby recruited the children as new members into the wife's matrilineal clan. Typically, a man's prestige and honour grow with his contributions to the matrilineal clan of his wife, and conversely he is shamed for failing to contribute[18]. Men's contribution to the clan, especially to the rearing of children of the matrilineal clan, is often referred to as 'paternal nurture' by ethnographers because it enables the children's and wife's matrilineal clan, who reciprocate it out of a sense of obligation to the father and his clan (Clay 1977, 1986; Wagner 1986; but see also Strathern 1988). As such, it seemed fitting that a New Ireland man recruited Bougainvillean children and cared for them as members of his wife's clan. He won social respect far and wide because the Bougainvillean child could call him father.

New Irelanders said that their obligations to Bougainvillean children would flourish into their adulthood, finding their fullest expression in the activities undertaken by the child's adoptive matrilineal clan in his or her name. For example, as an adult grieving his dead father, the child would keep his or her obligations to the man who had adopted and cared for him, by encouraging his clan to work collectively at the ceremony, recalling that all should recognise the gifts of the deceased father. The clansmen of the now grown-up children would then carry gifts of pigs, prepare a dance presentation or present a funeral sculpture to honour the dead man. Foster (1995) writes of the matrilineal clan as a social agent: 'It is an instance of deliberate collective action through which agents define relations of similarity amongst themselves – bind themselves as a group – by differentiating themselves from other persons likewise grouped as similar to each other' (1995: 14). He argues that fathers aim to create the social agency of the wife's matrilineal clan, especially as displayed in the ritual process.[19] Seen as reproductive acts, a father's many actions and gifts can nurture the agency of entire clans acting in concert, sometimes to honour him. New Ireland clans – and potentially Bougainvillean clans – would flourish with the gifts of New Ireland fathers.

Obligation as a Moral Value of Future Bougainvillean and PNG Citizens

New Irelanders nurtured Bougainvillean children as future citizens when they 'legalised' adoptions, and thereby enabled their education. As I have shown, legalising adoptions made social relations even more fluid because the children and parents could call on yet another round of relatives by invoking specific clan names. I think this is why New Irelanders and Bougainvilleans gave many reasons for adoptions. Some clans reasoned that the future was unknowable; Bougainvillean children might never be able to return home and they needed kin in New Ireland. Some reasoned that someone had to step in for the present because the state had made it impossible for the child's natal clan to wield authority over the behaviour of the child, as it normally would in modern PNG.[20] For the present, the New Ireland matrilineal clan adopted the child to correct the errors of the PNG government. New Irelanders reasoned that the government had jeopardised the Bougainvillean child's future by thwarting the normal care and responsibilities of parents' clans living amidst strife, and simply by shrugging off the duty to provide social services. New Irelanders augmented the father's customary gifts with the gift of legal fees for the adoption of the Bougainvillean child into his wife's New Ireland matrilineal clan, who would be empowered with legal responsibility for the child's well-being. Ultimately, with the finalising of the legal adoption in New Ireland, they felt also that the PNG government would recognise its duty to provide care for children.

Children were adopted legally to both augment and distinguish the customary obligations of the matriliny to the child and honour the care given by the father's own clan and the rest of the community. Richards (1936) showed a long time ago that there was nothing natural about membership within matrilineal clans, but that people always created kinship ties.[21] In contemporary PNG, matrilineal affiliations at a great distance succeeded when people used legal mechanisms to adopt children to underline and enhance the customary power of clan membership, based on the obligations of the matrilineage to attend to the deportment of its children and youth, and on the belief that the supervision of the matrilineage would enable the child to grow up properly. In all of these legal debates, parental natal obligations to nurture the child disappeared under the shadow of the larger claim made on the child's right to grow up as a member of a clan in modern Papua New Guinea.

The Bougainvillean adoptions arranged across the region creatively used relationships between fathers, the matrilineal clan and the government, first to alter the difficult limits placed on daily life initiated by the crisis, and then to stimulate the peace process. Throughout that decade, two processes complemented each other. As fathers stretched and multiplied the number of their relationships beyond the village to rise to the challenges from the state, everyday kin politics in the village established the obligations of adults, and even of the state, to children as clanspersons and future citizens. Fathers in the villages thereby reproduced social values that enabled children's rights, first by helping others to realise the capacity of social relations, and then by enabling them to keep their obligations to each other, even if this meant seeking legal provisions of the state for their adoption.

In many respects, the changes in the work of giving paternal care in New Ireland certainly did not arise simply because of the crisis. The situation of Bougainvillean children in New Ireland highlights a widely felt change in the region. Indeed, requirements for men to be fathers in New Ireland have changed with the restructuring of international aid and its effects on the state's budget after the financial losses of the Bougainville crisis. In the contemporary period when the state aimed to reorganise social services and meet the variable flow of funds from the national coffers to social services, fathers planned to donate their own work to the development of schools, health care and government offices, or in setting up their own *bisnis* (private 'companies'). In this flurry of activity, the vast number of connections spread each father's work a bit more widely and thinly than before. This effect of structural adjustment on 'paternal nurture' spun fathers into rapid activity as they took on more social obligations than the day permits in order to plan for their children. Fathers had to find ways of linking that child's future up to new groups in order to enable the child and the child's clan in the future. The typical father networked and thereby extended his functions as an adult man. He joined regional government, paid school fees to the village school, supported the village aid post by fixing its roof, went to church and repaired the minister's water tank, or associated with national politicians in order 'to make connections'. He thought he was opening relationships, communications or pathways of exchange between those new groups and his child's clan, so as to enable the child's clan to call upon those new social groups and services in the future.

In the midst of this intense contemporary activity, New Ireland fathers scrutinised the ability of a national government to keep up with them. Could government provide social services in return equal to the scale of practical work that they have given to the government, the school and the health centres? Since independence in 1975, parents have measured the government's credibility in terms of its record of shouldering the burden of providing social services. At meetings of the village, where adults consulted together weekly about the implementation of new policies for the community, senior men and women openly argued that a lawful democratic government must provide for modern citizens, who, in turn, undertook their duties to care for children. They said that providing health care and schooling for children would be a first step towards legitimating the state's existence (Sykes 2001). They extended their general argument that the government is a partner in the work of social reproduction by pointing to the particulars of the circumstances of the crisis facing Bougainvillean children in the region, and argued that reciprocal nurture should be given by the government, the father and the matrilineal clans.

It is remarkable that adoptions in these years, when money and services seemed hard to find, were completed, but it was not only out of concern for Bougainvillean children. Joshua and Betty made a more complex series of decisions to seek legal adoption of Bougainvillean children into Betty's clan. Because Betty's own clan lacked many young men in it, they looked forward to strengthening it with the addition of the two little boys. In the past it often occurred that a matrilineal clan might adopt children, especially girls, in order to add to its numbers over a generation when few clanswomen bore children, and so they sought to do the same. In this case, the courts supported the adoption of the boys by Betty's matrilineal clan on the grounds that it facilitated both the boys' longer-term residence in New Ireland and Betty's clan power of customary legal authority in the everyday life of the boys, thereby supervising the boys' moral life. The legal decision supported the rule of customary law in the matrilineal society of the village, which Joshua and Betty reported as a good solution.

The contemporary problem was how to enforce the reciprocal practice of honouring paternal care and thereby to effect transformations of that norm of social behaviour to transcending actions of father and children, but also their clans, and even hopefully the national government.[22] The children's clan acknowledges the ethical action of a man, most commonly at the time of his funeral. Conventionally, at a funeral for a mature man, his children gave shell wealth and pigs and organised ritual dances in order to publicly honour his name and history. Affectionate memories moved children to make funerals for the father, but the most important work of the funeral ritual aimed to publicly recognise the role that a father played in the life of the children's clan, as well as in the personal life of the child. A child should remember the father's gifts at the time of his death, and mobilise his or her clan to show respect for the dead man who was the father of them all. A question remained: how would a Bougainvillean matrilineal clan be moved to remember the New Ireland man who made extraordinary gifts to the clan, such as the payment for legal adoption of a Bougainvillean child into it? This is a matter for future research.

The Obligation to Restore Social Services and Citizens' Rights to Access Them

The historical record shows that the PNG government initially moved slowly to restore services to Bougainville after 1994, when the international delegations first recommended they do so, after which progress accelerated towards peace. The PNG government's response

(Kaputin 1999) came after the exposure of human rights abuses (Taleo-Havini 1995, 1996); after international organisations had chided the government for failing in its democratic duty to its citizens (Amnesty International 1994); and after the report of a visiting delegation asked what the PNG government planned to do in order to build peace in Bougainville (UNDP 1993, 1998). However, lobbying and argument about human rights did not succeed in fully restoring services. Instead, Bougainvilleans accessed social services in two ways: first, by becoming generous hosts to the Papua New Guineans who came to fulfil the state's obligation to rebuild schools and hospitals; and, secondly, by entering into legal adoptions, a social action that acknowledged the value of meeting obligations.

By upholding obligation as a moral value, some New Irelanders and Bougainvilleans demonstrated that, by taking responsibility into their own hands that they had shamed the government for its failure to meet obligations to reopen hospitals and schools, and had thereby provoked them to speed up the work in restitution of services. Local leaders and villagers in New Ireland stepped into the government's place and claimed responsibility for the failed leadership they had once supported, saying that they 'pitied' the national government in its time of weakness. Individual men and matrilineal clans shouldered the burden of responsibility to provide the Bougainvillean children with access to education and health care in their own province, in an attempt to rectify the problems that Chan as a New Ireland-born leader had created. Although no one worked collectively or organised the effort, New Irelanders repeated the process of adopting Bougainvillean children many times across the villages of the province. While eschewing state paternalism, New Irelanders argued that a legitimate state, like a good father, should raise citizens by setting up new schools and hospitals. Although the government led by Chan had failed them, some New Ireland village leaders said that they would legitimate with votes any government that could meet obligations to raise the clans and their children.

New Irelanders acted directly within the existing structures of both kinship and democratic politics by holding obligation to be a moral value. They mobilised regional political structures in sympathy for the Bougainvilleans and in the attempt to repair inter-provincial relationships. The Bougainvilleans' businesses had closed down, their trade had been embargoed, their social services cut and local development plans thwarted. Initially Bougainvilleans worked alone to recover the loss of finances, jobs and commercial services with the closure of the mine in the NSP, but failed. Subsequently, throughout the 1990s the restructuring of international aid budgets magnified their struggle to secure access to services for their children because the region already lacked the private resources to fill the occasional budget shortfall.[23] For some time, children, fathers and mothers within their clans tried to fulfil what were once State social services of education and health. Later, in 1997, when New Irelanders arrived in Bougainville as the first PNG civil servants – the teachers, doctors and nurses – to step forward for the reconstruction of health and education, the state failed to support their work; resources did not arrive, salaries werenever paid. Without state support, individual New Irelanders met the obligations with a human face and rescued the state from its embarrassment by carrying on with the help of individual Bougainvilleans, who fed the New Irelanders while they rebuilt schools and hospitals. Sadly, the few provisions made by the government to support Bougainvilleans with services depended on the individual goodwill of the civic employees to carry on, while their pay materialised much later than did the services they provided on behalf of the state.

Bougainvilleans' commitment to inter-provincial adoption of their children is an example of direct political action, in which they sustained access to state health and education by meeting obligations to each other, whether as clanspersons or as citizens of region, province or nation. Across the region, the earlier expressions of anger, tension and disagreement, so much a part of the Bougainville crisis,[24] changed to active commitment to meet obligations within and across the matrilineal clans and the state as a peaceful 'pathway to the future'. Bougainvilleans demonstrated commitments to children's well-being, but in an apparently unfamiliar way. Elders grieved that some of the older youth remain in jungle retreats because they are still at odds with the mining company and the PNG government.[25] Mature Bougainvilleans sent some children away to relatives in other provinces in the Islands Region. Here I have described how some Bougainvilleans reasoned that it was necessary to give their children for adoption so that they would come back to participate in the reconstruction of Bougainville.

After the crisis, New Guinea Islanders continued to value citizens' obligations to each other. Papua New Guineans of the Islands Region met obligations by completing adoption processes within customary relations during structural adjustments to the PNG economy, and even after the violent conflict.[26] The values sustaining matrilineal clans of Bougainville persisted from times before the crises amongst those who moved to town or went to work on either copra or oil palm plantations across the islands of New Ireland and New Britain or in copper mining on Bougainville Island.[27] Relatives had regularly consulted over affairs of their extended in kin in either place.

A recent documentary (Chamberlain 1999) proposes a more radical perspective on obligation as valued in social action. Francis Ona, leader of the Bougainvillean revolutionary separatist movement, asks: 'Just what obliges people to recognise the PNG State, and thereby justify its existence?' His companions argued that a state that does not provide social services has no reason to exist. Other Bougainvilleans often said that they would have been better off without the establishment of the government, given that budgets fluctuated and the state's capacity to provide services for its citizens has been severely limited. The leaders of the independence movement lead by the Bougainvillean Revolutionary Army (BRA) argued that they did not seek to make a new state in Bougainville, but did seek recognition from the state for the integrity of their life ways and the chance to live a life of self-sufficiency.[28] These men and women argued that, when the state facilitates the erosion of indigenous resources in favour of mining companies with international partners sharing in the profits, the state exists only for shadowy reasons.

New Irelanders' involvement in the Bougainvillean peace process showed that by meeting obligations to sustain a social life (as opposed to what they say and write in contracts and agreements), people across the region could enjoy moral politics and achieve the constitutional ideal of good government, if the government met its own obligations to citizens. When lobbying by human rights groups failed, direct political action by Papua New Guineans sustained the peace process.[29] If these actions – including actions towards the living, the unborn and dead relatives – spoke louder than tricky words,[30] then eventually the state did meet its obligations to Bougainvilleans when drafting a constitution for Bougainvillean autonomy (UNPO 2004), freeing Bougainvilleans to meet their obligations to each other by a referendum in June 2005.

Obligation as a Moral Value

Mauss made clear that people created moral order by clarifying a shared concept of peace, harmony and well-being in meeting obligations (Mauss 1931). As I commented in the introduction, Mauss added that the concept of harmonious social life, the social good, could be taught to the younger generation by discussion and negotiation, not simply by inculcation. In this case, Bougainvilleans and New Irelanders focused on the value of obligation in determining who should provide care for the children, as exemplified by the father's nurturing care and gifts for his child. With their direct actions to provide Bougainvillean children with social services where the state failed, New Guinea Islanders reminded state politicians, mining company officials and civil servants that the government could keep to its obligations to the citizenry.

I showed that the Bougainvilleans' concern that the state should keep it obligations to citizens, including the future generation of Papua New Guineans, had spread to New Ireland with their adoptions of Bougainvillean children. New Irelanders learned that good government must have a human face. The state cannot meet its obligations to citizens through the established government offices, institutions and civil servants. Criticism of the failure of men and women to meet obligations does not expose corruption so much as humiliate some politicians as bad fathers or failed big men (see Clark 1997 for different variations on this). Public disapproval does not show a loss of trust in government, as some have argued (Foster 2002; Giddens 1991). Instead, condemnations provoke people to achieve good government by asking the New Ireland people who fill bureaucratic and political offices to meet their obligations to other Papua New Guineans with a human and personal face. In the case described in this chapter, New Irelanders and Bougainvilleans made claims on the government. Now, can the PNG government legitimate its existence by acting as a nurturing father, by providing basic social services and by enabling Papua New Guineans to keep their obligations to their relatives, friends and, in this case particularly, the next generation?[31]

I have described the different forms of obligation that enjoined New Guinea Islanders to participate in the Bougainvillean peace process whereby their moral reasoning enabled their nurturing acts. Adopting an obligation, which is an action expressing a person's moral reasoning, can be seen in the reciprocal cultivation of social life amongst Papua New Guineans of the Islands Region. Notably, social life entrenches moral reasoning about how to keep obligations, and presents this value as a capacity of social action. It becomes more apparent from the perspective of the triad of partners keeping the obligations. In overseeing the legal adoption processes, the state clarifies within the law those services that it offers to children of clans. It stands in relation to the child as if it were a partner to the father's nurturing role in the life of his wife's matrilineal clan. Making adoption a legal process puts the government as the provider of social services into the lives of Papua New Guineans as a provider of the means of access to modern lifestyles in a contemporary world. The legitimate government should see that the child's health care and schooling are available if that child is to grow through its relationships and cultivate adult responsibilities. Sometimes government fails; and sometimes clans take up the work of governance. If children grow to adulthood through keeping obligations as kin, as friends and as citizens, then the state may be said to have met its obligation to enable children to grow up.

Notes

Acknowledgements. I thank members of UCL Social Anthropology Departmental Seminar, the EHESS Seminaire des Anthropologies des Systèmes Mondiaux and the Max Planck Institute Workshop, 'Rethinking Morality' for suggestions on written drafts. As ever, I err in misusing their advice. I thank the people of the villages of the Lelet Plateau with whom I have lived, and the students and teachers in New Ireland secondary schools for their help.

1. In earlier years liberals debated standardising financial currency in order to free trade from political regulations and socialists argued that states should protect the basic needs of their citizens within an international market society.
2. I thank my colleagues in our discussions with Chris Gregory, and acknowledge that the idea that morality could become a new gold standard draws deeply on his use of the concept of value and standards of value in his book *Savage Money* (Gregory 2004).
3. The PNG customary adoption process, working with national laws, was predisposed to encompass the changes to the delivery of education and health services precipitated by the Bougainville crisis. The case is exemplary to current concerns.
4. Mauss had argued that the moral basis of 'tribal'society (a society comprised of the interrelations of many clans), like modern society (an equally complex organisation), coheres when members foster, discuss and adapt social relationships, such as the parental/filial relation, to the work of social regeneration. I am grateful to Susanna Narotzsky for pointing out this feature of Mauss's work. Mauss's short essay 'Cohesion Sociale dans les Sociétés Polysegmentaires' is not translated. Misunderstandings are my own.
5. The island provinces of Manus, New Ireland, East New Britain, West New Britain, and the North Solomons comprise the geopolitical region.
6. People of the PNG Islands Regions successfully used the established national law as it was intended. PNG family law was adopted largely from Australia, and then adjusted to meet the conditions of social life in clans, as is common across the country (Luluaki 1990). A striking contrast exists between legal adoption, in which the court acts to sever the child from birth parents in the interest of securing the legal claims of the adoptive parents, and inter-provincial adoption in PNG, where legal agreements between clans do not sever ties between natal clans and children, but simply record them.
7. The different parties to any adoption in post-colonial nations – the state, the clans, the child and the birth parents – all face the difficulties of defining the child's interests, especially after the United Nations Convention on the Rights of the Child (1989). Ethnographers show that the key issues in establishing children's rights include: first, the recognition of children's dependence on families to protect them as citizens (Stephens 1995; Sargent and Scheper-Hughes 1998; Gailey 1999a, b; Helleiner 2003; Sharp 2003); secondly, that the comparison of customary forms of adoption falters on definitions of Euro-American categories of jurisprudence (Bodenhorn 1988; Carsten 1991; see also McKinnon and Franklin 2001; Bowie 2004); and, thirdly, that Euro-American legal adoption focuses on the rights of parents (Goody, J. 1969; Goody, E. 1982; Zelizer 1985), in contrast with customary forms of adoption, which focus on children's interests in keeping kin (Carroll 1970; Brady 1976). Modell (1994, 1998), Gailey (1999a), Stoler (2002) and Gershon (2003) argued that governmentality reshapes kinspersons into citizens. In contrast,

Demian (2001, 2004a,b) asks how Pacific people understand children's rights as post-colonial citizens.

8. Protests in Bougainville continued until the 2005 vote on autonomy.
9. The peacekeeping initiative (New Zealand, Australia, Fiji and Vanuatu) was successful for individuals involved. In comparison, see the personal account of the unsuccessful Canadian-led UN peacekeeping mission in Rwanda (Dallaire 2003)
10. Bougainvillean decisions echo habits of social mobilisation in other matrilineal societies. In Milne Bay women married spouses and adopted children, and thus maximised access to the use of land and traditional wealth (Weiner 1976).
11. A father pays for a legal adoption in New Ireland because he also wishes for conventional results under PNG family law for his and his wife's matrilineal clan. Adoption affiliates the child to the wife's matrilineal clan, in whose care the child resides. He or she has an appropriate clan name and also addresses all of his mother's kin from the particular calculus of his or her position in the mother's matriliny. Fathers say that the payment of legal fees is a gift to the matriline of the wife and mother of their adoptive child.
12. The father's gift of the payment of legal adoption costs does more than simply affect traditional social relations, largely because adoptions are made as part of the peace process. By using the mechanisms of the state as if it were only a new idiom of kinship, rather than an institution, New Irelanders were consciously engaging the complexity of social relations as the locus of moral action. Because of the legal adoption, it would be possible to find the children who left Bougainville and to hold the New Ireland clans accountable for their well-being.
13. I argue that clanship is a modality of sociality that people use to get access to citizens' rights, which they believe the state must provide out of moral and political obligations to citizens. I do not think that clanship is a latent form of citizenship.
14. This stands in contrast to societies where rights of inheritance are conferred across or within households.
15. Some new children were the offspring of marriages to women from outside NIP, who were brought back by their fathers so that they would grow up in the village and have access to land there.
16. Mandak make strangers into kin by asking them to participate in simple exchanges of small goods (Clay 1977).
17. Biological relations are never 'more real' than adoptive ones (Clay 1977).
18. A contemporary Islands Region rock song belittled the man who leaves his wife's children, wandering like a dog in the streets. The refrain asked who would remember him when he dies.
19. Clay (1992, 1986) describes the Mandak norm: a father enables the child to meet adult obligations.
20. Senior clansmen are legally accountable for children's behavior.
21. Richards (1936) described youth claims on 'mother rights' from the matrilineal clan.
22. Malinowski argued that reciprocity by the affinal clan, as carried out by the next generation, constituted a form of customary law (Malinowski 1935; Weiner 1992). According to that law, fathers should care selflessly for their children by looking after them with *mapula, lanavolo, nat-lo* (as different Austronesian languages name the ethos in which fathers use small gifts to express affection and paternity). According to Godelier (1999), neither Malinowski nor Weiner (1992) fully understood *mapula*. Mosko (2000) calls for a revision of the anthropological uses of the Trobriand concepts of personhood in order to address the issue.
23. Parent, clan and government kept mutual obligations to arrange school fees (see Sykes 2001).

24. For discussions of the history of the Bougainvillean crisis, see Oliver 1990; Polomka 1990; Filer 1992; Amnesty International 1993; Reagan 1996; Lea 1997; Ogan 1999; Pacific Islands Development Report 2002).
25. The BRA seeks compensation for damages to the matrilineal clan grounds, and injury to clan members.
26. Earlier anthropologists had debated matriliny's end (Oliver 1937, 1990; Ogan 1972; 2001 Nash 1974).
27. Zambian men left villages for wage work in mines and urban lifestyles, severing connections with their clan, both as a significant social unit and as a point of reference for moral deliberation (Ferguson 1999). In Sierra Leone, an entire generation has entered into violent struggle across their home region (Richards 1996).
28. Francis Ona, BRA leader, refused to participate in the work of forming an interim government (Chamberlain 2001).
29. Ultimately, obligation rather than human rights led to the success of the peace process. Throughout the 1990s, delegations of international visitors inspected the human rights record and supported the Bougainvilleans in their actions to see the restoration of social services (Amnesty International 1993, 1997a,b; UN Development Programme 1995, 1998; Australian Parliamentary Delegation 1994). No single delegation could enforce the delivery of state services; yet, each insisted that the state meet its obligations to provide these, even during the course of Bougainvillean deliberations with PNG government over their island's independence.
30. See Clay (1977, 1986); Wagner (1986).
31. Schools do not simply teach provincial children modern rights in the nation (Reed-Danahay 1986; Stambach 2000).

Chapter 10

BETWEEN FACTS AND NORMS: TOWARDS AN ANTHROPOLOGY OF ETHICAL PRACTICE

Mark Goodale

As correctly argued in the introduction to this volume, anthropologists have traditionally neglected morality as a topic for ethnographic study and ethnological theory. This major lacuna in the intellectual history is a peculiar one, and not without consequence, especially as twenty-first century anthropology tries to come to terms with a range of contemporary problems in which morality – and normativity more generally – is fundamentally implicated. These include the rise of transnational human rights after the end of the cold war, the increasingly aggressive campaigns of religious conversion being waged in new places and new ways in the developing world, the attempt to establish a real international legal regime through institutions like the International Criminal Court, and, more recently, the reframing of major military and political interventions – by the United States, for example – in the language of the moral crusade. But because anthropology has failed to produce – through its twisting theoretical turns – an epistemological framework for either explaining or understanding the increasing normativity of contemporary social life, anthropologists have come to the debates over these problems with their discursive quivers poorly stocked. The lack of sustained and broad anthropological engagement with the normative is compounded by the fact that anthropologists have been working at cross purposes. Scholars have developed quite robust traditions that are self-limited to areas like religion, law, politics and (more recently) human rights, without really considering that each of these more conventional focuses are, at least from certain perspectives, expressions of a more basic normativity: the social practices through which illusive values are rendered – or, perhaps, actualised – as standards of right conduct, visions of the good, legal prohibitions, and so on.

Yet this anthropological absence carries with it several unintended benefits: first, it means that the sudden interest in the normative unfolds non-paradigmatically, without the heavy burden of expectations; secondly, the anthropology of normativity (including morality) can be critical in the best of senses, because to answer the question 'Why not anthropology?' (in matters moral, for example) is, by extension, to ask questions like 'Why must values be opposed to facts?' or 'Is there a way in which norms can be understood as both an object worth of ethnographic attention *and* a category of social ephemera at the same time?' And, finally, as in other instances in which anthropology was late to the game – the anthropology of global systems or transnational networks, to mention two others – the recent concentrated attention to questions once thought beyond the pale comes with a delightful combination of vim and subversion. As the current volume shows so convincingly, anthropologists are beginning to offer answers to these questions that show remarkable potential, not least in how they point to a set of unifying threads – or, if you like, strings – that link apparently disparate forms of normative practice.

Of course anthropologists have not been completely absent from debates over the normative. Late in his career, Bronislaw Malinowski considered the relationship between morality and freedom in his *Freedom and Civilization* (1944), although the great father remains more widely known for leaving the veranda and deigning to help the natives build their canoes than for anything he had to say about morality. Moreover, there could very well have been a much more robust anthropology of normativity at the time scholars like Mary Douglas became neo-Durkheimians, but they were inspired by different ideas from the Frenchman's *oeuvre*. And the American anthropological philosopher David Bidney, who is credited with introducing what has come to be known (somewhat idiosyncratically, I am implying) as "humanism" into the discipline, certainly seemed to be addressing himself to a range of social-normative questions, most notably in his article 'Normative Culture and the Categories of Value', which appeared in this *Theoretical Anthropology* (1953). But, as I shall explain in more detail in the next section, his efforts, like those of Malinowski before him, to bring anthropological forms of knowledge to bear on moral and other normative questions – either in the abstract or in context – never got off the ground. In Bidney's case, he tried to bring anthropology closer to philosophy, an effort that was largely futile, although it did lead – by yet more twists and turns – to a fondness for poetry of all things among a small, but passionately devoted, cadre of American anthropologists.[1] As I will develop more fully below, Bidney would have done much better and his worthy efforts would have had a more lasting influence, had he attempted something like the opposite: to bring philosophy closer to anthropology, to suggest a way in which the very nature of normative enquiry could be re-established, to rethink what it means to ask and answer questions that transcend the empirical levels where the Malinowskian ethnographer plies her trade.

This chapter is in part both a reflection on this intellectual history and a kind of counter-discursive reading of it, a way of imagining what the anthropology of normativity would be like had the discipline been more willing to move in different epistemological directions and less willing to cede the conceptual high ground to those for whom the empirical is just an annoying distraction from the journey to and from the Platonic ether. To do this, I explore what it would mean to pursue an anthropology of normativity by first developing a version of what I have described elsewhere (Goodale 2006a) as an 'anthropological philosophy of human rights'. In other words, I consider the implications of bringing philosophy to anthropology. Next I illustrate these problems and possible solutions with reference to certain normative shifts in contemporary Bolivia. As we shall see, to argue for an alternative epistemological framework through which problems of values, morality, rights and norms can be understood is not simply to replace one artificially abstracted system with another. Instead, it is to conceptualise such a system, as we shall see, in terms of social practice, to anchor both its criteria and ultimate legitimacy in the messiness of everyday life. Normative questions are also, at times, real questions of life and death for social actors caught in any number of insidious webs. So there is also, unavoidably, an ethical dimension to this debate, one that must somehow be given new prominence. Finally, I end this chapter more prospectively by suggesting how what I call an anthropology of ethical practice modestly points the way towards new directions for research, critique and socio-political action.

Anthropology between Facts and Norms

Through the first part of the twentieth century, anthropology was the science of mankind, a self-understanding that had both epistemological and intellectual-historical consequences. This positioning was the result of a division of intellectual and academic labour that, with certain modifications, shaped the emergence of the discipline and its identity on both sides of the Atlantic. American cultural anthropologists might have been more heavily informed by the German historical school and developments within the wider Austro-Hungarian counter-enlightenment (Stocking 1996), while British sociocultural anthropology might have emerged under the sign of British empiricism (Stocking 1988; Goody 1995), but both were committed to the empirical study of culture and society, which was expressed in terms of those 'social facts' – to invoke an idea from yet another major disciplinary tradition at the time – through which illusive internal imaginaries were made manifest as objective things that could be studied scientifically. In other words, anthropology was committed to the observation, description and explanation of what fitted within the dominant post-Enlightenment scientific paradigm; the inevitable controversies – and there were many – took place within these circumscribed epistemological boundaries. And, of course, to draw boundaries like these is to define a range of phenomena that lie beyond as much as it is to define those that lie within. Without question, both specific normative problems, and, even more, those we might call meta-normative – that is, those that revolve around the nature of morality or values or law as such – were conventionally excluded from the domain of the science of mankind. The first kind of problem involved questions of feeling, belief and meaning that were perhaps, at some level, empirical, but very difficult – or, indeed, impossible – to observe, measure, predict and otherwise access through even the most expansive and creative applications of the scientific method. And the second were understood to be clearly non-empirical problems that fell within the rubric of philosophy and were thus subject to a completely different epistemology, one in which knowledge is produced through a deductive process of conceptual envisioning and the derivation of logical implications. Mathematics is perhaps the best example of this non-empirical epistemology, but other disciplines – theology, for example-are also dependent on it.

A good example of how this epistemological division of labour had profound consequences for anthropology – some intended, some not – is the case of American cultural anthropology and human rights. As I have described in much more detail elsewhere (Goodale 2006a, b, 2009a), UNESCO solicited an advisory opinion from Melville Herskovits, who later produced an official 'Statement on Human Rights' that was adopted by the Executive Board of the American Anthropological Association, then as now the largest association of professional anthropologists in the world. In his 'Statement' Herskovits rejected the idea of a declaration of universal human rights on a number of grounds. But the one that concerns me here is his assertion that the idea of human rights makes claims that are based on perceived universal values. The discipline of anthropology was being asked to evaluate this claim and, it was hoped, legitimate it. But Herskovits demurred. He explained that anthropology was a science committed to empirical observation and, as such, was simply unable to say anything either way about human rights, at least anything based on anthropological research itself. The formal engagement with values and their actualisation as norms was best left to the philosophers, theologians and others for whom non-empirical speculation was firmly and epistemologically grounded. The result of the 1947 'Statement' was that anthropological modes of enquiry played almost no role in the post-war development of human rights theory and practice until about the 1980s, when a small group of mostly American anthropologists undertook to transform the relationship between the discipline and human rights.[2] This they did through a series of special commissions that were constituted to investigate various accounts of human rights abuses against indigenous populations, mostly – coincidentally – in South America. This intense and passionate activism led to the creation of a permanent standing committee on human rights within the AAA and, in 1999, the promulgation of the 'Declaration on Anthropology and Human Rights', which clearly and unequivocally repudiated the 1947 Statement and outlined a set of essentially political rationales through which anthropologists could – and, indeed, must – use their knowledge of particular cultures to advocate greater protection of populations at risk.

But this radical realignment was not based on a new understanding that normative problems like human rights were now suddenly within those epistemological boundaries that had previously excluded them. Indeed, the dramatically reconfigured relationship between at least American anthropology and human rights was not, as I have said, grounded in a well-articulated epistemiological shift at all. Instead, a political decision was taken – or, perhaps, emerged over time – that it was no longer tolerable for the discipline to stand idly by as its subjects/informants/collaborators were victimised in any number of ways, even if the basis for this decision was ambiguous at best.

What this sounding from one current in the recent broader intellectual history of anthropology tells us, among other things, is that any reframing of the discipline's potential contribution to normative problems once thought beyond the pale has taken place not through epistemology but rather, we might say, against it. The emergence of an activist anthropology committed to the protection and support of international human rights, for example, must be seen in the light of contemporaneous waves of disciplinary self-critique that shook the halls of academic departments and set the pages of journals on fire throughout the 1980s. Although anthropologists on both sides of the Atlantic had always engaged in vigorous and, at times, contentious debates, these unfolded within a more general set of assumptions about what anthropology as a discipline could, and could not, do. But what distinguished the critical battles of the 1980s was the fact that some quarters suggested that the very idea of epistemology itself implied a discursive framework that served to exclude and marginalise. That is to say, with the dark shadow of certain continental post-structuralists hovering over them, at least some anthropologists were suggesting that any theory of knowledge tended to transmogrify into the dreaded master narrative. This meant, among other things, that even the mere gesture towards a different epistemological foundation through which anthropology could engage with normative problems was effectively foreclosed as a reactionary retreat into the Comtian citadel.

The problem with these two opposed currents – the one committed to anthropology as some version of the science of mankind, the other committed to an anti-epistemological deconstruction of it – is that they both exclude in different ways, but with equally profound effects, the possibilities of envisioning a new basis on which anthropology can address super-empirical problems without having to merely adopt a version of the philosophers' method. The real contribution to our understanding of the normative lies elsewhere, in a radically reconfigured approach to knowledge, one that unfolds in a conceptual space that draws from aspects of both poles of the classic fact-value spectrum without positioning itself anywhere between them. In other words, as I shall develop more fully in the chapter's final section, a different anthropological orientation to the normative can be pursued that combines the peculiar knowledge produced by the ethnographic encounter with normative practices with knowledge that transcends the empirical. Indeed, as I shall show, these two dimensions – what I shall call 'ethical practice' – are mutually and inseparably constitutive: a mere ethnographic understanding of normative practices is necessary but not sufficient, and the theorisation of normativity as such that is not grounded in actual normative practices is, ultimately, an intellectual (and perhaps ethical) house of cards.

Political Change and the Moral Imagination in Bolivia

Since 1999, Bolivia has been shaken by a series of political, economic, social and, most important, discursive upheavals whose meanings and implications are fraught with ambiguity. There is a conventional way of framing developments in contemporary Bolivia, one that is – as I have argued recently (Goodale 2006c) – more a mis-reading than anything else. The reasons for both this ill-conceived diagnosis and the potentially much more fruitful alternative to it illustrate certain dilemmas in the anthropology of normativity more generally. Although I am not able to give a full account of key developments in Bolivia's recent past (see Postero 2006; Goodale 2009b), the following synopsis should give a sense of what is most important for my purposes here. Between 1999 and 2005 the traditional political establishment in Bolivia – or at least the one that had emerged after the (apparently permanent) restoration of civilian rule in the early 1980s – was dismantled, piece by piece, partly through its own critical misunderstanding of broader currents flowing through the majority indigenous Bolivian body politic, but also as a result of wider transnational discursive shifts within which Bolivia was merely one seismic fault line.

A succession of old-school elites from all points on the conventional political spectrum – from Gonzalo Sánchez de Lozada to Hugo Banzer Suárez – continued with what is known in Bolivia (as elsewhere) as neoliberalism,[3] which meant, among other things, the development of business relationships with multinational corporations to take over the management of major public utilities (like water services), a focus on the exploitation of natural resources, in which foreign companies both assumed control over extraction and retained a major stake in future profits, and, perhaps most importantly, the robust embrace of human rights discourse at all levels, which included both the codification into national law of key international human rights instruments (like ILO 169 and CEDAW) and a seemingly bottomless receptivity to the work of transnational NGOs, most of whom had by the late 1980s reconceptualised their mission in terms of human rights.[4] At the same time, new political and social movements were crystallising in Bolivia, many anchored in new forms of indigeneity. The two most important were the Movement to Socialism (MAS) party, headed by Evo Morales, the former head of Bolivia's coca growers union, and the Indigenous Pachakuti Movement (MIP), under the leadership of Felipe Quispe, a former *katarista* who worked to position himself to the purer left of Morales and MAS.

As in the past, social unrest and resistance to the status quo apparently took the usual forms: marches through the streets of La Paz, Cochabamba and El Alto drenched in a sea of *wiphalas*; blockades of major national transportation arteries; running street battles with police and the army (which eventually massacred almost 100 people in El Alto in October 2003, in what quickly became known as Black October); the pall of tear gas and the whizzing of rubber bullets; the increasing unease of Bolivia's powerful ally to the north, which saw the prospects of relatively cheap natural gas imports disappearing with each passing week; and, finally, the millenarian assertions by leaders of the resistance that the moment had, at long last, come in which a new day would dawn for Bolivia's exploited indigenous majority. But, even though the forms of protest in Bolivia between 1999 and 2005 evoked memories of upheavals past, they ended in what is from a mere historical perspective a startling result: the election of Evo Morales to Bolivia's presidency in December of 2005 in what was – given the multiple candidates in the race – a landslide, in which middle-class *mestizos* and urban Bolivians joined with the rural and peri-urban indigenous majority to deal a crushing blow to Bolivia's *ancien régime*.

Yet, even if the political, social and legal momentum in Bolivia over the last six years has led in surprising directions, what is important here is to remember that the forms of this momentum are understood to be simply variations on a theme, the logical, if extreme, conclusion to the influence of centuries of identifiable structural factors. In other words, although extraordinary in every way, the election of Evo Morales and the defeat of the symbols of Bolivia's elite political establishment have not been seen as signs of an epochal rupture or the beginnings of an epistemic break beyond which only a completely new reality is possible. Rather, the marches and blockades and rubber bullets this time simply accomplished what they were always meant to accomplish: the giving to Bolivia's indigenous majority its world-historical due, the shift of Bolivia's modern trajectory on to the track from which it had long been derailed – the track of justice and *dignidad humana*. The final straw in this much longer historical process was the series of legal, political and economic reforms instituted during the late 1980s and through much of the 1990s that were hatched under the sign of 'neoliberalism'. The apotheosis of neoliberalism in Bolivia was about 1993 or 1994, the middle point of Gonzalo Sánchez de Lozada's first government, when middle-class and urban Bolivians suddenly had 'indigenous' on their lips and there was a growing sense – only among progressive intellectuals, as it turned out – that the creation of a pluricultural Bolivia was the key to breaking free from the seemingly unbreakable bonds that had historically kept the country from realising its true potential. But the creation of a multicultural Bolivia came with its own strings attached, including those that tied the transforming nation to transnational economic networks in both new and very old ways. And of course there were the ever-present and rapacious demands of Bolivia's landed elites, many of them based in the Santa Cruz region, who did not simply allow themselves to be swept away in the torrent of *wiphalas* and calls for the redistribution of land. If anything, they saw the decentralisation of the power to make decisions over public monies and lands – a key pillar of Goni's Law of Popular Participation – as an opportunity to exercise their own human rights (especially to acquire and increase property). So despite what were unarguably the best of intentions by at least some segments of Goni's cadres of progressive government officials, journalists and supportive academics, the reforms of the mid-1990s actually reinforced many of those structural factors they were meant to weaken.

All of this is nothing if not eminently conventional: long existing economic, political and social factors have worked to oppress Bolivia's indigenous majority, from the *norte de Potosí* to the forests of the Beni; these factors have formed the foundation of modern Bolivia, even if through the years they have taken different forms and have involved different sets of government, corporate and social actors; these factors are not mystifying or spiritual or abstract, but rather apprehensible through reason, material (endemic poverty, for example) and concrete, in that they express themselves in the form of social hierarchies, class prejudice, racism and the highly skewed distribution of wealth throughout the country; they are, taken together, the long-term cause of the pervasive disenchantment among Bolivia's indigenous populations and, more recently, the proximate cause of the upheavals over the last six years; and, finally, as keen observers of these types of structural factors, from Marx to Guevara, have long said, there will come a time when the world-historical system from which they ultimately emerge will no longer be able to sustain them and the political-economic version of Newton's third law will no longer be valid – when the forces of social change push hard enough there will not be anything to push back.

And of course there is a role for anthropology to play in tracking and explaining these processes, since they take the form of those social facts that are susceptible to the application of the discipline's latter-day version of the scientific method – ethnography; and, for those contemporary anthropologists who vehemently reject the scientific method and the totalising epistemology that justifies it, there is another response: the self-referential critique that is couched in the broadest and most amorphous of terms, so that developments in Bolivia come to look – to the extent they are referenced or, we might say, indexed at all

– suspiciously like developments in other parts of what James Ferguson (2006) has recently described as the 'neoliberal world order'. So, at least for the orthodox, anthropologists have a choice to make: either document and then try and understand the empirical manifestations of underlying structural factors – in the form of resistance, counter-resistance and even apathy – or ignore the empirical dimensions of contemporary Bolivia altogether. The problem is that both of these – admittedly starkly drawn – alternatives, which continue to characterise dominant trends in the discipline, are badly miscalculated to miss both the most important changes that are taking place in Bolivia today, and the long-term meaning of these changes. If the sheer fact of Evo Morales's election, or the presence of protesters in the streets or the cancellation of contracts with multinationals are all empirical (and social) facts that can be observed – after a fashion – described and explained, while the illusive values that shape these facts remain forever closed to ethnographic study (and thus open only to critical theorists, philosophers and perhaps literary realists), then we must conclude that socio-political change in contemporary Bolivia is actually taking place between these facts and values.

By this I very much mean to imply a new way of understanding the social ontology of actual sociocultural processes, one that is based on a different analysis of the spaces of normative engagement through which social actors across the range in Bolivia reclaim for themselves the meaning of modernity itself. They do so through a radical projection of the moral imagination, a complicated social act that has been – as I have suggested above – misinterpreted in conventional political and structural terms. The real action, as it were, is taking place in the conceptual, social and normative spaces between values and social action, between morality and political reform, between actual norms and social facts. There is no question that earlier periods of socio-political ferment in Bolivia have also unfolded at multiple levels. But what is so different about contemporary developments is that the underlying discursive framework has been so profoundly reconfigured, in particular in the way it makes transformations in subjectivity the ultimate basis of socio-political action. Keep in mind that for much of the last century, a completely different set of ideas motivated social and political actors in Bolivia by, in a sense, removing the problem of agency from historical processes. Bolivian peasants, miners, coca growers, rural schoolteachers, and all the other social classes for whom fundamental change was the regular rallying cry took comfort from the fact that their socio-political worldview put both the burden and the potential for system transformation on factors within the system itself. Moreover, because the potential for transformation was embedded in the national expressions of different factors within a broader world political-economic system, oppressed social actors in Bolivia could also take solace in the fact that these factors were impelling the system to its logical conclusion: its disintegration and evolution into something dramatically different, and more just.

But since the late 1980s Bolivia has undergone what I have described elsewhere as a liberal renaissance (Goodale 2009b). I very much mean to contrast this account of contemporary Bolivia with the discourse of neoliberalism in that I understand the rise of new indigenous parties and their self-articulation within a conventional liberal rights framework as evidence that Bolivia is undergoing a process of return more than anything else – a return to its origins in liberalism mediated by law. The liberalism vs. neoliberalism debate is perhaps tangential to my purposes here, but both ways of explaining Bolivia's contemporary epistemic condition underscore several key points, all of which indicate the need for a new way of understanding recent socio-political developments. First, with the coming of the human rights discourse to Bolivia in the late 1980s, the historical externalising of system transformation was brought to a grinding halt. No longer would social actors look outside themselves for both the causes and meanings of social change. Rather, the idea of human rights effectively internalised the impetus for change and, in a way, circumscribed it within the boundaries of personhood itself. In other words, the idea of human rights – as distinct from any second-order legal or bureaucratic manifestations of this idea – makes subjectivity both the alpha and omega of what we might describe as moral progress. What is so peculiar from an intellectual-historical perspective is that the kind of development of human rights consciousness that is so important to much of the contemporary international and transnational political and social landscape takes places one person at a time without any assumptions about how this internal normative revolution is supposed to add up. Another way of saying this is that the rebirth of liberalism in Bolivia is essentially monadic in the Leibnizian sense: each person is a little mirror of the moral universe, indivisible, complete and, to the extent to which each person's humanness is the source of human rights, immortal, in that everyone is – from this perspective – an actualised expression of a more universal human essence. This is a far cry from the competing social ontologies in Bolivia that made the individual an essentially powerless cog in a historically fragile machine; it was only en bloc, as social classes, as ethnic groups or, much broader still, as 'the oppressed' that individual Bolivians could be said to exercise agency. In contrast, the most recent iteration of liberalism in Bolivia – the version that expresses itself with perhaps the most historical force and clarity – makes the moral subject almost hyper-agentive.

Secondly, to understand current socio-political change in Bolivia as unfolding first (and last) at the level of the moral imagination, and not within those political-economic structures that had always seemed paradoxically to both exclude and encapsulate Bolivian modernity at the same time, is to adopt an explanatory framework that is startlingly non-teleological. Liberalism (or neoliberalism, for that matter) is anchored in a set of assumptions about the moral and social world, of course, and some of these assumptions imply movement of some kind. For example, if human beings are, ultimately, rational beings whose purpose is to clear away the range of social, political and legal obstacles to the actualisation of this rationality, then 'progress' can be defined as the forward movement towards this existential ideal. And the spread of human rights discourse in places where such a vision of the moral and political universe was either submerged (as in Bolivia) or absent altogether can be seen as a kind of progression in the late-modern drive to make dignity and autonomy pillars of the human condition. But all of this is a long way from the intensely teleological theories of history that have structured much of Bolivia's historical self-understanding since at least the early twentieth century. For most of the last century, Bolivia's contested modernity was rolling on through that process of dialectical inevitability that provided what Rorty (2000) has described as 'social hope' at the same time it seemed to dehumanise the meaning of history itself.[5] If people had a social role to play, it was only as understood in the *longue durée*, as the sum total of clicks on the historical dial, as symbolic actors in a series of increasingly purer epochal syntheses. The moral and discursive revolution that is emerging in contemporary Bolivia, in contrast, has no defined end point; it is, in Kantian terms, an end unto itself. Its purposes are realised every time another indigenous activist invokes the idea of human rights or speaks of the 'essential dignity' of Bolivia's indigenous populations. In a way, both the greatest potential and danger in this new transformation of the moral imagination in Bolivia result from the fact that it is, quite literally, going nowhere.

And, finally, the kind of alternative understanding of current socio-political developments in Bolivia I am proposing here reinterprets the socio-political itself. Instead of seeing social and political spheres as prior to and determinative of the more ambiguous – and difficult to apprehend – levels of the moral and (more broadly) normative, I want to propose something like a categorical reversal of these relationships. With the coming of Bolivia's (neo)liberal epistemic moment over the last twenty years, in which certain ideas about personhood have taken on new, and fundamental, importance, the moral imaginary has become the primary lens through which the meanings of socio-political change are refracted. By moral imaginary I mean those socio-cognitive spaces in which individuals within collectivities construct their own visions of life, what Grace Jantzen (2001) has described as 'the habitus of our ethical attitudes and actions'. So there is something like an order of normative priority, as I would like to understand it, although it is not my intention to offer a formal theory of the normative. But, just for the sake of argument, we can understand values to be the most general set of necessarily contested and dynamic principles from which people can and do derive meaning. Within the symbolic anthropological literature, the equivalent of values would be what Sherry Ortner (1973) described as 'summarizing key symbols'. Norms would be the first step towards giving values some social shape, although they still exist below and prior to the more formal institutional sphere. Ethical practices, or what Jantzen calls 'ethical attitudes and actions', are norms as social practice, and by social I mean anything beyond the internal imaginings of the individual mind.[6] There are other ways of dividing the conceptual pie and other permutations; for example, morality could be seen, within this schema, as institutionalised ethical practices; laws would occupy the most formal, bureaucratic end of this normativity continuum; and so on.[7] But what is most important for my purposes here is the fact that the real revolution in contemporary Bolivia is taking place somewhere between values and ethical practices. New understandings of citizenship, the transformative impact of human rights discourse and what I have called elsewhere indigenous cosmopolitanism are shifting the nature of Bolivia's modern trajectory, and these developments must be tracked in these ambiguous and illusive sub-political-economic normative spaces. But how can this be done, by anthropologists or others? And what would a project like this mean for the 'anthropology of moralities'?

Toward an Anthropology of Ethical Practice

In this final section I want to both draw together the different theoretical arguments and speculate on what they might mean for a reconfigured anthropology of moralities/normativity. I began the chapter by making what I think is the fairly non-controversial observation that earlier anthropology failed to develop an epistemology of the normative that was distinct from dominant alternatives of the time, most notably those based in law and philosophy that were anchored in deductive, non-empirical or logical procedures. Although the sociologist Emile Durkheim had developed several ways of integrating the empirical with the normative, and Durkheim was obviously influential to at least some early and mid-twentieth-century anthropologists (particularly in France and Great Britain), his work on social norms, law and regulation did not inspire anthropologists in the way his other writings (most notably about religion) did. This anthropological reluctance to consider the problems of normativity (including morality) more robustly was related to the early commitment to a very orthodox – and thus narrow – self-understanding of the discipline as the science of mankind. This meant, among other things, that the range of topics that was understood to fall within the disciplinary rubric was circumscribed by, in the first instance, what could be observed or derived at the empirical level. This is not to say that anthropologists were bound by a rigid Humean empiricism or that they engaged in debates over the accuracy of sense perceptions, but there was a general agreement that certain aspects of the human experience were clearly outside the empirical – even understood broadly – and therefore beyond the anthropological pale. The normative was only accessible to anthropologists as scientists as second-order phenomena, for example, when underlying values were eventually codified into legal codes. And, even here, what was accessible was not the nature or meaning of the values as norms themselves, but rather their expression within observable forms of legal or political practice. The later disciplinary auto-critique, in which the scientific self-understanding was nearly problematised out of existence, did not bring anthropology any closer to developing alternative frameworks for apprehending and conceptualising the normative. If anything, the possibility of developing such new approaches was made even more unlikely, especially since much of the new critical anthropology was devoted to destabilising just the kind of generalised social theory – beyond the theory of critique itself – that is necessary in order to create an alternative framework to the normative that synthesises empirical and, say, philosophical epistemologies.

But, as we saw through the illustrative sounding from contemporary Bolivia, the consequences of this epistemological myopia for anthropology have been profound. And, I would argue, the consequences have been equally profound for the more general understanding of normativity itself, since the historical absence of anthropology's peculiar forms of methodological and critical engagement from debates over legal subjectivity, human rights and values, among others things, has negatively shaped the way these illusive and largely non-empirical dimensions of the moral imaginary have been (mis)understood. For example, as I have argued elsewhere (Goodale 2006c), many scholars, especially those committed to ethnography and other forms of empirical engagement, have largely misread Bolivia's emergent revolution, one that is unfolding primarily at the level of the moral imagination. An understandable – in light of the intellectual history – obsession with social-structural relations of power within Bolivia and the transnational political-economic structures in which they are embedded has meant, among other things, that the internalised spaces of social change in contemporary Bolivia have been ignored in favour of what is believed to be a more concrete and fundamental, reality. Indigenous Bolivians might be thinking of themselves in profoundly different ways, this dominant line of reasoning goes, including as citizens of a new global community of human rights bearers. But all of this is framed as a kind of superstructural gloss that obscures the more basic relations of economic and social power. What about poverty? Rates of literacy? Infant mortality? The problem of domestic violence? These are understood as the real sites of struggle, the real indicators of either social transformation or inertia.

Looking forward, I would argue that a new synthesis can be envisioned that would allow anthropology to make different kinds of contributions to understanding the role and meaning of the normative in social life. It brings together insights from the empirical, critical and philosophical traditions in a way that creates new possibilities for the anthropology of normativity, but it is really directed beyond disciplinary debates, especially since the underlying stakes involved are so consequential for many social actors for whom the practice of normativity goes to the heart of many basic struggles over identity, meaning and even the sustainability of life itself. I would describe this synthesis, or potential ordering principle, as the anthropology of ethical practice. As I have already explained, ethical practices are locations on a broader spectrum of normativity in which conceptually and ontologically illusive values are given different forms of expression in practice. These expressions could take the form of legal processes, debates over morality, arguments about the relationship between culture and human rights, and so on; what is most important is that those most basic frameworks of subjectivity, values, are rendered or actualised in a way that can be apprehended for analytical, political or other purposes. The key problem – and point of intervention – revolves around apprehension: if values rendered as ethical practices provide a window into the what Jantzen and others have also described as the 'moral imaginary', how is one to gain access to them? What does (or might) 'apprehension' mean in this context?

The first point to remember is that values without ethical practices are, in a sense, incomplete, but so are ethical practices taken in isolation, as a kind of fact that is susceptible to empirical study. In other words, I am making a claim that is both ontological and methodological at the same time. Values and ethical practices do not exist in a kind of linear relationship; rather, they are what I shall call 'co-instantiative'.

They exist, that is to say, in their co-instantiation, their co-expression. And, since values, as such, cannot be expressed except through ethical practices, we must think of them ontologically in a way that does not give priority to either location on the normativity spectrum. To make the idea of co-instantiation the core of an anthropology of ethical practice is necessarily to owe a debt to other scholars of social practice, especially Habermas, who has articulated several similar theories of what we might call communicative normative action. In his monumental study of law and democracy, for example, Habermas (1996) examines law through what he calls 'co-original' systems of both knowledge and action (and public and private autonomy), systems that, while distinct, coexist in that communicative realm in which social categories (ideally) are given both legitimacy and potentiality. But the co-originality thesis is too dichotomous for my purposes here: co-instantiation is a way of theorising the relationship between values and ethical practices that avoids having to make this conceptual distinction without giving up the ability to make other, more fruitful ones, for example, between the internalised nature of individual moral identity and the social nature of morality (another form of ethical practice).

And, finally (and more pragmatically), how would an anthropologist translate this idea into her own professional practice? How does one – methodologically – encounter this moment in which values and ethical practices are co-expressed? There is obviously an important empirical dimension to this process, one for which conventional ethnography is happily well placed. But, since ethical practices are examined in part as they co-instantiate values as well, how are the meaning and contours of these values to be read through these practices? Here it is necessary for the anthropologist to retreat, in a sense, into her own moral imaginary, without retreating so far that she is forced to simply assert (or deduce) the meaning and contours of the particular values. I envision this, again, methodologically, as a kind of non-philosophical critique or process of sustained reflection, one that is informed by everything the anthropologist knows about the broader social context in which normativity plays itself out. In other words, ethnography is not nearly enough, since the kind of internalised dynamics that form such an important part of normativity are beyond the scope of direct perception; yet this fact should not then necessarily lead us to either escape into various metaphysical approaches to normativity or simply to wait for the second- and third-order empirical dimensions of it to emerge. Rather, the anthropology of ethical practice calls for the projection of the analytical imagination in a way that captures the complicated in-betweenness of the values/ethical practice relationship.

In many ways, an epistemological language does not yet exist that would allow us to describe these normative spaces with any degree of precision. But anthropologists – like the contributors to this volume – who are turning to problems of morality, rights and values with renewed interest and creativity are in a good position to help build such an analytical grammar.

Notes

1. Even though Bidney's efforts to establish a proper – meaning informed by the criteria of an essentially deductive contemporary philosophy – theoretical anthropology modelled on those titans of *reine Vernunft* came to naught, his willingness to abandon the need for ethnography seemed to open the epistemological floodgates, so that a journal like *Anthropology and Humanism*, which has been associated with students of Bidney like Bruce Grindal and Dennis Warren, now features all manner of experimental writing, including poetry, some of which has a difficult time passing for either poetry or anthropology.
2. As I have argued elsewhere (Goodale 2009a), it is questionable whether the earlier founding of Cultural Survival, Inc. (1972) by the anthropologist David Maybury-Lewis and his wife Pia was a first sign of the realignment that was to begin about fifteen years later. Even though CS later focused its work on behalf of indigenous peoples through a human rights lens, its earlier organisational statements point to other grounds for justifying action.
3. This description is not meant to be self-consciously naive, but rather to signal that 'neoliberalism' is actually a much more complicated problem than indicated by its elevation into the pantheon of apparently self-evident propositions – like Globalisation – that are too obvious now to even mention. In Bolivia, neoliberalism is almost universally used as a simple historical marker, a way of describing a moment in the recent Bolivian past that has either run its course – as Postero (2006) argues – or which continues to characterise at least some aspects of post-2005 Bolivia. As I argue in this chapter, what is best understood as the discourse of neoliberalism in Bolivia (a discourse that includes the vigorous critique of it – both within and outside the country) obscures more than it reveals about Bolivia's actually existing emergent revolution.
4. There is, of course, in fact a two-step process here that I gloss over in this description. Bolivia first ratified a series of important international human rights instruments (ILO 169 in 1991 (the third country to do so after Norway and Mexico) and CEDAW in 1990) and then 'reglemented' them by converting them into domestic law, a process that left the frameworks more or less intact. After *reglementación*, the Bolivian government went further (more steps) by creating new ministries and vice-ministries that were charged with ensuring that the spirit of, say, CEDAW was followed through a series of ever more specific steps, like the establishment of legal clinics – the *Servicios Legales Integrales*, or SLIs – that were meant to provide a resource for women victims of domestic violence-cum-human rights abuses.
5. I realise that this joining of Rorty's idea of social hope with the more utopian social hope that was supposed to flow from the inevitability of dialectical materialism can only be ironic, since Rorty himself would be horrified to see his 'postmodernist bourgeois liberalism' associated with a social vision that would be considered

fundamentally opposed to it. But I'm sure the great ironist would not mind this jarring identification, especially since he has made a career of developing his many profound insights in part by juxtaposing the idea systems of others in often unexpected ways, often against their wills!

6. And to talk about the normative is simply a way to describe any (or all) of this continuum between values and ethical practice.

7. As I have done even within this chapter, the moral is also a perfectly acceptable way of describing points anywhere east of values on this spectrum.

REFERENCES

Abu-Lughod, L. 1999 [1986]. *Veiled Sentiments: Honor and Poetry in a Bedouin Society.* Berkeley: University of California Press.

Allen, N.J. 1998 'Louis Dumont (1911–1998)'. *JASO* 29(1): 1–4.

Amnesty International. 1993. *PAPUA NEW GUINEA "Under the Barrel of a Gun" – Bougainville 1991–1993.* AI Index: ASA 34/05/93.

_____. 1997a. *Bougainville – International Action Essential as Violations Continue.* AI Index: ASA 34/03/97.

_____. 1997b. *Papua New Guinea: Bougainville: The Forgotten Human Rights Tragedy* AI Index: ASA 34/01/97.

Anand, S.A. and P. Chandra. 2001. 'Adoption Laws: Need for Reform'. *Economic and Political Weekly* 21 September: 3891–93.

Appadurai, A. 1996. *Modernity at Large: Cultural Dimensions of Globalization.* Minneapolis and St Paul: Minnesota Press.

Ariés, P. 1962. *Centuries of Childhood.* Harmondsworth: Penguin Books.

Aristotle: *Poetics* (transl. by Butcher, S.H.), http://classics.mit.edu/Aristotle/poetics.html (accessed 23 October 2005).

Aronsson, J. 1999. 'Homosex in Hanoi? Sex, the Public Sphere, and Public Sex', in W. Leap. (ed.) *Public Sex/Gay Space.* New York: Columbia University Press, pp. 203–23

Artaud, A. 1988. 'The Theatre of Cruelty', in S. Sontag (ed.) *Selected Writings of Antonin Artaud.* Berkeley: Berkeley University Press pp. 242–51.

Auer-Falk, N. 1990. 'Exemplary Donors of the Pali Tradition', in Sizemore, R.F. and D.K. Swearer (eds) *Ethics, Wealth and Salvation. A Study in Buddhist Social Ethics.* University of South Carolina Press pp. 124–43.

Australian Parliamentary Delegation. 1994. *Bougainville: A Pacific Solution Report of the Visit by the Australian Paliamentary Delegation to Bougainville.* Canberra: Australian Government Publishing Service.

Barnes, R.H., D. De Coppet and R.J. Parkin (eds). 1985. *Contexts and Levels: Anthropological Essays on Hierarchy.* Oxford: *JASO*.

Battistella, E.L.1990. *Markedness: The Evaluative Superstructure of Language.* Albany: State University of New York Press.

Bauman, Z. 1988. *Freedom.* Minneapolis: University of Minnesota Press.

Baumard N. and D. Sperber. 2007. 'La Morale', *Terrain* 48 : 5–12.

BBC. 1999. 'World: Asia-Pacific Saving Vietnam's Youth'. 12 January.

Beattie, J. 1964. *Other Cultures.* London: Routledge and Paul.

Beidelman, T.O. 1993. *Moral Imagination in Kaguru Modes of Thought.* Washington: Smithsonian Institution Press

Bélanger, D, Khuat Thi Hai Oanh, Liu Jianye, Le Thanh Thui and Pham Viet Thanh 2003. 'Are Sex Rations at Birth Increasing in Vietnam?' *Population-E* 58 (2): 231–50.

Bélanger, D. and Khuat Thu Hong. 1996. *Youth, Premarital Sexuality, and Abortion in Hanoi Region*. Hanoi: UNFPA.

Bidney, D. 1953. *Theoretical Anthropology*. New York: Columbia University Press.

Biesele, M. 1997. 'An Ideal of Unassisted Birth: Hunting, Healing, and Transformation among the Kalahari Ju/'hoansi', in R.E. Davis-Floyd and C.F. Sargent (eds), *Childbirth and Authoritative Knowledge. Cross-Cultural Perspectives*. Berkeley: University of California Press. pp. 474–92.

Binyon, M. 1983. *Life in Russia*. Hamilton.

Bizot, F. and F. Lagirarde. 1996. *La Pureté par les mots*. Bangkok: Ecole Française d'Extrême Orient.

Blake, W. 1975. *The Marriage of Heaven and Hell*. Oxford: Oxford University Press

Bodenhorn, B. 1988. 'Whales, Souls Children and Other Things that are Good to Share: Core Metaphors in a Contemporary Whaling Society'. *Cambridge Anthropology* 13: 1–19.

Borenstein, E. 1999. 'Suspending Disbelief: "Cults" and Postmodernism in Post-Soviet Russia', in A.M. Barker (ed.) *Consuming Russia: Popular Culture, Sex, and Society since Gorbachev*. Durham: Duke University Press.

Boundteun, A. 2003. *Khu mue gantheetsanaa lueang phaventsandoon* (Handbook for the chanting of the Vessantara story). Unpublished manuscript. Vientiane [in Lao].

_____. 2004. '*Vetsandoon gap sivit khun lao*' (Vessantara and his Relation to the Life of the Lao). unpublished manuscript. Vientiane [in Lao].

Bourdieu, P. 1991. *Language and Symbolic Power*. Cambridge: Harvard University Press.

_____. 1992. *The Logic of Practice*. Cambridge: Polity Press.

Bowie, F. (ed.). 2004. *Cross-Cultural Approaches to Adoption*. London: Routledge.

Bradley, A.C. 1950. *Oxford Lectures on Poetry*. London: Macmillan.

Brady, I. (ed.). 1976. *Transactions in Kinship: Adoption and Fosterage in Oceani*. ASAO Monograph 4. Honolulu: University of Hawaii Press.

Brown, S.D. 2002. 'Michel Serres – Science, Translation and the Logic of the Parasite', *Theory, Culture and Society*. 19(3) pp. 1–27.

Brubaker, R. 1984. *The Limits of Rationality: An Essay on the Social and Moral Thought of Max Weber*. London: Routledge.

Bruner, E.M. 1986. 'Experience and Its Expressions', in V. Turner and E. Bruner. (eds). *The Anthropology of Experience*. Urbana: University of Illinois Press.

Burman, E. 1996. 'Local, Global or Globalized? Child Development and International Child Rights Legislation'. *Childhood* (3): 45–66.

Butler, J. 1997. *The Psychic Life of Power*. Stanford: Stanford University Press.

_____. 2003. *Kritik der ethischen Gewalt*. Adorno Vorlesung 2002. Frankfurt: Suhrkamp Verlag

_____. 2004. *Undoing Gender*. New York and London: Routledge.

Caiani-Praturlon, G. 1991. 'Adoption in a Framework of Child Welfare Legislation', in E.D. Hibbs (ed.) *Adoption: International Perspectives*. Madison: International Universities Press.

Cameron, D. and D. Kulick. 2003. *Language and Sexuality*. Cambridge: Cambridge University Press.

Carrithers, M. 1992. *Why Humans Have Cultures: Explaining Anthropology and Social Diversity*. Oxford: Oxford University Press.

_____. 2005. 'Anthropology as a Moral Science of Possibilities'. *Current Anthropology* 46 (3): 433–56.

Carroll, V. (ed.). 1970. *Adoption in Eastern Oceania*. ASAO Monograph 1. Honolulu: University of Hawaii Press.

Carsten, J. 1991. 'Children in Between: Fostering and the Process of Kinship on Pulau Langkawi, Malaysia', *Man* (NS) 26: 425–43.

Carsten, J. 2004. *After Kinship.* Cambridge: Cambridge University Press.

Caruth, C. 1996. *Unclaimed Experience: Trauma, Narrative, and History.* Baltimore: Johns Hopkins University Press

Chamberlain, M. (Producer). 2001. *Coconut Revolution.* London: Stampede Films.

Clark, J. 1997. 'Imagining the State, or Tribalism and Arts of Memory in the Highlands of Papua New Guinea', in T. Otto and N. Thomas (eds). *Narratives of Nation in the South Pacific.* Amsterdam: Harwood, pp. 65–90.

Clay, B. 1977. *Pinikindu.* Chicago: University of Chicago.

———. 1986. *Mandak Realities.* Piscataway: Rutgers University Press.

———. 1992. 'Other Times Other Places: Agency and the Big Man in Central New Ireland', *Man* (NS) 27: 719–33: 101–11.

Cohen, P.T. 1983. 'A Bodhisattva on Horseback: Buddhist Ethics and Pragmatism in Northern Thailand', *Mankind* 14(2).

Colby, D. 2001. *HIV Knowledge and Risk Factors among Men who Have Sex with Men in Ho Chi Minh City, Vietnam.* Seattle: University of Washington.

Collier, J., M.Z. Rosaldo and S Yanagisako. 1992. "Is There a Family? New Anthropological Views" in B. Thorne and M. Yalom (eds). *Rethinking the Family: Some Feminist Questions.* Boston: Northeastern University Press, pp. 71–91

Collins, S. 1998. *Nirvana and Other Buddhist Felicities. Utopias of the Pali Imaginaire.* Cambridge: Cambridge University Press.

Comaroff, J. and J. Comaroff. 1999. 'Occult Economies and the Violence of Abstraction: Notes from the South African Postcolony', *American Ethnologist* 26: 279–303.

Cone, M. and R. Gombrich. 1977. *Perfect Generosity of Prince Vessantara: A Buddhist Epic.* Oxford: Oxford University Press

Conley, A. 2000. *Child Welfare in a Changing Romania 1989–1999.* Boston: Boston University Senior Theses.

Crapanzano, V. 2004. *Imaginative Horizons: An Essay in Literary-Philosophical Anthropology.* Chicago: University of Chicago Press.

Cunningham, H. 1995. *Children and Childhood in Western Society since 1500.* Harlow: Longmans.

D'Andrade, R. 1995. *The Development of Cognitive Anthropology.* Cambridge: Cambridge University Press.

Das, V. 2001. 'Stigma, Contagion, Defect: Issues in the Anthropology of Public Health'. Paper at the 'Stigma and Global Health Conference', Maryland, USA.

Dear, P. 1995. *Discipline and Experience: The Mathematical Way in the Scientific Revolution.* Chicago: University of Chicago Press

Deleuze, G. and F. Guattari. 2002. *A Thousand Plateaus: Capitalism and Schizophrenia.* London: Continuum.

Dallaire, R. 2003. *Shake Hands with the Devil: the Failure of Humanity in Rwanda.* Toronto: Random House

Demian, M. 2001. 'Disputing, Damage versus Disputing Ownership in Suau', in L. Kalinoe and J. Leach (eds) *Rationales of Ownership.* New Delhi: UBS Publishers.

———. 2004a. 'Transacting in Rights, Transacting in Children: a View of Adoption in Papua New Guinea', in F. Bowie, F. (ed.) *Cross-Cultural Approaches to Adoption.* London: Routledge.

———. 2004b. 'Custom in the Courtroom, Law in the Village: Legal Transformation in Papua New Guinea', *Journal of the Royal Anthropological Institute* 9.

Derrida, J. 1992. *Deconstruction and the Possibility of Justice.* New York: Routledge.

———. 1996. *The Gift of Death.* Chicago: Chicago University Press.

Desjarlais, R. 1997. *Shelter Blues: Sanity and Selfhood Among the Homeless.* Philadelphia: University of Pennsylvania Press.

'Dilemma Seventy-first. Vessantara's Giving'. in *The Questions of King Milinda*, [1890] translated by T.W. Rhys Davids, Sacred Books of the East, Vol. 35/36 http://www. sacredtexts.com/bud/sbe36/sbe3606.htm#fn_292 [accessed 20 October 2005].

Do Thi Ninh Xuan. 1997. 'To Prevent and Combat Social Evils: A Contribution to Women's Progress.', in Le Thi and Do Thi Binh (eds). *Ten Years of Progress: Vietnamese Women from 1985 to 1995*, pp. 287–97. Hanoi: Women's Publishing House.

Douglas, M. 1991. *Purity and Danger: An Analysis of the Concepts of Pollution and Taboo*. London: Routledge.

Dumont, L. 1977 *From Mandeville to Marx: The Genesis and Triumph of Economic Ideology*. Chicago: University of Chicago Press.

_____. 1979. 'The Anthropological Community and Ideology', *Social Science Information* 18 (6): 785–817.

_____. 1980. *Homo Hierarchicus: The Caste System and its Implications*, transl. M. Sainsbury, L. Dumont and B. Gulati, Chicago: University of Chicago Press.

_____. 1985. *Essais sur l'individualisme. Une perspective anthropologique sur l'idéologie moderne*. Paris: Seuil.

_____. 1986 *Essays on Individualism: Modern Ideology in Anthropological Perspective*. Chicago: University of Chicago Press.

Durkheim, E. 1953 [1906]. *Sociology and Philosophy*. London : Routledge

_____. 1973. *Moral Education: A Study in the Theory and Application of the Sociology of Education*. New York: Free Press.

Edel, A. 1962. Anthropology and Ethics in Common Focus. *Journal of the Royal Anthropological Institute* 92: 55–92.

Edel, M. and A. Edel. 1968 [1959]. *Anthropology and Ethics. The Quest for Moral Understanding*. Cleveland: The Press of Case Western Reserve University.

Efroymson, D., V.P.N. Thanh and N.Q. Trang. 1997. *Confusions and Contradictions: Results of Qualitative Research on Youth Sexuality*. Programme for Appropriate Technology in Health Canada.

Egge, J. 2002. *Religious Giving and the Invention of Karma in Theravada Buddhism*. Richmond, Surrey: RoutledgeCurzon.

Eisenstadt, S.N. 1982. 'The Axial Age: the Emergence of Transcendental Visions and the Rise of the Clerics'. *Archives Européennes de Sociologie* 23 (2): 294–314.

Elster, J. 1999. *Strong Feelings, Emotion, Addiction and Human Behaviour*. Cambridge: MIT Press.

Etkind, A.M. 1996. 'Psychological Culture', in D.N. Shalin (ed.) *Russian Culture at the Crossroads: Paradoxes of Postcommunist Consciousness*. Boulder: Westview Press.

Evans, G. 1998. *The Politics of Ritual and Remembrance – Laos since 1975*. Honolulu: University of Hawai'i Press.

Fabian, J. 1983. *Time and the Other*. New York: Columbia University Press.

Faubion, J. 2001a. *The Shadows and Lights of Waco: Millennialism Today*. Princeton: Princeton University Press.

_____. 2001b. 'Toward an Anthropology of Ethics: Foucault and the Pedagogies of Autopoiesis', *Representations* 74: 83–104.

Ferguson, J. 1999. *Expectations of Modernity: Myths and Meaning of Urban Life on the Zambian Copper Belt*. Berkeley: University of California Press.

_____. 2006. *Global Shadows: Africa in the Neoliberal World Order*. Durham: Duke University Press.

Filer, C. 1990. 'The Bougainville Rebellion, the Mining Industry, and the Process of Social Distintegration in Papua New Guinea', *Canberra Anthropology* 13(1):1–39.

Formoso, B. 1992. 'Le bun pha w:et des Laos du nord-est de la Thaïlande', *BEFEO* 79(2): 233–60.

Foster, R. 1995. *History and Social Reproduction in a Melanesian Society.* Cambridge: Cambridge University Press.

———. 2002. 'Bargains with Modernity in Papua New Guinea and Elsewhere', in B. Knauft (ed.) *Critically Modern.* Bloomington, Indiana: University of Indiana Press.

Foucault, M. 1978. *The History of Sexuality,* Vol. 1. Harmondsworth: Penguin Books.

———. 1980. 'Truth and power', in *Power/Knowledge: Selected Interviews and Other Writings 1972–1977,* ed. C. Gordon. New York: Pantheon Books.

———. 1984. *The Foucault Reader,* ed. P. Rabinow. New York: Pantheon Books.

———. 1988. 'Two Technologies of the Self', in M.L. Luther, H. Gutman and P. H. Hutton (eds) *Technologies of the Self: A Seminar with Michel Foucault.* London: Tavistock, pp. 16–49.

———. 1991. 'Governmentality'. In G. Burrell, C. Gordon and P. Miller (eds) *The Foucault effect: Studies in Governmentality.* London: Harvester/Wheatsheaf.

———. 1997. *Ethics,* ed. P. Rabinow. London: Penguin Books.

Fournier, M. 2005. *Marcel Mauss.* Princeton: Princeton University Press

Franklin, B. 2000. *Expanding Horizons: Changing Gender Roles in Vietnam.* Hanoi: Women's Publishing House.

———. (ed.) 2002. *The Handbook of Children's Rights: Comparative Policy and Practice.* London: Routledge.

Gabaude, L. 1991. 'Controverses modernes autour du Vessantara-Jataka', *Cahiers de l'Asie du Sud-Est.* 29/30: 51–73.

———. 2003. *'Le don ou dana comme fenêtre sur les mentalités bouddhistes thaïes',* paper presented at the conference 'Buddhist Legacies in Southeast Asia'. Bangkok : Ecole française d'Extrême-Orient.

Gailey, C. 1999a. 'Seeking Baby Right: Race, Class, and Gender in US International Adoption', in M. Dalen, A.-L. Rygvold and B. Saetersdal (eds). *Mine- your - ours and theirs: Adoption, changing kinship and family patterns.* Oslo: University of Oslo Press.

———. 1999b. 'Rethinking Child Labour in an Age of Capitalist Restructuring', *Critique of Anthropology,* 19 (2): 115–19.

Gammeltoft, T and Nguyen Minh Thang. 2000. *Our Love Has No Limits.* Hanoi: Nha Xuat Ban Thanh Nien.

Ganes, M. ed. 1992. *The Radical Sociology of Durkheim and Mauss.* London. Routledge.

Geertz, C. 1973. *The Interpretation of Cultures.* New York: Basic Books.

———. 1984. 'Anti Anti-Relativism', *American Anthropologist* (NS) 86:2: 263–78.

———. 1985. *Local Knowledge. Further Essays in Interpretative Anthropology.* New York: Basic Books

———. 1986. 'Making Experience, Authoring Selves', in V. Turner and E. Bruner (eds). *The Anthropology of Experience.* Urbana: University of Illinois Press

———. 2005[1972]. 'Deep Play: Notes on the Balinese Cockfight', *Daedalus* 134(4): 56–86.

Gell, A. 1998. *Art and Agency: an Anthropological Theory.* Oxford: Clarendon Press.

Gender Education Group. 1996. *Results of Group Interviews with Youth on Reproductive Health Issues in Da Lat, Nha Trang, Da Nang, and Ho Chi Minh City.* Hanoi: Institute of Sociology.

Gershon, I. 2003. 'Knowing Adoption and Adopting Knowledge', *American Ethnologist* 30 (30): 438–46.

Gibson, A. 1999. *Postmodernity, Ethics and the Novel. From Leavis to Levinas.* London and New York: Routledge.

Giddens, A. 1991. *Modernity and Self Identity: Self and Society in the Late Modern Age.* Stanford: Stanford University Press.

Gillis, J. 1996. *A World of their Own Making: Myths, Ritual and the Quest for Family.* Cambridge: Harvard University Press.

Gluckman, M. 1955. *The Judicial Process Amongst the Barotse of Northern Rhodesia*. Manchester: Manchester University Press.

_____. 1963. *Order and Rebellion in Tribal Society*. London: Cohen and West.

Godelier, M. 1999. *The Enigma of the Gift*. transl. Nora Scott. Chicago: University of Chicago Press.

Goffman, E. 1963. *Stigma: Notes on the Management of Spoiled Identity*. Englewood Cliffs: Prentice Hall.

Gombrich, R.F. 1995 [1971]. *Buddhist Precept and Practice. Traditional Buddhism in the Rural Highlands of Ceylon*. London and New York: Kegan Paul.

Goodale, M. 2006a. 'Toward a Critical Anthropology of Human Rights', *Current Anthropology* 47(3): 485–511.

_____. 2006b. 'Ethical Theory as Social Practice'. *American Anthropologist* 108 (1): 25–37.

_____. 2006c 'Reclaiming Modernity: Indigenous Cosmopolitanism and the Coming of the Second Revolution in Bolivia'. *American Ethnologist* 33(4): 634–49.

_____. 2009a. Surrendering to *Utopia*: The Anthropology of Human Rights. Stanford: Stanford University Press.

_____. 2009b. *Dilemmas of Modernity: Bolivian Encounters with Law and Liberalism*. Stanford: Stanford University Press.

Goody, E. 1982. *Parenthood and Social Reproduction: Fostering and Occuptional Roles in West Africa*. Cambridge: Cambridge University Press.

Goody, J. 1969. 'Adoption in Cross Cultural Perspective', *Comparative Studies in Society and History* 11: 55–78.

_____. 1995. *The Expansive Moment: African Anthropology in Britain 1918–1970*. Cambridge: Cambridge University Press.

Gregory, C.A. 1982. *Gifts and Commodities*. London: Academic Press.

_____. 2004. *Savage Money*. London: Harwood.

Habermas, J. 1996. *Between Facts and Norms: Contributions to a Discourse Theory of Law and Democracy*. Cambridge, MA: MIT Press.

Hallisey, C. and Hansen, A. 1996. 'Narrative, Sub-ethics, and the Moral Life. Some Evidence from Theravada Buddhism', *Journal of Religious Ethics*, 24 (2): 305–28.

Hallisey, C. 1996. 'Ethical Particularism in Theravada Buddhism'. *Journal of Buddhist Ethics* 4(1).

Harris, C. 2004. *Control and Subversion: Gender Relations in Tajikistan*. London: Pluto Press.

Hauschild, Th. 2005. 'Ethos and Ethics'. Conference paper presented at the Max Planck Institute Conference 'Rethinking Moralities', 15–16 December 2005.

Heim, M. 2003. 'The Aesthetics of Excess', *Journal of the American Academy of Religion* 71 (3): 531–54.

Helleiner, J. 2003. 'The Politics of Traveller "Child Begging" in Ireland', *Critique of Anthropology* 23 (1): 11–34.

Hewlett, B.S. 1991. *Intimate Fathers: the Nature and Context of Aka Pygmy Paternal Infant Care*. Ann Arbor: University of Michigan Press.

Hibbets, M. 2000. 'The Ethics of Esteem', *Journal of Buddhist Ethics*, Vol. 7(1).

Hollis, M. and S. Lukes eds. 1982. *Rationality and Relativism*. Oxford: Blackwell.

Howell, S. 1997a. 'Introduction', in S. Howell. (ed.) *The Ethnography of Moralities*. London: Routledge, pp. 1–22.

_____. ed. 1997b. *The Ethnography of Moralities*. London: Routledge

_____. 2003a. 'The Diffusion of Moral Values in a Global Perspective', in Th. H. Eriksen (ed.) *Globalization: Studies in Anthropology*. London: Pluto Press.

_____. 2003b. 'Kinning: Creating Life-trajectories in Adoptive Families', *Journal of the Royal Anthropological Institute* (N.S.) 9 (3): 465–84.

_____. 2006a. *The Kinning of Foreigners: Transnational Adoption in a Global Perspective*. Oxford and New York: Berghahn Books.

_____. 2006b. 'Changing Moral Values about the Family: Adoption Legislation in Norway and the US'. *Social Analysis*, 50 (3): 146–63.

Humphrey, C. 1997. 'Exemplars and Rules', in S. Howell (ed.) *The Ethnography of Moralities*. London: Routledge, pp. 25–47.

Ingold, T. 2000. *The Perception of the Environment: Essays in Livelihood, Dwelling and Skill*. London: Routledge.

Jantzen, G. 2001. 'Flourishing: Towards an Ethic of Natality', *Feminist Theory* 2 (2): 219–32.

Jaspers, K. 1953. *The Origin and Goal of History*. Transl. M. Bullock. New Haven: Yale University Press.

Johnson, K., H. Banghan and W. Liyao. 1998. 'Infant Abandonment and Adoption in China'. *Population and Development Review* 24 (3): 469–510.

Jory, P. 2002. 'Thai and Western Buddhist Scholarship in the Age of Colonialism: King Chulalongkorn Redefines the Jatakas', *Journal of Asian studies* 61(3).

Kant, I. 1971. *Doctrine of Virtue: Part II of the Metaphysic of Morals*. Philadelphia: University of Pennsylvania Press.

Kaputin, J. 1999. *Crisis in the North Solomons Province: Report of the Special Committee Founded by the National Executive Council*. Honourable J. Kaputin, Chairman. Port Moresby: National Parliament.

Karimov, I. 1992. *Uzbekistan: The Road of Independence and Progress*. Tashkent: Izdatelstvo Uzbekiston.

_____. 1993. *Building the Future: Uzbekistan – Its Own Model for Transition to a Market Economy*. Tashkent: Izdatelstvo Uzbekiston.

_____. 1995. *Uzbekistan: Along the Road of Deepening Economic Reform*. Tashkent: Izdatelstvo Uzbekiston.

_____. 2001. 'Will and Faith: A Test of our Faith', in *Islom ziyosi ozbekim siyimosida* (The Light of Islam in our Uzbek Form), Tashkent: Tashkent Islamic University, pp. 169–82.

Kawamura, L.S. 2004. 'Paramita (Perfection)', in R.E. Buswell (ed.) *MacMillan Encyclopedia of Buddhism*. New York: Macmillan.

Kharkhordin, O. 1999. *The Collective and the Individual in Russia*. Berkeley: University of California Press.

Khuat Thu Hong. 1998. *Study on Sexuality in Vietnam: The Known and Unknown Issues*. Hanoi: Population Council.

Kligman, G. 1992. 'Abortion and International Adoption in Post-Ceausescu Romania'. *Feminist Studies* 18 (2).

_____. 1998. *The Politics of Duplicity: Controlling Reproduction in Ceausescu's Romania*. Berkeley: University of California Press.

Klima, A. 2002. *The Funeral Casino: Meditation, Massacre, and Exchange with the Dead in Thailand*. Princeton: Princeton University Press.

Koret, P. 1996. 'Past and present Lao Perceptions of Traditional Literature', in J. Butler-Diaz (ed.) *New Laos, New Challenges*. Temple, Arizona: Arizona State University Program pp. 109–26.

Koroteyeva, V. and E. Makarova. 1998. 'The Assertion of Uzbek National Identity: Nativization or State-Building Process?' In T. Atabaki and J. O'Kane (eds) *Post-Soviet Central Asia*. London: Tauris Academic Studies.

Kotkin, S. 1995. *Magnetic Mountain: Stalinism as a Civilization*. Berkeley: University of California Press.

_____. 2001. *Armageddon Averted: The Soviet Collapse 1970–2000*. Oxford: Oxford University Press.

Ladwig, P. 2008 'Between Cultural Preservation and This Worldly Commitment: Modernisation, Social Activism and the Lao Buddhist Sangha', in Y. Goudineau and

M. Lorillard (eds) *Nouvelles recherches sur le Laos*. Collection études thématiques. Paris: Ecole Française d'Extrême-Orient pp. 465–90.

Laidlaw, J. 1995. *Riches and Renunciation: Religion, Economy, and Society among the Jains*. Oxford: Oxford University Press.

———. 2002 'For an Anthropology of Ethics and Freedom', *Journal of the Royal Anthropological Institute* 8 (2): 311–32.

Lambek, M. 1996. 'The Past Imperfect: Remembering as Moral Practice'. In P. Antze and M. Lambek (eds) *Past Tense: Cultural Essays in Trauma and Memory*. New York: Routledge pp. 235–54.

———. 2000. 'The Anthropology of Religion and the Quarrel between Poetry and Philosophy'. *Current Anthropology* 41 (3): 309–20.

———. 2002. 'Nuriaty, the Saint and the Sultan: Virtuous Subject and Subjective Virtuoso of the Postmodern Colony'. In R. Werbner (ed.) *Postcolonial Subjectivities in Africa*. London: Zed Books.

Lea, D. 1997. *Melanesian Land Tenure in a Contemporary and Philosophical Context*. Lanham: University Press of America.

Leenhardt, M. 1947. *Do Kamo. La Personne et le Mythe dans le Monde Mélanésien*. Paris : Gallimard

Le Kha Phieu. 2001. *Vietnam Entering the 21st Century: Selected Speeches and Writings of the General Secretary of the Central Committee of the Communist Party of Vietnam*. Hanoi: Gioi Publishers.

Le Thi Nham Tuyet. 1999. *The Role of the Family in the Formation of Vietnamese Personality*. Hanoi: Gioi Publishers.

Lévy-Bruhl, L. 1951 [1911]. *Les fonctions mentales dans les sociétés inférieures*. Paris: PUF.

Ljunggren, B. 1997. 'Vietnam's Second Decade under *doi moi*: Emerging Contradictions in the Reform Process?', in B. Beckman, E. Hansson, and L. Román (eds) *Vietnam: Reform and Transformation*. Conference Proceedings. Stockholm: Center for Pacific Asia Studies p. 9–37.

Lobacheva, N.P. 1989. 'Znachenie obshini v jizni semi (po materialam svadebnoi obriadnosti khoresmskikh yzbekov)', In N. Palagina (ed.) *Etnicheskaya istoria i traditsionnaya kyltura narodov srednei azii i kazakhstana*. Nukus: Izdatescvo Karakalpakistan.

Løgstrup, K. 1989. *Norm und Spontanität. Ethik und Politik zwischen Technik und Dilettantokratie*. Tübingen: Mohr.

———. 1997 *The Ethical Demand*. Notre Dame: University of Notre Dame Press.

Luang phavetsandoon phasa lao – phasa angkit. 2002. (The Story of Vessantara Lao – English), unpublished manuscript., Luang Phrabang [parts in Lao, no author]

Luluaki, J. 1990. 'Customary Family Law in Yangoru: Implication of Legal Pluralism in Papua New Guinean Society'. PhD Dissertation, University of Cambridge.

Luhmann, N. 1990. *Essays on Self-Reference*, New York: Columbia University Press.

MacIntyre, A.C. 1981. *After Virtue: a Study in Moral Theory*. Notre Dame: University of Notre Dame Press.

Mai Thuc. 1997. 'On the Model of Women's Participation in the Fight against Prostitution', in Le Thi and Do Thi Binh (eds) *Ten Years of Progress: Vietnamese Women from 1985 to 1995*. Hanoi: Women's Publishing House.

Malinowska-Sempruch, K., J. Hoover, and A. Alexandrova. 2004. 'Unintended Consequences: Drug Policies Fuel the HIV Epidemic in Russia and Ukraine', in K. Malinowska-Sempruch and S. Gallagher (eds) *War on Drugs, HIV/AIDS and Human Rights*. New York: International Debate Education Association.

Malinowski, B. 1935. *Crime and Custom in Savage Society*. London and New York: Routledge.

_____. 1944. *Freedom and Civilization*. New York: Roy Publishers.

Manderson, M. and P. Liamputtong Rice. 2001. *Coming of Age in South and Southeast Asia: Youth, Courtship, and Sexuality*. Copenhagen: Curzon/NIAS Press.

Marr, D. 1981. *Vietnamese Tradition on Trial 1920–45*. Berkeley: University of California Press.

_____. 1997. 'Vietnamese Youth in the 1990s'. *The Vietnam Review*, 2: 288–354.

Marriage and Family Law No. 22/2000/QH10. 9 June 9 2000. *Official Gazette*, No. 28. 31 July 2000. Hanoi: National Assembly of Vietnam.

Massicard, E. and T. Trevisani. 2003. 'The Uzbek Mahalla: Between State and Society', in *Central Asia: Aspects of Transition* T. Everett-Heath (ed.) New York: Routledge Curzon.

Massumi, B. 2002. 'Translator's Foreword: Pleasures of Philosophy', in G. Deleuze and F. Guattari. *A Thousand Plateaus: Capitalism and Schizophrenia*. London: Continuum pp. ix–xvi.

Mauss, M. 1931. 'La cohésion sociale dans les sociétés polysegmentaires'. Communication presented to the Institut français de sociologie. *Extrait du Bulletin de l'Institut français de sociologie I*. Accessible at URL: http://www.uqac.ca/zone30/Classiques_des_sciences_sociales.

Mauss, M. 1990 [1925]. *The Gift*. London: Routledge.

McKinnon, S. and S. Franklin. 2001. *Relative Values: Reconfiguring Kinship Studies*. Durham and London. Duke University Press.

McNally, S. 2003. '*Bia Om* and Karaoke: HIV and Everyday Life in Urban Vietnam', in L. Drummond and M. Thomas (eds.) *Consuming Urban Culture in Contemporary Vietnam*. London: Routledge Curzon, pp. 110–23

Melosh, B. 2002. *Strangers and Kin: The American Way of Adoption*. Cambridge: Harvard University Press.

Mensch, B S., W.H. Clark and Dang Nguyen Anh. 2002. *Premarital Sex in Vietnam: Is the Current Concern with Adolescent Reproductive Health Warranted?* Working Papers, No. 163. Population Council, Policy Research Division.

Miller, P. and N. Rose. 1991. 'Governing Economic Life', in G. Burchell, C. Gordeon and P. Miller (eds) *The Foucault Effect: Studies in Governmentality*. London: Harvester/Wheatsheaf.

Modell, J. 1994. *Kinship with Strangers Adoption and Interpretations of Kinship in American Culture*. Berkeley: University of California Press.

_____. 1998. 'Rights to the Children: Foster Care and Social Reproduction in Hawai'i', in S. Franklin and H. Ragoné (eds) *Reproducing Reproduction: Kinship, Power and Technological Innovation*. Philadelphia: University of Pennsylvania Press.

Moody-Adams, M. 1997. *Fieldwork in Familiar Places: Morality, Culture and Philosophy*. Cambridge: Harvard University Press.

Moryakova, E. 1998. 'Mahallah: the Traditional Muslim Neighbourhood Community in the Development of Uzbek Civil Society'. In D. Dornish, P. Elvin and R. Kania (eds) *Post-Communist Transformations: A New Generation of Perspectives*. Warsaw: IfiS Publishers.

Mosko, M. 2000. 'Inalienable Ethnography: Giving While Keeping and the Trobriand Case', *Journal of the Royal Anthropological Institute* 6 (3): 377–96.

Nash, J. 1974. 'Matriliny and Modernisation: The Nagovisi of South Bougainville'. Canberra and Port Moresby: *New Guinea Research Bulletin* 31.

Ngo Thi Ngan Binh. 2004. 'The Confucian Four Feminine Virtues (*tu duc*)', in L. Drummond and H. Rydstrøm (eds) *Gender Practices in Contemporary Vietnam*. Singapore: Singapore University Press, pp. 47–74.

Nguyen Khac Vien. 1975. 'Confucianism and Marxism in Vietnam'. In D. Marr and J. Werner (eds) *Tradition and Revolution in Vietnam*. Berkeley: Indochina Resources Center pp. 15–52.

Nguyen-vo Thu-huong. 1998. 'Governing the Social: Prostitution and the Question of Liberal Governance in Vietnam during Marketization'. Doctoral Dissertation, University of California, Irvine.

Nietzsche, F. 1994. *On the Genealogy of Morality*, transl. C. Diethe. Cambridge: Cambridge University Press.

Nussbaum, M.C. 1998. Morality and emotions, in E. Craig (ed.) *Routledge Encyclopedia of Philosophy online-edition*, http://www.geocities.com/Athens/Rhodes/3724/Cytrix/cdrom5/Routledge_morality_emotion.htm (accessed 19 September 2005).

———. 2001. *Upheavals of Thought*. Cambridge: Cambridge University Press

Obeyesekere, G. 1981. *Medusa's Hair: An Essay on Personal Symbols and Religious Experience*. Chicago: University of Chicago Press.

Ogan, E. 1972. 'Business and Cargo: Socio-economic Change among the Nasioi of Bougainville'. *New Guinea Research Bulletin* No. 44. Port Moresby and Canberra: Institute for Applied Social and Economic Research.

———. 1999. 'The Bougainville Conflict: Perspectives from Nasioi'. *Technical Report Discussion Paper 99/3, State, Society and Governance in Melanesia Project, RSPAS, ANU.*

Ogan, E. 2001. 'The Nasioi of Papua New Guinea', in J. Fitzpatrick. (ed.) *Endangered Peoples of Oceania: Struggles to Survive and Thrive*. Santa Barbara: Greenwood Press, pp. 106–21.

Ohnuma, R. 1997. 'Dehadana: The 'Gift of the Body' in Indian Buddhist Narrative Literature'. PhD dissertation, University of Michigan.

———. 2004. 'Jataka', in R.E. Buswell (ed.) *MacMillan Encyclopedia of Buddhism*. New York: Macmillan pp. 400–1.

———. 2005. 'Gift', in D.S. Lopez (ed.) *Critical terms for the study of Buddhism*. Chicago: Chicago University Press pp. 103–23.

Ojo, O. 1990. 'Understanding Human Rights in Africa', In J. Berting et. al. (eds) *Human Rights in a Pluralistic World: Individuals and Collectivities*. London: Meckler Westport.

Oliver, D. 1937. *A Solomon Island Society*. Cambridge: Harvard University Press.

———. 1990. *Black Islanders*. Melbourne: Hyland House.

Ong, A. 1997. *Flexible Citizenship*. Chapel Hill: Duke University Press.

Ortner, S. 1973. 'On Key Symbols', *American Anthropologist* 75 (5): 1338–46.

Ott, K. 2001. *Moralbegründungen. Zur Einführung*. Hamburg: Junius.

Oushakine, S.A. 2004. 'The Flexible and the Pliant: Disturbed Organisms of Soviet Modernity', *Cultural Anthropology* 19 (3).

Pacific Islands Development Programme Report. 2002. 'Bougainville Wins Praise from UN in Peace Deal', in *Pacific Islands Report*. Honolulu, Hawaii: East–West Center.

Panther-Brick, C. 2000. 'Nobody's Children? A Reconsideration of Child Abandonment', in C. Panther-Brick and M.T. Smith (eds) *Abandoned Children*. Cambridge: Cambridge University Press.

Parish, S. M. 1994. *Moral Knowing in a Hindu Sacred City: An Exploration of Mind, Emotion, and Self*. New York: Columbia University Press.

Paxson, M. 2005. *Solovyovo: The Story of Memory in a Russian Village*. Bloomington: Indiana University Press.

Penn, H. 2002. 'The World Bank's View of Early Childhood', *Childhood* 9 (1): 118–32.

Pesmen, D. 2000. *Russia and Soul*. Ithaca: Cornell University Press.

Phan Thi Vang Anh and Pham Thu Thuy. 2003. 'Let's Talk about Love', in L. Drummond and M. Thomas (eds) *Consuming Urban Culture in Contemporary Vietnam*. London: Routledge Curzon, pp. 202–19.

Pharo, P. 2004. *Morale et sociologie, le sens et les valeurs entre nature et culture*. Paris: Gallimard.

Polomka, R.1990. *Bougainville: Perspectives on a Crisis*. Canberra: Research School of Pacific Studies, Australian National University.

Population Council. 1997. *A Study of Vietnamese Youth's Decision Making for Health and HIV/AIDS Prevention in Kien Giang and Quang Ninh Provinces*. Hanoi: Population Council

Postero, N. 2006. *Now We Are Citizens: Indigenous Politics in Postmulticultural Bolivia*. Stanford: Stanford University Press.

Potter, S.H. 1988. 'The Cultural Construction of Emotion in Rural Chinese Social Life', *Ethos* 16 (2): 181–208.

Quan Le Nga. 2000. *Communication and Advocacy Strategies: Adolescents' Reproductive and Sexual Health*. Hanoi: UNFPA.

Rajavaramuni, P. 1990 'Foundations of Buddhist Social Ethics', in R.F. Sizemore and D.K. Swearer (eds) *Ethics, Wealth and Salvation. A Study in Buddhist Social Ethics*. Columbia: University of South Carolina Press pp. 35–43.

Rasanayagam, J. 2002. 'Spheres of Communal Participation: Placing the State within Local Modes of Interaction in Rural Uzbekistan', *Central Asian Survey* 21: 55–70.

Rassudova, R. 1969. 'Zanyatiya naceleniya'. In G. Vasileva and B. Karmisheva (eds) *Etnograficheskie Ocherki Uzbekskovo Selskovo Nacelenia*. Moscow: Nayka.

Reagan, T. 1996. *The Bougainville Conflict Origins and Development, Main Actors, and Strategies for its Resolution*. Port Moresby: Faculty of Law, University of Papua New Guinea.

Reed-Danahay, D. 1986. *Education and Identity in Rural France: the Politics of Schooling*. Cambridge: Cambridge University Press.

Reinhorn, M. 2001. *Dictionnaire laotien–français*. Paris: Librairie You-Feng.

Retta, M. 2001. *On the Rights of the Child*. Addis Ababa: Federal Supreme Court Juvenile Justice Programme (1), pp. 9–10, 28–31.

Richards, A. 1936. 'Mother-right Among the Central Bantu', in E.E. Evans-Pritchard, R. Firth, B. Malinowski and I. Schapera (eds) *Essays Presented to C.G. Seligman*. London: Kegan Paul and Trench, Trubner and Company pp. 267–80.

Richards, P.1996. *Fighting for the Rainforest: War, Youth and Resources in Sierra Leone*. London: International African Institute.

Ricoeur, P. 1988. *Zeit und Erzählung*, Vol. 1. Munich: Wilhelm Fink.

———. 1991. *Zeit und Erzählung*. Vol. 3. Munich: Wilhelm Fink.

Ries, N. 1997. *Russian Talk*. Ithaca: Cornell University Press.

Rivkin-Fish, M. 2004. '"Change Yourself and the Whole World Will Become Kinder": Russian Activists for Reproductive Health and the Limits of Claims Making for Women', *Medical Anthropology Quarterly* 18 (3).

Robbins, J. 1994. 'Equality as a Value: Ideology in Dumont, Melanesia and the West'. *Social Analysis* 36: 21–70.

———. 2003. 'On the Paradoxes of Global Pentecostalism and the Perils of Continuity Thinking'. *Religion* 33 (3): 221–31.

———. 2004a. 'The Globalization of Pentecostal and Charismatic Christianity'. *Annual Review of Anthropology* 33: 117–43.

———. 2004b. *Becoming Sinners: Christianity and Moral Torment in a Papua New Guinea Society*. Berkeley: University of California Press.

———. 2005. 'Introduction – Humiliation and Transformation: Marshall Sahlins and the Study of Cultural Change in Melanesia', in J. Robbins and H. Wardlow (eds) *The Making of Global and Local Modernities in Melanesia: Humiliation, Transformation and the Nature of Cultural Change*. Aldershot: Ashgate, pp. 3–21.

Rogers, D.J. 2004. 'An Ethics of Transformation: Work, Prayer, and Moral Practice in the Russian Urals, 1861–2001'. Doctoral Dissertation, Department of Anthropology, University of Michigan.

Rorty, R. 2000. *Philosophy and Social Hope*. New York: Penguin.

Rose, N. 1999. *Governing the Soul: the Shaping of the Private Self*. London: Free Association Books.

Rosen, S. and D. Marr. 1999. 'Chinese and Vietnamese Youth in the 1990s', in A. Chan, B. J. Tria Kerkvliet and J. Unger (eds) *Transforming Asian Socialism: China and Vietnam Compared*. Lanham, Boulder and New York: Rowman and Littlefield Publishers, pp. 176–203.

Roy, O. 2000. *The New Central Asia: The Creation of Nations*. London: I.B. Tauris.

Rydstrøm, H. 2001. 'Like a White Piece of Paper: Embodiment and the Moral Upbringing of Vietnamese Children', *Ethnos* 66 (3): 394–413.

_____. 2002. 'Sexed Bodies/Gendered Bodies: Children and the Body in Vietnam', *Women's Studies International Forum* 25 (3): 359–72.

_____. 2003. *Embodying Morality: Growing Up in Rural Northern Vietnam*. Honolulu: University of Hawai'i Press.

_____. 2004. 'Female and Male "Characters": Images of Identification and Self-Identification for Rural Vietnamese Children and Adolescents'. In L. Drummond and H. Rydstrøm (eds) *Gender Practices in Contemporary Vietnam*. Singapore: Singapore University Press, pp. 74–96.

Sahni, I.P. 2005. 'Review Essay: Max Weber Today'. Canadian Journal of *Sociology* Online Sept.–Oct: 1–15.

Sargent, C. and N. Scheper-Hughes. 1998. *Small Wars*. Berkeley: University of California Press.

Schrift, A. 2001. 'Logics of the Gift in Cixious and Nietzsche', *Angelaki. Journal of Theoretical Humanities* 6 (2): 113–24.

Schroeder, R. 1992. *Max Weber and the Sociology of Culture*. London: Sage.

Schubel, V.J. 1999. 'Post-Soviet Hagiography and the Reconstruction of the Naqshbandi Tradition in Contemporary Uzbekistan', in E. Özdalga (ed.) *Naqshbandis in Western and Central Asia: Change and Continuity*. Istanbul: Swedish Research Institute.

Scott, J. C. 1985. *Weapons of the Weak: Everyday Forms of Peasant Resistance*. New Haven: Yale University Press.

_____. 1992. 'Experience', in J. Butler and J.W. Scott (eds) *Feminists Theorize the Political*. New York: Routledge.

Senft, G. 2002. *Field Manual 2002*. Unpublished manuscript. Max Planck Institute for Psycholinguistics, Nijmegen.

Serres, M. 1982. *The Parasite*. Baltimore: Minnesota University Press.

Sharp. L. 2003. 'Labouring for the Colony and Nation: the Historicized Political Consciousness of Youth in Madagascar', *Critique of Anthropology* 23 (1): 75–91

Shields, A. 2004. *Creating Enemies of the State: Religious Persecution in Uzbekistan*. Human Rights Watch Pbl.

Shweder, R. 1991. *Thinking through Cultures*. Cambridge: Harvard University Press.

Simpson, B. 2004. 'Impossible Gifts: Bodies, Buddhism and Bioethics in Contemporary Sri Lanka', *Journal of the Royal Anthropological Institute* (N.S.) 10(2): 839–59.

Smith, B.L. (ed.). 1978. *Religion and Legitimation of Power in Thailand, Laos, and Burma*. Chambersburg: Anima Publications.

Soucy, A. Dec. 2000/Jan. 2001. *Adolescent Reproductive Health Campaign in Vietnam*. Hanoi: UNFPA.

Spiro, M. E. 1971. *Buddhism and Society: A Great Tradition and its Burmese Vicissitudes*. Berkeley: University of California Press.

Stambach, A. 2000. *Lessons from Mount Kilimanjaro*. London: Routledge

Stephens, L. 1995. *Children and the Politics of Culture*. Ann Arbor: Michigan University Press.

Sterett, S.M. 2002. 'Introductory Essay', *Law and Society Review* 36 (2): 209–26.

Stevenson, P. 2002. *Language and German Disunity. A Sociolinguistic History of East and West in Germany, 1945–2000*. Oxford: Oxford University Press.

Stivens, M. 2002. 'The Hope of the Nation: Moral Panics and the Construction of Teenagerhood in Contemporary Malaysia', in L. Manderson and P. Liamputtong (eds) *Coming of Age in South and Southeast Asia: Youth, Courtship and Sexuality.* London: Curzon, pp. 188–207.

Stocking, G. 1988. *Functionalism Historicized: Essays on British Social Anthropology.* Madison: University of Wisconsin Press.

_____. 1996. *Volksgeist as Method and Ethic: Essays on Boasian Ethnography and the German Anthropological Tradition.* Madison: University of Wisconsin Press.

Stoler, A. 2002. *Carnal Knowledge and Imperial Power: Race and the Intimate in Colonial Rule.* Berkeley: University of California Press.

Strathern, M. 1988. *The Gender of the Gift: Problems with Women and Problems with Society in Melanesia.* Berkeley: University of California Press.

Strauss, C. and N. Quinn. 1994. 'A Cognitive/Cultural Anthropology', in R. Borofsky, R. (ed.) *Assessing Cultural Anthropology.* New York: McGraw-Hill.

Svendsen, L. 2004. *Kineseren fra Konigsberg – Immanuel Kant (1724–1804).* Oslo: Transit Forlag.

Sykes, K. 2001. 'Paying a School Fee is a Father's Duty'. *American Ethnologist* 28 (1): 1–27.

Taleo-Havini, M. 1995. *A Compilation of Human Rights Abuses Against the People of Bougainville 1989–1995,* Vol. 1. Erskineville, Sydney: Bougainvillean Freedom Movement.

_____. 1996. *A Compilation of Human Rights Abuses Against the People of Bougainville 1989–1996,* Vol. 2. Erskineville, Sydney: Bougainvillean Freedom Movement.

Tambiah, S.J. 1970. *Buddhism and Spirit Cults in North-East Thailand.* Cambridge: Cambridge University Press.

_____. 1977. *World Conqueror and World Renouncer,* Cambridge: Cambridge University Press.

_____. 1985. *Culture, Thought, and Social Action: An Anthropological Perspective,* Cambridge: Harvard University Press.

Taylor, C. 1989. *Sources of the Self: The Making of the Modern Identity.* Cambridge: Harvard University Press.

_____. 2002. *Varieties of Religion Today: William James Revisited.* Cambridge: Harvard University Press.

Thang Van Trinh. 2003. 'On Parent–Adolescent Communication about Sex and HIV/AIDS Issues in Thai Binh Province, Vietnam'. MA thesis, Chapel Hill, University of North Carolina.

Throop, C.J. 2003. 'Articulating Experience'. *Anthropological Theory* 3 (2): 219–41.

Truong Trong Hoang. 1998. 'Sexual Behavior Relating to HIV/AIDS Prevention and Influential Factors among Unmarried Young Males in Ho Chi Minh City, Vietnam'. MA thesis, Mahidol University.

United Nations Development Program (UNDP) 1993. *Rehabilitation and Reconstruction of Bougainville: A Needs Assessment and Program Proposal.* Report of a UN Inter-agency Mission to Bougainville.

United Nations Development Program 1998. *Rehabilitation and Reconstruction of Bougainville: A Needs Assessment and Program Proposal.*Report of a UN Inter-agency Mission to Bougainville.

UNPO 2004. Autonomous Bougainville a Step Closer Unrepresented Nations and Peoples Organization http://www.unpo.org/news 21 December 2004.

Van der Veer, P. 2000. '"The Enigma of Arrival": Hybridity and Authenticity in the Global Space', in P. Werbner and T. Modood (eds) *Debating Cultural Hybridity: Multi-Cultural Identities and the Politics of Anti-Racism.* London: Zed, pp. 90–105.

Van der Waal, K. 1990. 'Collective Human Rights: a Western View', in J. Berting, P. Baehr, J.H. Burgers and C. Flinterman (eds) *Human Rights in a Pluralistic World: Individuals and Collectivities*. London: Meckler Westport.

Vedder, H. 1942. *Am Lagerfeuer der Anderen*. Windhoek: Meinert.

Vetsantarasadok (phen khamgoon). (The Vessantarajataka in Poetry). 1972. Vientiane [in Lao, no author].

von Hinueber, O. 1998. *Entstehung und Aufbau der Jataka-Sammlung. Studien zur Literatur des Theravada-Buddhismus*. Stuttgart: Franz Steiner.

Wagner, R. 1977 'Analogic Kinship: A Daribi Example', *American Ethnologist* 4 (4): 623–42.

_____. 1981 [1975]. *The Invention of Culture*. Chicago: University of Chicago Press.

_____. 1986. *Asiwinarong*. Princeton: Princeton University Press.

Weber, M. 1946. *From Max Weber: Essays in Sociology*, transl. H.H. Gerth and C.W. Mills. New York: Oxford University Press.

_____. 1949. *The Methodology of the Social Sciences*, transl. E.A. Shils and H.A. Finch. New York: Free Press.

Weiner, A. 1976. *Women of Value, Men of Renown*. Austin: University of Texas Press.

_____. 1992. *Inalienable Possessions*. Berkeley: University of California Press.

Weiner, J.F. 2001. *Tree Leaf Talk: A Heideggerian Anthropology*. Oxford: Berg.

Werner, J. 2004. 'Managing Womanhoods in the Family: Gendered Subjectivities and the State in the Red River Delta in Vietnam', in L. Drummond and H. Rydstrøm (eds) *Gender Practices in Contemporary Vietnam*. Singapore: Singapore University Press, pp. 26–47.

Widlok, T. 2004a. 'Sharing by Default? Outline of an Anthropology of Virtue'. *Anthropological Theory* 4: 53–70.

_____. 2004b. 'Needs and Virtues. An Anthropological Exploration of the Relationship between Morality and Necessity'. Unpublished. Habilitationsschrift, University of Cologne.

_____. 2006. 'Speakers are Ephemeral, Language Documentation Endures?', Unpublished paper held at the DOBES Conference 15–16 June 2006, Nijmegen, the Netherlands.

Wieschiolek, H. 1999. 'Separation Through Unification: Changing Cultural Models in an East German Company', in M. Rösler and T. Wendl (eds) *Frontiers and Borderlands: Anthropological Perspective*. Frankfurt (Main): Peter Lang, pp. 211–24.

Williams, B. 1973. *Problems of the Self*. Cambridge: Cambridge University Press.

Williams, R. 1983 [1976]. *Keywords: A Vocabulary of Culture and Society*. New York: Oxford University Press.

Wilson, B. 1970. *Rationality*. Oxford: Blackwell.

Wongthes, M. 2000. 'The Gift of the Body as the "Gift of Knowledge": Body Donation in Thailand', MPhil thesis in Social Anthropology, University of Cambridge.

Yurchak, A. 1997. 'The Cynical Reason of Late Capitalism: Power, Pretense and the Anekdot', *Public Culture* 9: 161–88.

_____. 2003. 'Soviet Hegemony of Form: Everything Was Forever, Until It Was No More', *Comparative Studies in Society and History* 45: 480–510.

Yuval-Davis, N. 1997. *Gender and Nation*. London: Sage.

Zelizer, V.A. 1985. *Pricing the Priceless Child: The Changing Social Value of Children*. New York: Basic Books.

Zigon, J. 2007. 'Moral Breakdown and the Ethical Demand: a Theoretical Framework for an Anthropology of Moralities'. *Anthropology Theory*, 7(2): 131–50.

_____. 2008. *Morality. An Anthropological Perspective*. Oxford: Berg.

_____. 2009. "Morality Within a Range of Possibilities: A Dialogue With Joel Robbins", Ethnos, vol. 74, no. 2.

NOTES ON CONTRIBUTORS

Mark Goodale, Associate Professor of Conflict Analysis and Anthropology , George Masson University, USA
He is the author of *Surrendering to Utopia: An Anthropology of Human Rights*, Stanford: Stanford University Press (2009) and *Dilemmas of Modernity*, Stanford: Stanford University Press, 2008, the editor (with June Starr) of *Practicing Ethnography in Law, New Dialogues, Enduring Methods*, New York: Palgrave Macmillan, 2002, the editor (with Sally Engle Merry) of *The Practice of Human Rights: Tracking Law Between the Global and the Local*, Cambridge: CUP, 2007, the editor of *Human Rights: An Anthropological Reader*, Oxford: Blackwell, 2008 and coeditor of *Mirrors of Justice: Law and Power in Post-Cold War Era*, Cambridge: CUP, 2009. He conducted fieldwork in Bolivia.

Monica Heintz, Associate Professor in Social Anthropology, University of Paris Ouest – Nanterre La Défense, France
She is the author of *'Be European, recycle yourself!' Changing Work Ethic in Romania*, Muenster: LIT, 2006, and the editor of *Weak State, Uncertain Citizenship: Moldova*, Berlin: Peter Lang, 2008. She conducted fieldwork in Romania and in the Republic of Moldova.

Signe Howell, Professor of Social Anthropology, University of Oslo, Norway
She is the author of *The Kinning of Foreigners*, Oxford: Berghahn Books, 2006; editor of *The Ethnography of Moralities*, London: Routledge, 1997; editor (with Roy Willis) of *Societies at Peace: Anthropological Perspective*, London: Routledge, 1989; editor (with Stephen Sparkes) of *The House in Southeast Asia*, London: Routledge Curzon, 1999; author of *Society and Cosmos: Chewong of Peninsular Malaysia*, Oxford: OUP, 1984; editor of *For the Sake of Our Future: Sacrificing in Eastern Indonesia*, Leiden: Research School CNWS, 1996. She carried out fieldwork in Malaysia and Norway.

Patrice Ladwig, Research Fellow, Max Planck Institute for Social Anthropology, Germany

He is the author of *Death Rituals among the Lao: an Ethnological Analysis*, Berlin: SEACOM. 2003. Patrice Ladwig has studied Social Anthropology and Sociology at the University of Edinburgh and the EHESS, Paris, and obtained his M.A. from the University of Muenster, Germany. He carried out fieldwork on urban Buddhism in Vientiane, Laos, and has completed his PhD ('Ethics, gifts and the state: Buddhism in postreform Laos') at the University of Cambridge.

Johan Rasanayagam, Lecturer in Social Anthropology, University of Aberdeen, UK

Johan Rasanayagam studied Arabic at the University of Durham and has compeleted his PhD in Social Anthropology at the University of Cambridge. He conducted fieldwork in Uzbekistan. He was the guest editor of the special issue *Post-Soviet Islam: An Anthropological Perspective*, *Central Asian Survey* 25 (3) (2006), and author of 'Healing with spirits and the formation of Muslim selfhood in post-Soviet Uzbekistan', *Journal of the Royal Anthropological Institute*, 12(2) (2006): 377–93.

Joel Robbins, Professor and Chair in Social Anthropology, University of California at San Diego, USA

He is the author of *Becoming Sinners: Christianity and Moral Torment in a Papua New Guinea Society*, Berkeley: University of California Press, 2004; editor (with David Akin) of *Money and Modernity: State and Local Currencies in Melanesia*, Pittsburgh: University of Pittsburgh Press, 1999; editor (with Holly Wardlow) of *The Making of Local and Global Modernities in Melanesia: Humiliation, Transformation and the Making of Cultural Change*, Aldershot: Ashgate, 2005. He carried out fieldwork in Papua New Guinea.

Helle Rydstrøm, Associate Professor in Social Anthropology, University of Lund, Sweden

She is the author of *Embodying Morality: Growing Up in Rural Northern Vietnam*, Honolulu: University of Hawai'i Press, 2003, and the editor of *Gendered Inequalities in Asia: Configuring, Contesting, and Recognizing Women and Men*. Copenhagen: NIAS Press (2009) and (with Lisa Drummond) of *Gender Practices in Contemporary Vietnam*, Singapore: Singapore University Press, 2004. She is also the editor (with Trinh Duy Luan and Wil Burghoom) of *Rural Families in Transitional Vietnam*, Hanoi: Social Sciences Publishing House (2008). She conducted fieldwork in Northern Vietnam.

Karen Sykes, Professor of Social Anthropology, University of Manchester, UK

She is the author of *Arguing with Anthropology: An Introduction to Critical Theories of the Gift*, London: Routledge, 2005; the editor of *Cultural Property in the New Guinea Islands Region*, New Delphi: UBS Publishers' Distributors, 2000 and of *Ethnographies of Moral Reasoning: Living Paradoxes of a Global Age*, Palgrave Macmillan, 2008. She conducted fieldwork in Papua New Guinea.

Thomas Widlok, Professor, Radboud Universiteit Nijmegen, the Netherlands

He is the author of *Living on Mangetti: Bushman Autonomy and Namibian Independence*, Oxford: OUP, 2000, and the editor (with Tadesse Gossa) of *Property and Equality*, Oxford: Berghahn Books, 2004. He conducted fieldwork in Namibia and Australia.

Jarrett Zigon, Assistant Professor, University of Amsterdam

Jarrett Zigon is the author of *Morality: An Anthropological Perspective*, Oxford: Berg, 2008 and of several articles on the anthropology of morality in such journals as Ethos, Anthropological Theory, and Ethnos. He conducted fieldwork in Russia.

INDEX

www.ingramcontent.com/pod-product-compliance
Lightning Source LLC
Chambersburg PA
CBHW060036030426
42334CB00019B/2357